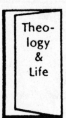

Theo-
logy
&
Life

THEOLOGY AND LIFE SERIES

Some New and Recent Titles

Other Titles in Preparation

Creation
and Redemption

GABRIEL DALY O.S.A.

Michael Glazier
Wilmington, Delaware

ABOUT THE AUTHOR

Gabriel Daly, OSA is a lecturer in Systematic and Historical Theology at Trinity College, Dublin and at the Irish School of Ecumenics. His publications include *Transcendence and Immanence: A Study in Catholic Modernism and Integralism* and *Asking the Father: A Study of the Prayer of Petition.*

First published in 1989 by Michael Glazier, Inc.,
1935 West Fourth Street, Wilmington, Delaware 19805,
by arrangement with Gill and Macmillan Ltd., Dublin.
© 1988 by Gabriel Daly, OSA.

Library of Congress Cataloging-in-Publication Data
Daly, Gabriel.
    Creation and redemption.

    Includes bibliographical references.
    1. Creation.   2. Redemption.   I. Title.
BT695.D35   1989   233'.1   89-24622
ISBN 0-89453-748-2

Printed in Great Britain.

Cover Design by Lilian Brulc.

Contents

Preface

THIS book owes much to the many discussions I have had over the years with colleagues, students, and friends about the topics which feature here. I am especially indebted to Dr Werner Jeanrond who read the typescript with his customary thoroughness and made several helpfully incisive suggestions. Both he, Professor Sean Freyne, and the Reverend Professor Enda McDonagh alerted me to passages which needed modification and clarification and in general gave me valuable advice and encouragement.

I have tried to avoid jargon and the unnecessary use of technical terms. There are, however, words and phrases which, though technical, can hardly be avoided in a book such as this. I have therefore included a short glossary for ease of reference.

The whole earth is our hospital
Endowed by the ruined millionaire,
Wherein, if we do well, we shall
Die of the absolute paternal care
That will not leave us, but prevents us everywhere.

T. S. Eliot, Four Quartets

Introduction

T. S. ELIOT's image of the earth as our hospital embodies a truth which is central to the theological relationship between creation and salvation. To be human is to find oneself amongst the walking wounded, constantly in need of healing, forgiveness, acceptance, affirmation, reinvigoration and hope. Any man, woman, or child who is denied these manifestations of love will be damaged as a person. No one can be human on his or her own. Consequently no one can be saved on his or her own. We are members one of another. Human interdependence necessarily implies the need for salvific relationships.

There is a long Christian tradition which ascribes all this to sin. While there can be no doubt that sin aggravates the damage done by destructive natural processes, these processes precede the commission, and even the possibility, of personal or social sin and have been traditionally treated in Christian theology under the rubric of 'original sin'. Chapters 6 and 7 will consider them.

The need to love and to be loved precedes morality. Refusal to love constitutes the essence of sin. To be denied love is the final tragedy, because all other manifestations of tragedy are redeemable by love. The faith-inspired insight that God is love controls all else in Christian theology. Salvation is the effect that divine love has upon men and women when they discern that love in the works of creation and welcome it as God's gift and invitation. The need to be saved precedes the commission of sin.

Human need for salvation stems in large measure from the painful fact that human beings are both continuous and discontinuous with the physical world from which they have

1

evolved. Much traditional Christian theology has emphasised the discontinuity, whereas contemporary theology, conscious of the need for ecological responsibility and the demands of cosmic thinking, emphasises all that our species has in common with the rest of creation. The difficult and sometimes abrasive relationship between what we have in common with the rest of nature, on the one hand, and what makes us different from the rest of nature, on the other, sets up a condition which is in need of healing and reconstruction. In Chapters 2 and 3 we shall consider how the emergence of *homo sapiens* produces a crisis for nature itself, precisely because in *homo sapiens* nature becomes conscious of itself and its own processes.

Beings who achieve self-awareness, the ability to love, and the power of abstract thought, while retaining their roots in physical and pre-human biological creation, present philosophers and theologians with the challenge of avoiding two extremes. The first is that of a reductionism which would see in human beings nothing but a more complicated arrangement of physical, chemical, and biological elements. The opposite extreme is a supernaturalism which would define human beings totally in terms of their spiritual nature while disregarding their physical and biological character and their place in Earth's ecosystems.

Nature, as a continuous process, is characterised, then, by a fascinating interrelationship between continuity and stability on the one hand and discontinuity and mobility on the other. This interrelationship is particularly evident in the evolution of living species as they adapt to their environment; but it is prefigured in the atomic and sub-atomic world where the random interplay of particles contributes in a mysterious way to their organisation into more complex forms of energy and matter. The process is one of differentiation and diversification, as units divide and sub-divide and then re-associate in systemic interrelationships. At each point in development something is lost and something gained. As nature evolves from the inorganic to the organic it loses some of its previous unity and simplicity and gains new and more complex possibilities. This process culminates, on planet earth, in a species which arrives at consciousness, self-awareness, and a freedom of action impossible to lower forms of life. With that development something radically new happens to nature, something unparalleled in earlier developments. In *homo sapiens* nature becomes conscious of itself. Because of the autonomy which comes with this consciousness these new beings, men and women, have tended to forget their origins and to emphasise what separates them from the rest of nature. The ecological crisis facing our planet today is alerting our species to the dangers of trying to live as if we had no responsibilities towards the rest of creation. It is teaching us to look more closely at the continuity which exists between us and all other denizens and components of the planet we share. Ecological necessity invites theological reflection; and that reflection focuses on the interrelationship between human identity with nature and human differentiation from other elements within nature.

The word 'saved' suggests being in a situation consequent upon another situation in which it would be better not to have been in the first place. There is the suggestion of *faute de mieux* about being saved, with the implication that an existence which does not give rise to an occasion for being saved is a better and more desirable kind of existence than one which does. Salvation, however, needs to be seen as something positive and valuable in its own right. Being saved forges a bond between the one who saves and the one who is saved. This bond is one of the deepest relationships that can occur between two people. It gives rise to a host of attendant and related experiences such as gratitude, love, friendship, fidelity, and resolve to respond in kind. Being saved is normally a condition of relieved delight which often more than compensates for the distress and danger which occasioned it. Salvation, in short, is a blessing in its own right and not merely a happy ending to an otherwise regrettable occurrence. That is why it should not be relegated in its entirety to a future life after death. This earthly life is shot through with salvific instances which demand to be recognised as such by faith. Grace is not an abstract or invisible entity granted by God directly and without mediation. It always coexists with tangible realities and is mediated by those realities. There is no such thing as a grace which is grace and nothing else. There are only graced persons, events, and things. If we wish to discover and encounter grace, we must turn to the created world, because it is the created world which supplies the materials and occasions that become the vehicles of grace.

In traditional Christian theology the word 'salvation' is often so inextricably bound up with the word 'sin' as to suggest that without sin there would be no need for salvation. Of course much depends on how one understands 'sin' in this connection, but in almost every instance there is the suggestion of fault, culpability, and possibly even a felt need for punishment. Yet in the liturgy of Easter night we find the daring oxymoron, O *felix culpa*, 'O happy fault that merited such and so great a redeemer'. Some of the Church Fathers can be found writing in effect that there had to be an illness so that there might be a physician. These examples of positive evaluation of what it means to be saved are relatively rare and, in the Western Christian tradition at least, almost totally overshadowed by a forensic and penal view of what it means to be human. Salvation is therefore seen not as a condition desirable in its own right but rather as a merciful expedient designed by an offended God to save from perdition the erring species known to anthropology as *homo sapiens*.

One effect of this penal view of salvation was the separation of the theology of creation from the theology of salvation. Although creation was regarded as good, coming as it does from the hands of God, this fact was coupled with the implicit and highly questionable premise that what is good is in no need of salvation. If creation groans for salvation, as St Paul claims, then according to the penal view it can only be because of sin. I wish to contend that the scope of salvation includes, but far exceeds, the scope of sin. We are saved not merely from our sins but also from the alienating effects (or, better, side-effects) of the creative process. Salvation is therefore an ambiguous, multi-layered idea, and the ambiguity arises out of the experience of being human.

Being human is one of nature's modes of existence. We shall consider this mode of existence at several points in the book. Here it is enough to note the ambiguity inseparable from the fact of enjoying an existence which is characterised by mind, freedom, conscience, and a desire which is transcendental—that is, always pointing beyond itself to a horizon

4

which is never reached in this world. In human beings nature itself arrives at consciousness and the knowledge of good and evil. In human beings nature cries out for redemption. For reasons which we shall later consider, evolving nature reaches a point where it needs salvation, healing, and reconciling. Some, but by no means all, of that need stems from human wrongdoing, and therein lies the ambiguity. Culpability there is in plenty; but there is also tragedy and mystery. The prospect of salvation is built into the very concept of a creation which flowers in intelligence and freedom. It simply will not do to make sin the source of so much that is sheerly human. The fact is that in many human situations culpability resists both accurate attribution and accurate measurement and is frequently mingled with tragedy.

In Chapter 9 we shall consider how our Christian forebears represented to themselves the salvific achievement of Jesus through his life, death, and resurrection. We shall note how biblical, patristic, and medieval soteriology employed a variety of models or analogues in order to structure the experience of redemption. Some of these models and analogues continue to speak authentically to us today while some have lost their cultural relevance. In Chapter 10 we shall ask how soteriology can be made culturally relevant to our age without losing anything essential to its perennial meaning or doctrinal integrity.

A good deal is being written today on the relationship between science and theology. Theologians who are not scientists can feel understandably hesitant about entering an arena where they may make technical mistakes and commit professional solecisms. They may have noticed certain theological gaucheries in the comments of some scientists and wish to avoid reciprocation. The fact that in earlier ages science and religion cultivated a mutually abrasive relationship can further deter a theologian from entering what has for long been a war zone. These fears, though understandable, should not be rationalised into a theological excuse for leaving science to the scientists. We are fortunate today that there are competent scientists writing books for the interested lay man and woman. These books enable non-professionals to gain some insight into what the specialists are doing and saying.

Questions about the existence and meaning of the universe are controlled and directed by our own experience, which is itself part of the phenomenon we are examining. These questions are ultimately neither scientific nor theological; they are philosophical, as, for example, when we pause to wonder why there is anything rather than nothing, or whether natural processes are shaped by purpose. Here we might with profit recall Paul Tillich's view that philosophy provides the common ground for dialogue between science and religion.[1] If the very exigencies of contemporary science are pointing scientists in the direction of philosophy, few theologians will wish to claim that theology can or ought to try to seclude itself from philosophical enquiry. What is important in all this is that the field of philosophical enquiry be, and be seen to be, neutral ground where neither scientist nor theologian should make preemptive demands on the other.

Since there is a long and not always creditable history of religious apologists making tendentious use of selected items of scientific information, I am concerned not to appear to be implying that science is now discovering God. Even if a scientist is prepared to use the word 'God', what he or she understands by that word may be very different from what the Judaeo-Christian religion has traditionally meant by it. Significantly, some scientists, such as Fritjof Capra, conduct their dialogue not with Judaeo-Christianity but with Eastern mysticism. It is up to the Western theologian to show that this dialogue need not be restricted to faiths which have a strong gnostic component. Inconvenient though it may seem, Jews and Christians are committed to the conviction that God must be sought and found in history as well as in nature. No historically based faith can hope for the easy ride which science is prepared to offer to faiths which are lived and practised in a spiritual realm beyond the reach of historical and scientific criticism.

The theologian, then, should look to science not for apologetical material to be used in religious argument, but for a contemporary description of how the universe came to be what it is. This description, albeit provisional, will help to delineate an area of agreed reference for believer and non-believer alike. Furthermore, the delineation of this area will serve as a

6

reminder to theological enquirers that we have no business looking to divine revelation for information about the physical, chemical, or biological character of the universe. If the Scriptures appear to be offering such information, it will be a sign that we are reading them from a false perspective. When the author of Genesis comments on the rainbow after the Flood, he is telling us nothing about the physical origin of rainbows. What he *is* telling us is a matter for anthropological and theological speculation. There is more to rainbows than what can be learnt from a study of the physics of light. Poets have as much right as physicists to speak of rainbows. If a religious poet finds in a rainbow a symbolic assurance of God's care for the world, no physicist can properly say him nay. If, however, a religious believer instructs us that on the evidence of Genesis we must hold that there were no rainbows before a historically specifiable flood, we do not need to be physicists to reject the instruction. Such a person would simply be misusing a sacred text.

It is therefore of the utmost importance that we recognise from the outset that religious discourse does not operate in the same manner as scientific discourse. Theologians and scientists contemplate the same universe, but they do so from different perspectives and with different methodologies. God, who is at the centre of theological enquiry, is never a scientific datum or hypothesis. To make him such would be to offend against both sound theology and sound science. Scientific method proceeds by way of hypothesis, through observation and measurement, to provisional verification or ultimate falsification of the original theory. Hypotheses are often put forward to account for and accommodate newly discovered phenomena. Such accommodation may demand a change of paradigm or perspective from which to view the evidence. The universe observed by Newton was observed by Einstein with different paradigms.

Here it is worth noting that scientists employ the word 'theory' in a specialised sense. Scientific theories are always open to falsification. More pertinently, they are also open to replacement by other theories which accommodate the evidence better. Such replacement does not necessarily prove that former theories were simply false. New paradigms give new insights into the functioning of the universe. Theologians have no business disregarding the theories advanced by scientists at any particular moment merely on the grounds that they are provisional, replaceable, and even falsifiable. Anything that is discovered or postulated by science about the cosmos is potentially of interest and importance to theologians. There is something sadly inappropriate about believers desperately trying to ferret out a credible biologist who appears to be challenging the theory of evolution.

A concluding comment on terminology may help to guard against possible misunderstandings. The words 'salvation' and 'redemption' are employed throughout the book as virtual synonyms, though each is, of course, derived from a distinct original model. In both cases the metaphor is inert, though it can be partially revived by conscious advertence to the etymological derivation of each: 'Salvation' speaks of being made safe, while 'redemption' speaks of rescue from captivity. In Chapter 9 we shall examine these and other soteriological terms.

Words which describe the situation from which we hope to be saved tend to be overshadowed by the sheer ubiquity and indiscriminate reference of the word 'sin' (cf. Chapter 6). Few other theological terms have been expected to do such heavy all-purpose duty. It is so tied to the idea of culpability that it lacks the power to suggest tragedy, ambiguity, or ambivalence. I shall therefore employ the word 'alienation' when I wish to suggest that the condition from which we desire and need to be saved includes, but extends well beyond, the area of moral failure and culpability.

I have therefore chosen the word 'alienation' with full advertance to its ambiguity. I wanted a word with sufficient width of reference to cover the phenomenon whereby a unified entity undergoes a process of fragmentation, a parting of ways, a differentiation which can be either necessary and morally neutral (e.g. birth, adolescence, leaving home, death) or contingent and morally wrong (e.g. enmity, warfare, social and industrial exploitation). More than that, I wanted a word which would describe the fracturing of a previous unity *in order that* a more organised and complex form of life might take place (Chapter 7). In effect I wanted a word with multi-layered reference and consequent ambiguity. 'Alienation' is a word with the etymological force of 'making other', 'separating', 'dividing', 'estranging', 'distanciating', 'dissociating', 'differentiating'. 'Alienation' has been used by Hegelians, Marxists, Freudians, and Existentialists, each with their own characteristic reference. In everyday language to be alienated is to feel excluded and disaffected, no longer part of some society, enterprise, or initiative to which one formerly belonged or subscribed.

Alienation, in the morally neutral sense of separation or distanciation, is potentially either good or bad. The process can lead, often painfully, to growth and a new level of life, or it can fester into hostility and aggression. The word itself is an effective antonym to 'reconciliation', and its very ambiguity is part and parcel of human experience. An inherently ambiguous situation demands an appropriately ambiguous word to describe it. The claim that alienation precedes, but goes on to overlap with, morality is essential to the argument of this book. The fact that 'alienation' can be employed in such different contexts as Marxism and psychoanalysis alerts us to its analogical character. The theological imagination, when it is alive to the uses (and limitations) of analogy, can see the value of a word that has as its antonym the word 'reconciliation', one of the more culturally enduring terms in the vocabulary of Christian soteriology.[2]

A theology of creation and salvation could consistently begin with consideration of the human condition and ascend thence to a consideration of God. I have chosen, however, to begin with a reflection on God, but to do so in a way which recognises that the reality of God is always mediated to us through our own experiences and is therefore vulnerable to constant distortion. The reality of God is always approached, in prayer or in theological reflection, through the images we form. If we fail to recognise this, we easily fall into an unwitting idolatry which takes the image for the reality. The Holy Spirit is the supreme iconoclast, for she is the Spirit of Wisdom and the earnest of eventual vision.

The reader will notice that St Augustine features prominently at certain points of the book. This is hardly surprising, given the topic in hand. The common phrase

'Augustinian pessimism', however, makes one last preliminary comment advisable. Along with many other Christians today I cannot follow Augustine in his estimate of sin and damnation, when these are seen to outweigh God's salvific intentions. On the other hand I believe that Pelagian optimism about the human condition is ultimately the most depressing of doctrines, as soon as one reckons with one's divided self, one's failed opportunities, and the ambivalent character of whatever good one may do.

Man, as Pascal has put it, is the glory and the scandal of the universe. The scandal precedes the glory; and forgiveness is the link between them. It was a man who gave his fellow men and women definitive assurance that our God is a saving and therefore forgiving God. Christians recognise in the man, Jesus of Nazareth, the perfect human expression of divinity. Chapters 4 and 5 are therefore devoted to the mystery of Jesus Christ who is the mediator not only between God and humankind, but also between creation and its fulfilment.

Pierre Teilhard de Chardin, profoundly aware of the importance for faith of a recognition that creation is evolutionary, saw in Christ the fulfilment of evolution and designated him 'Omega Point'. This Teilhardian insight is remarkably consonant with certain Pauline and early patristic texts which treat Christ as a cosmic figure. There is a cosmic Christ, however, only because there was a historical man, Jesus from Nazareth, who lived in a historically specifiable time and place. This therefore poses the question of how history and culture are to be related to nature and to God. The earthly Jesus belongs to time and place, while the risen Christ belongs to the realm of ultimate fulfilment. It is the *crucified* Christ who is raised to new life; and this glorious truth makes the cross, when lit by the resurrection, an assurance of salvation and a manifestation of divine forgiveness.

1

In The Beginning God

THERE is a scene in Joseph Heller's novel, *Catch 22*, which portrays an argument between the hero, Yossarian, and one of his girlfriends. Neither of them believes in God, but they are celebrating Thanksgiving. Yossarian proclaims that there is little to be thankful for anyway and then launches into a tirade against God which upsets his girlfriend.

> 'What the hell are you getting so upset about?' he asked bewilderedly in a tone of contrite amusement. 'I thought you didn't believe in God.'
> 'I don't,' she sobbed, bursting violently into tears. 'But the God I don't believe in is a good God, a just God, a merciful God. He's not the mean and stupid God you make Him out to be.'
> Yossarian laughed and turned her arms loose. 'Let's have a little more religious freedom between us,' he proposed obligingly. 'You don't believe in the God you want to, and I won't believe in the God I want to. Is that a deal?'[1]

The zany illogicality of this scene raises a matter of profound importance to any discourse about God. No one, saint or sinner, believer or unbeliever, has an uninterpreted, objectively faithful, idea or image of the God they do or do not believe in. A really consistent unbeliever would hardly find it necessary, as some combative atheists do, to attempt to refute such arguments as may be advanced in favour of God's existence. Even to name God is to have a concept or image of what the word might mean. St Anselm's ontological argument for the existence of God has been refuted many times, but it refuses to lie down, mainly because, although its inclusion is derived from a logical flaw, its first premise is irrefutable: God is 'something than which nothing greater can be thought'. God is *by definition* beyond the limits of human thought, or, more accurately, God is the unexperienced superlative of any quality that can be thought of. That no one can see God and live is the constant message of Judaeo-Christian religion. All human apprehension of God is indirect, selective, distorted—in short, profoundly interpretative. God as he really is can be approached only through the concepts and images which we have formed of him. These images and concepts can range from the sentimental to the horrible.

If Feuerbach and Freud, in proclaiming that God is the projection of man on to an infinite screen, had meant no more than that our *image* of God is the infinite projection of our own human experience, they would have been proclaiming a truth which any reflective believer could applaud. Like so many believers, however, they failed to distinguish between image and reality. The statement 'I believe in God' has no content or reference until the believer is able and ready to tell us what sort of God he or she believes in. There are images of God in writings, sermons, and other kinds of religious discourse which, if the image were identical with reality, would make atheism more attractive than belief.

As it it, the believer has warrant for practising a genuine agnosticism about the reliability of even the most celebrated images and concepts of God which reach us from the specu- lative and imaginative minds of others. Our image of God is always partial, selective, wayward, and distorted. It is coloured by our changing moods, shaped by our passing enthusiasms, chipped at by our fears, preoccupations, and distastes. There are times when we may wonder whether our own subjectivity has not totally obscured God as he really is. We do indeed pray to God as he really is, but it is always through the filter of an image of greater or lesser distortion.

This is the principal difference between prayer and theology. Prayer is addressed to God as he is in himself. Theology is concerned with the proper management of the concepts and images which are our means of talking about him. The two activities are distinct though closely interrelated. Prayer can afford to rest almost completely in the apophatic—that is, in

12

tranquil acquiescence in what we do not know about God. Prayer cannot dispense with the distorted concepts and images which are the common coin of our discourse about God, but it can afford to discount them, or adjust them, or use them as it sees fit. Prayer can afford, even welcome, an impressionistic approach to the images and concepts traditionally employed as vehicles for reaching God. Theology does not have the same freedom of action. It has to work with more precise instruments and therefore it cannot repose in prayerful impressionism.

We always, even the most cognitively abstract among us, humanise the God we worship or speak about. If we are wise, we recognise that this is so and we learn to cultivate a little modesty, a little tolerance, and a great deal of humour and irony. 'If you have understood, then it is not God', said Augustine crisply. We shall meet Augustine later, and it may strike us that his God seems to be a rather severe and intimidating being. When, for example, he is prepared to consign large numbers, including unbaptised infants, to hell, his understanding of God may strike us as horribly misplaced. At such moments we may need to remind ourselves that this is *Augustine's* God, not God as he is in himself. I single out Augustine here, because he dominates the Christian theology of pilgrimage, and because, as von Hügel said of John Henry Newman, we think his thoughts and share his images without necessarily being aware that we are doing so. Augustine gave Christian theology in the West much of its language, many of its images, and some of its lasting preoccupations. There is a grandeur about his vision of God which has rarely been equalled; but there is also a terrible harshness which chills us and forces us to cry out, 'That is not the sort of God I believe in'. When we read him, however, we must be prepared to pay the price of seeing God through the eyes of a theological genius by remembering that we are also seeing God through the eyes of a fifth-century Romanised African living the latter half of his life in a world that was breaking up, profoundly and uncomfortably aware of his own passionate nature, of his misspent youth, and of his chequered intellectual and spiritual development. Augustine's God is awesome, loving, and terrifying by turns. Omnipotence, however, wins out over every other attribute.

13

It is also the attribute which tends to overshadow all thought and discourse about creation. Our image of God will naturally control our image of how he acts in the world, and this ought to be carefully noted at the outset of any treatment of the theology of creation and salvation.

Omnipotence, the power to do anything that can be done, is a concept full of dangers even for the most practised of theologians. Simply thinking about the notion of omnipotence can bring out the megalomaniac in any of us. 'Whatever he wills he does' is in such contradiction to human experience that the human mind can scarcely take it in. The imagination staggers drunkenly under the images of unlimited power. Human will and desire, conscious of being constantly thwarted, luxuriate vicariously in the thought of infinitely unshackled power and limitless possibility. It is all too easy to let fantasy take over when we contemplate omnipotence. There have been Christian philosophers who construed divine omnipotence in a way which absolved God of the restraints even of logic, rationality, morality and self-consistency. In point of fact, much talk about omnipotence is little more than an exercise in formal logic, a moving of counters around a board without any emotional commitment. Theologically there are, however, greater dangers than that of mere logic-chopping. By use of the concept of omnipotence one can paradoxically place limits on what God can do, if he is not to forfeit his omnipotence. When omnipotence is linked to immutability, many *a priori* conceptual restraints are placed upon divine action. Divine attributes, i.e. *a priori* ontological abstractions such as omnipotence, omniscience, immutability, and impassibility are derived mentally from human experience, stripped mentally of their human imperfections, and then predicated of God in an 'eminent', i.e. infinite, way. They not merely maximise divine power to infinity, but they also antecedently rule out any divine action deemed not to be in keeping with one or other of the attributes. As we shall see, this essentialist language has far-reaching implications for the theology of creation. An immutable God who creates is a very tricky mental construct, rather like an athlete throwing a javelin while wearing a strait-jacket.

Far more pertinently, an omnipotent God who subjects

14

himself in any way to the vagaries and imperfections of an evolving universe is in grave danger of losing his claim to divinity. Yet certain religious philosophers have felt it necessary to escape from the rigid absolutes of Greek philosophy, because the God who results from such philosophical premises seems to them to emerge as a bundle of abstract superlatives devoid of life, love, or attractiveness. Thus the God of the Process philosophers is conceived of as a dialectical correction to the cosmic tyrant who stands apart from, and remains unaffected by, the world he has created.

Before considering the contribution to theology of Process thought, let us examine the concept of omnipotence a little further. It is, as we have noted, derived from the experience of human capability and its limitations. There is more than a touch of the ontological argument about the conclusion that a God without omnipotence would not be God: By common consent the power to do all things enters into the very definition of God. God is that than which nothing more powerful can be thought. In short, God is unsurpassable *by definition*. Therefore if we place limitations on God's capacities, we simply create a space to be filled by a being whose capacities are *un*limited. What, however, is a limitation on omnipotence? Or rather, can one distinguish between a limitation which is compatible with deity and a limitation which is not? Logical impossibilities belong to the kind of limitation which does not infringe upon deity. To say that God cannot make a square circle or cause himself not to exist is no limitation on his power. Omnipotence cannot mean the power to perform logical impossibilities, i.e., acts which entail intrinsic contradictions. If God decides (the word is of course anthropomorphic) on a specific course of action, for example to create beings who are intelligent and free, he accepts the logical, and therefore necessary, limitations of his decision.

He cannot, for example, will a creature who has real freedom of choice and at the same time ensure in advance that that creature will necessarily do everything that he or she could and should do. Human freedom is not an ontological limitation on God's omnipotence, though it may provide philosophers and theologians with other challenging problems.

The long and often arid debates about predestination and

freedom are witness to the human mind's limitations in handling both concepts. Ability or willingness to live with paradox has not usually marked the labours of essentialist metaphysicians. The problems entailed by the concept of omnipotence are raised in an acute and painful form by the phenomenon of evil, as we shall see. These problems in turn arise out of any consideration of the universe as it actually exists. Could its physical laws be different, given that God has a purpose in creating it? Did evolution have to take the course it did, e.g., through natural selection? Has God determined in advance the precise stages from initial cosmic explosion down to the emergence of *homo sapiens*; or does he give his creation a general direction while leaving the concrete working out of the details partly to the random processes of nature, and finally to the unpredictabilities of human freedom in decision and action?[2]

Questions of this sort have a reference both to the universe as creation and to God as creator. If the physical processes which are the subject of scientific investigation reveal a high degree of randomness operating within the laws of nature, does this not say something to the theist about God's action in the world? Does it not in a sense prepare the reflective believer to face the formidable questions which arise when we come to consider our own species, *homo sapiens*? Is there not some sort of analogy between random physical forces and human actions which are the product of free choice? There are, of course, scientists who maintain that what we call randomness or chance is simply a phenomenon of whose causes we are at present ignorant, just as there are philosophers for whom human freedom of choice is an illusion. However, scientific consensus increasingly favours the view that many physical processes are genuinely random and that future research will not uncover and force a return to a now undisclosed determinism of the older mechanical type.

Determinism in fact governed scientific attitudes until Niels Bohr showed that light could be understood and treated as either wave-like or particle-like, but not at the same time, and that each function complemented the other. Certain experiments revealed it as wave-like, other experiments as particle-like. Function, relationship, and the contribution of the observer are all part of the phenomenon. Quantum physics shows that the observer in a very real and objective sense influences what he or she observes. The experimenter is inescapably part of the experiment. Quantum theory, therefore, makes it impossible for one to envisage a universe which is physically predetermined always to behave in a certain way, given certain conditions, as Laplace had maintained. It does not, however, remove the problems associated with attempts to harmonise determinacy with freedom. What it does is to suggest that questions of freedom and determinacy are indissolubly linked to the restrictions of space and time. If timelessness and omnipotence are divine properties, then the conclusion would seem to be that freedom as we understand it in its myriad of contexts is a concept without meaning when applied to God. This is analogous to Paul Davies's remark that 'cause and effect are temporal concepts, and cannot be applied to a state in which time does not exist; the question ["What happened before the big bang"] is meaningless'.[3]

The concept of time has constituted an endlessly fertile topic of philosophical reflection since men and women began to ponder the meaning of their existence. The basic existential questions, Where did we come from? and Where are we going? inevitably prompt further questions about the nature of time, as St Augustine saw so clearly. Platonist that he was, Augustine contemplated the eternity, and therefore the time-lessness, of God, but he was consequently in awe of the mystery of time. He 'knows' what it is, until he has to explain it to a questioner.[4] We live our lives within the dimensions of past, present, and future. Only the present, however, actually exists.

> At any rate it is now quite clear that neither future nor past actually exists. Nor is it right to say there are three times, past, present and future. Perhaps it would be more correct to say: there are three times, a present of things past, a present of things present, a present of things future. For these three exist in the mind, and I find them nowhere else: the present of things past is memory, the present of things present is sight, the present of things future is expectation.[5]

17

Therefore I see time as in some way extended. But do I see it? Or do I only seem to see it? Thou wilt show me, O Light, O Truth.[6]

It is therefore, he concludes, by the mind that I measure time. He apostrophises his mind thus:

> In you, I say, I measure time. What I measure is the impress produced in you by things as they pass and abiding in you when they have passed: and it is present. I do not measure the things themselves whose passage produced the impress; it is the impress that I measure when I measure time. Thus either that is what time is, or I am not measuring time at all.[7]

The problem of determinism and freedom was of course much canvassed in patristic and medieval Christian theology. It poses logical, psychological, philosophical, theological, and ethical enigmas of inexhaustible fertility and complexity. In classical Thomism it forms part of a much wider system of thought about God. The Thomistic conception of God commands a good deal of respect among theologians and philosophers, even among those who find it necessary to dissent at least in part from it. The principal reason for dissent is the seemingly static and abstract character of Thomas's God. God is the being whose essence it is to exist. God is pure act, necessary and impassible. His perfections are identical with his being. He exists *a se*, that is, he has no need of anything or anyone outside himself. Because he is infinite perfection, he cannot be influenced by any being outside himself. He is impassible, that is, although he is active in the world, he is himself untouched, unaffected, unmoved by any being outside himself. God knows everything by knowing himself. He is not really related to his creatures: any relationship between a creature and God is real only on the part of the creature. This vision of God has its own magnificence, its internal consistency, and its elevated view of God's transcendence and utter difference from his creation.

Pascal was later to depict this God as the product of philosophers and one to be sedulously contrasted with the God of Pascal's own mystical experience, the God of Abraham,

Isaac, and Jesus Christ. But Pascal's God, in turn, may suggest a degree of irresponsibility in the face of reason which is also finally unsatisfactory. There is no need to traverse again the well-trodden ground of biblical God versus the God of Greek philosophy. The biblical writers did not hesitate to portray a God who felt, who could be passionate, who was, in short, actually affected by what his creatures did. Scholastic theology was able to explain away the seeming imperfections of the biblical God more or less as figures of speech; but it never dealt successfully with the *philosophical* problems thrown up by the notion of a God who, though absolutely self-sufficient, could nevertheless be a creator.

> The basic metaphysical difficulty of Thomas's view of creation is that a God who is wholly necessary is supposed to create a world which there was no necessity for him to create, and in which there is real contingency, freedom and evil and ignorance.[8]

The difficulty raised by Keith Ward here is a formidable one. A necessary being turns out on reflection to be a remarkably circumscribed being. Moreover, the God of classical theism is so self-sufficient as to give the impression of being 'the supreme case of self-centred egoism...a sort of eternal Narcissist'.[9] Fear of attributing to him any quality or disposition which would suggest need or vulnerability prevented classical theism from applying to him qualities like unfeigned and real compassion. Compassion, praiseworthy in a human being, would be an ontological defect in a God whose being and actions are necessary and totally self-orientated. The Bible, of course, has no such metaphysical scruples. The biblical God possesses and exercises a wide variety of emotions such as joy, anger, compassion, tenderness, all of which are, without unseemly mental gymnastics, strictly incompatible with the God of classical philosophy in whom such qualities must be seen as defects.

It is hardly surprising that in the twentieth century there should have been a philosophical reaction against classical theism among those for whom theism remained important. The reaction bore especially upon the notion of creation and the relationship between God and world. Three factors have played a notable part in bringing it about. (1) Liberal Protestantism and scientific biblical criticism have drawn attention to the discrepancies between hellenistic and biblical theism. (2) The flowering of atomic and sub-atomic physics is revealing a cosmos of startling and beautiful complexity which is marked above all by movement and the wonders of systemic interrelationship. (3) Advances in psychology, anthropology, and sociology have revealed complexities, ambiguities, and ambivalences in human individual makeup and social relationships. Consequently, theologians are having to reckon with a far more mysterious relationship between God and human kind than was apparent in earlier ages.

Classical theism simply seemed incompatible with each of these factors. Some of this reaction goes under the general label of 'Process thought'. It would be incorrect to suppose that Process theology and philosophy are uniform in their approach. Process thinkers share certain preoccupations, but they can differ from one another both in terminology and in points of emphasis.

The term 'Process' is intended primarily to suggest dissatisfaction with the static interpretation of reality which was characteristic of post-Socratic Greek philosophy. The protest is less against essentialism as such than against the role played by essentialism in establishing the canons of theistic orthodoxy among Christians. Both historical and existentialist thinking are a challenge to exclusive essentialism. Process thought, however, aims at more than merely challenging essentialism in Christian thinking.

John Cobb and David Griffin in their book, *Process Theology: An Introductory Exposition*, specify five concepts, or images, of God which are unacceptable to Process thinkers, including the two philosophers principally associated with the school, Alfred North Whitehead and Charles Hartshorne. These are: *God as Cosmic Moralist*, i.e. one whose primary concern it is to lay down moral rules for mankind and to keep a careful watch on men and women with a view to rewarding the good and punishing the bad; *God as the Unchanging and Passionless Absolute*, i.e. a being who has no real relationship with his creatures and is unaffected by what happens in the lives of his creatures; *God as Controlling Power*, i.e. a supreme being who determines all that happens in the world; *God as Sanctioner of the Status Quo*, i.e. one who underwrites the prevailing socio-political situation at any given moment in history; and *God as Male*, i.e. not just as one to whom male titles and pronouns are attributed, but one who is considered as the infinite embodiment of characteristics often regarded as specifically male. Cobb and Griffin signalise this God as 'totally active, controlling, and independent, and wholly lacking in receptiveness and responsiveness. Indeed, God seems to be the archetype of the dominant, inflexible, unemotional, completely independent (read "strong") male.'[10]

Many theologians sympathise with much of this indictment and tend to agree that whatever or whoever God is, he/she/it is not like *that*. Others, however, are moved to protest that we have here a popular caricature of classical theism. In the matter of constructing concepts and images of God there is no accounting for tastes. As I have already remarked, it is always theologically pertinent to ask Whose God are we dealing with? and What preoccupations is he made to embody? One can hardly deny, however, that classical essentialist theism is difficult to reconcile with the Bible's view of God, with revelation considered in its historical mode, and, today, with the universe that is being discovered by contemporary science. Some kind of reaction was to be expected, and Process thought is one such.

It postulates what it calls 'dipolarity' in the divine nature. Whitehead described the two poles as 'primordial' and 'consequent'. In his primordial nature God is 'free, complete, primordial, eternal, actually deficient and unconscious'. This primordial nature has to be given concrete expression in God's 'consequent' nature, which is 'determined, incomplete, consequent, everlasting, fully actual and conscious'. These two sides to God's nature are inseparable, according to Whitehead. They are two poles within the one being. Between them they set up a process of becoming in which pure possibilities become actualities. Charles Hartshorne describes the two poles of the divine nature as (a) the abstract essence of God and (b) his concrete actuality. Santiago Sia, a specialist in Hartshorne's thought, explains Hartshorne's conception of dipolarity:

21

Hartshorne's doctrine of a changing-immutable God is based on his doctrine of a dipolar God. God in Hartshorne's philosophy has two aspects or poles, an abstract pole and a concrete pole. Neither can be comprehended apart from the other. The abstract aspect of God is what is absolute, immutable and independent while the concrete aspect is what is relative, changing and dependent. The concrete aspect *includes* the abstract and not the other way around. Unless one appreciates this distinction and this asymmetrical relationship between the two poles or aspects, much of what Hartshorne has to say regarding God's relativity and his immutability will fail to enlighten us.[11]

In his concrete actuality, then, God is fully responsive to the world, to its random processes and especially to the freedom which the cosmos achieves in men and women. By his consequent (Whitehead) or actualised (Hartshorne) nature God enters into a real relationship with his creatures, respects their freedom, shares their feelings and emotions, and is limited by their limitations. According to both Whitehead and Hartshorne 'God is not before but *with* all creation'. Creation is not a divine afterthought. It is the nature of God to be a creator.

Christian theologians are divided in their response to Process thought. Some see it as a valuable and helpful attempt to avoid the rigidities of classical theism. Others feel either that it lacks internal consistency or that the God it presents lacks the characteristics which belong by definition to the concept 'God'. The problem is basically one of the relationship between a necessary being on the one hand and a contingent creation on the other. Some theologians are uncomfortable with the emphasis placed by Process theology on the necessity of creation. There is something ironic in the sense (often indefinable) which one has that it is human vulnerability which stirs compassion and gives a real depth to relationships which would otherwise be shallow, conventional, or determined by power and selfish interest. The irony is that we tend not to want a God who is too vulnerable or not sufficiently in control of the world which poses so many problems for us. Such a God appears to fail an essential test of divinity.

The classical theists, for all that they appear to have constructed a distant and unfeeling God, have the merit at least of leaving us with a God who really knows what he is doing and is really and masterfully in charge of the world. It almost seems as if the principle of analogical predication of human characteristics of God breaks down here. It is precisely the lack of omnipotence which makes human beings tolerable and approachable. Omnipotence is a disturbingly unattractive attribute in prospect, yet a God without it would fail the first test of deity: 'whatever he wills he does'. Is it theologically possible to reconcile omnipotence with such characteristics as compassion, wonder, aesthetic delight, humour and irony, all of which can seem to be the direct result of fallibility, finitude, and vulnerability, and to do so without recourse to dipolarity?

Perhaps the best expedient is to see Process theology less as a finished position than as a needed corrective to certain elements in classical theism. This expedient is adopted by John Macquarrie, who in his book, *In Search of Deity*, advances the concept of 'Dialectical Theism', which is designed to correct the imbalance he detects in traditional theism.[12] The word 'dialectical' applies here to the clash of ostensible opposites, like transcendence and immanence. Transcendence describes God's otherness and distance from his creation, while immanence describes his presence and his indwelling of creation. Classical theism emphasised divine transcendence, often to the point of distortion, while leaving it to the mystics to concern themselves with God's immanence. To be sure, God's ubiquity was affirmed, but it was often a curiously extrinsic ubiquity, more suggestive of the spy satellite than of a warm, interior, receptive and collaborative presence. Macquarrie applies his dialectic to a number of attributes. Here I single out one pair which is especially relevant to the theology of creation, namely, impassibility and passibility.

The doctrine that God is pure act has normally led to the conclusion that he cannot be acted upon or influenced in any way by what occurs in creation. He is sufficient to himself; he is under no necessity to create; when he does create, it is totally out of beneficence; he has all to give and nothing to receive. This may be good theistic ontology, but it almost inevitably suggests something cold, lacking in attractiveness and in the power to feel with others. Impassibility is a predominantly intellectual construct which excludes genuine vulnerability precisely because it excludes the power to feel and to be influenced. It is therefore widely felt to be in need of dialectical correction. Macquarrie is obviously aware of what he sees as the weakness of Process theology: it saves God's vulnerability, but it appears to do so at the expense of his power and of his ultimate control of all that is. In effect Macquarrie puts forward a theory of theistic *kenosis* whereby God freely chooses to create and, having done so, accepts the inevitable consequences of his creative act. This is anthropomorphic language, to be sure; but it is no less valid for that, when it is deployed in full critical awareness of what one is doing.

> In creating an existent other than himself, and in granting to that existent a measure of freedom and autonomy, God surrendered any unclouded bliss that might have belonged to him had he remained simply wrapped up in his own perfection. In creating, he consents to know the pain and frustration of the world. All this needs to be strongly asserted against the teaching of divine impassibility presented in traditional theism.[13]

Macquarrie's thesis safeguards the ontological omnipotence of God by showing how an all-powerful being can exercise his power without logical incoherence by choosing to take into himself a vulnerability which, precisely because it is freely chosen, is a strength rather than a weakness. A notable theological benefit of this kind of thinking is that it lends itself to further development in christology and soteriology. It accommodates itself to the Pauline doctrine of Christ's self-emptying. It is therefore a very important conceptual means for bringing the theology of creation into close and fruitful relationship with the theology of salvation. A creative God is thus more easily seen as a saving God. Salvation, which is all too easily construed as a kind of divine afterthought in traditional theism, here becomes of a piece with creation. To create is to prepare the way for salvation. More than that, creation envisages salvation as its gracious crown. If one appreciates this, one has no difficulty in claiming with joy that merely to be human is to be in need of being redeemed.

Redemption can thus be seen as an ideal rather than as a mere rescue operation without which we would have been better off.

'Dialectical Theism' also helps us to face, and even wrestle with, the problem of evil. Of course it does not pretend to resolve the problem, but it softens the harsh dilemma in which the problem is so often expressed: Either God *could* remove the evil but does not choose to do so, and therefore can be seen to be unloving; or, he is loving but *cannot* remove the evil and therefore can be seen to lack the power of action and hence not to be God. We shall consider this matter further in Chapter 8, but it is worth noting in the present context that at least the dilemma of having to choose between omnipotence and love can be relieved by observing (a) that God can freely allow his omnipotence to be limited by (b) 'granting a measure of freedom and autonomy' to creation and by (c) 'consenting to know the pain and frustration of the world'. For the Christian the problem of evil can never be taken in isolation from the cross of Christ; nevertheless the cross of Christ must not be deployed as an automatic answer to the scandal of innocent suffering. The fact that God in Christ shares in the horror of innocent suffering does not remove the scandal of the fact that innocent suffering actually exists in a world created by a good God; but it does prompt the believer to accept in faith and hope that the problem *has* an eschatological answer, however difficult that answer may be to discern in this life.

God's voluntary self-limitation, coupled with his active involvement in what is happening in his creation, provides the nearest thing we have to a key to the purpose of creation and to the presence of evil in that creation. It does not solve the problem, but it makes the mystery habitable by faith. The scandal remains, so that it is always possible, and often fitting, for the believer to wrestle with God, to ask in prayer why things are this way and not otherwise, and to protest about the empirical inequality of suffering and its distribution. Such protest may, however, serve also to remind us of our own human part in so many of the world's evils. Acquiescence in the will of God should never be supine, nor can it dispense the reflective believer from the hard slog of trying to make sense of it all. God does not take offence or regard us as unfaithful when we question and protest, provided that in the end we accept that some matters lie beyond the comprehension of our limited intellects. Meaning is the final grace; but meaning never dispenses with mystery. When our pilgrimage is over, we shall know God as beatifically incomprehensible and infinitely lovable, because we shall know all that we are capable of knowing as creatures. Our incapacity will remain, but it will no longer be a burden, because there will no longer be false gods to torment it.

In the meantime, however, the quest for meaning involves the reflective believer in some seemingly insoluble problems. One of the most intractable questions that face the modern theologian is the *mode* of God's action in the world. There are two groups for whom this matter appears to raise no serious difficulties: (1) those who, like the Deists, deny that God does in fact act in the world or who, like Rudolf Bultmann, make a radical distinction between personal, or existential, knowledge, on the one hand, and scientific, or empirical, knowledge on the other, and who reject out of hand the possibility of establishing any link between God and physical happenings in the world; (2) those who experience no difficulty in attributing this or that physical event to the direct intervention of God and who can be heard making some such remark as 'I was not afraid, because I knew that God would protect me', or 'if you pray hard, God will get you that job'. There are serious arguments to be brought against both these views.

The first case may be described as non-interventionist. It refuses to ascribe directly to God any influence on physical or historical events. The difficulty with this position is that, in giving the world its secular autonomy, it in effect segregates God completely from his creation. Bultmann states the matter thus: 'This is the paradox of faith, that faith "nevertheless" understands as God's action here and now an event which is completely intelligible in the natural or historical connection of events'.[14] This view reduces God's action in the world to a subjective human, albeit faith-inspired, interpretation. It leaves unanswered the question of whether God does really and objectively act in the world he is creating. A God who does not act *in some way* within his creation, apart from starting everything off, is a God who is not present in his creation; and a

God who is not present in his creation is in effect a God who has died.[15] No historical religion would be possible under such conditions. Christianity is committed to the conviction that God is present to, and acts in, the world, though the *mode* of that presence and action is extremely difficult to conceptualise or imagine.

The second case might be described as unrestrained interventionism. On the surface it appears to be impressively pious. It is prepared to find God everywhere, less as a steady, continuous, though intangible, presence than as someone who enters into or withdraws from the action as the occasion demands. Some forms of this interventionism express themselves in a preoccupation with miracles. This is not merely a 'God of the gaps' but the God of much popular piety. The theologian has no business condescending to this kind of piety. It often expresses a deep and loving faith which can put the theological sophisticate to shame. It is a subjectively effective way of maintaining human contact with God. For all its lack of sensibility and refinement, it clearly satisfies some of the deeper pre-reflective religious instincts which are often un-reached by reasonable belief. Its drawbacks, however, are formidable and possibly dangerous to thoughtful faith and hope. It leaves too many serious questions unanswered—for example, Why does God not protect Lucy, a careful driver in her mini, complete with St Christopher medal, from being run down and killed by Tom, a careless lorry-driver who hasn't said a prayer in years and who escapes the crash unhurt? Such questions are innumerable and are often met by the pious but hardly satisfactory answer that God has his own reasons for granting or refusing succour and favours.

That God *can* intervene in the physical chain of cause and effect is not at issue. That he *does* so intervene is a different matter. That he is present to, and cares for, his creation is one thing. The mode of his presence and caring is quite another. We live in a world which is autonomously, if only partially, explicable in physical terms from a scientific standpoint. As Laplace remarked, God is not a hypothesis to be invoked whenever we lack a scientific explanation for some phenomenon. To utilise God as an explanatory principle in matters which are the proper concern of science is simply to invite ultimate rejection of the divine presence and action, as one phenomenon after another is finally explained by a satisfactory theory.

Those who appeal to God's immediate physical action in the world are not necessarily appealing to God as a hypothesis in Laplace's sense. They may be saying no more than that God breaks into the sequence of cause and effect to bring about an event which would not otherwise have happened. This sort of intervention is normally described as 'miraculous'. The basic problem turns on what we mean by 'miracle'. Underlying every understanding of miracle is the pervasive question of causality. What does it mean to say that one event *causes* another? John Cobb has rightly pointed out that although scientists tend to avoid the *word* 'cause', they do not thereby avoid reference to the *idea* to which the word refers.[16]

Aristotle's classification of causality into efficient, material, formal, and final serves to alert us to the width of scope possible to the concept. It is, of course, efficient causality which has traditionally had primary importance in the minds of those who speak of God as cause. Precisely because efficient causality, when applied to God, is so difficult to reconcile with real freedom on the part of the creature, some theologians have advocated its abandonment as a theological tool. The efforts of theologians like Moltmann and Pannenberg to find alternatives to the concept of efficient causality are not finally persuasive, if only because the concept always seems to return under another name. It is better surely to accept the paradox of affirming *both* divine causality on the one hand *and* chance and freedom on the other.

A distinction between primary and secondary causes is crucial to the Thomistic position: an effect proceeds simultaneously from two causes. God as primary cause acts in such a manner as to leave untouched the autonomy of secondary causes. Curiously, post-Enlightenment liberal theology held the same view, though it expressed it in less philosophically rigorous terms. The liberals, of course, would not allow that God intervenes in the physical world without mediation. Liberal emphasis on the immanence of God in his creation schools one to find God at work in all that happens. This leaves unanswered the question of how God acts specifically in one event as distinct from another. There is fairly widespread agreement among theologians that God should not be thought of as one cause alongside others; and this conviction is already, if partially, enshrined in classical theism's distinction between primary and secondary causality. That distinction, however, does not remove the problem of how historically specific events can be attributed to God without making him a cause alongside other causes.

Karl Rahner accepts the paradox of this. 'By definition God does not seem able to be within the world.' ' If he wanted to appear in his world, he apparently would immediately cease to be himself: the ground of everything which appears but which itself does not appear.'[17] The problem as Rahner sees it is less how God acts in the world than how historically situated men and women can make contact with God while not treating him as a 'categorical object', i.e. as a being alongside other beings. In short, how can one meet, know, and love 'the ground of our being'? Rahner's answer to this question has its point of departure in 'transcendental experience'. Men and women encounter God as the horizon which encompasses and draws them on beyond every concrete experience. God is the dynamic principle in life and he manifests himself in the depth experiences which come to us from life, in the mind's quest for meaning, and in the heart's restless reaching out towards a beyond which is encountered prospectively in the experience of our subjectivity but never apprehended as a graspable object. God approaches men and women in and through created beings. Men and women are made aware of this approach through their experience of transcendence as horizon and their encounter with the depth dimension of everyday human experience. The experience of creatureliness, the 'sting of contingency', as von Hügel called it, is the felt presence of God as the absolute future of man. It cannot be objectified categorically or empirically. It is encountered, experienced, and lived as dependence, contingency, hunger for infinity. It is embodied in every element which points beyond itself to the being of God himself.

From all this Rahner draws an important conclusion about God's action in the world:

A special 'intervention' of God, therefore, can only be understood as the historical concreteness of the transcendental self-communication of God which is *already* intrinsic to the concrete world.[18]

Concrete, categorical, historically specific encounters with God are manifestations of God's already transcendental presence and action in the world. Revelation is the historical categorisation of God's primordial immanence in the world. It thematises and makes concrete what is already transcendentally present. It of necessity particularises and, because it is historical, it also relativises. It is part and parcel of the scandal offered to the mind by any particularised manifestation of what one knows to be universal.

The Word is with God from eternity, is present to all creation, but becomes incarnate at a particular time and place and as the culmination of a particular history. This particularising of the universal offended the Greek mind. We find Justin Martyr wrestling with it as he reflects on the infant Jesus and tells himself in shocked awe, 'The *Logos* cried like any other baby'. It is this 'scandalous particularity' which removes salvation from the realm of gnostic generalities and gives it a history which is co-extensive with the history of the human race. All of saving history is particularised in the person and life of Jesus the Christ, so that what he achieves in the course of one short and perfect human life may have a universal cosmic significance and reference.

Rahner therefore rightly refuses to segregate the events of salvation history from the events of universal secular history. Whereas Oscar Cullmann claims that the events of salvation history constitute a swathe cut from the course of universal history by God himself, Rahner affirms the universal scope of salvation which can be found in all history but which is given an explicit interpretation in Judaeo-Christian history. Jesus Christ is thus the interpretative centre not only of Christian history but of universal human history. Rahner's point is that if God is not experienced transcendentally in the dynamism of human existence, he will hardly be experienced in any specific historical events, since these events, however salvific in themselves, presuppose for their efficacy an experienced need for what they graciously offer. There must be a search before there can be a finding; a journey before there can be an arrival; a readiness to travel in hope through darkness before there can be a homecoming to the realm of light. There must be a hunger and thirst for the divine before the would-be believer can respond in faith to what God offers in the person, teachings, and actions of Jesus the Christ. In short, there must be an openness to the presence and action of God in creation before there can be a salvific response to what he discloses in the life, teaching, death, and resurrection of Jesus of Nazareth.

Willingness to find God present everywhere may prompt the naïve believer to find him in a constant stream of miracles, even though in being thus found God is reduced to the status of one being among others. For many modern reflective believers such naïveté is not an honest option, if by 'divine action' is meant an intervention in the physical chain of secondary causes. Such cognitive honesty does not, however, have to mean an experienced absence of God. The reflective believer too can find God everywhere, not as a being among beings, a secondary cause among secondary causes, but as a pervasive presence which under certain circumstances and in a mysterious manner becomes concretely present in historical persons, things, places, and events. Otherwise how could Christians proclaim as the most central truth of their faith that 'God was in Christ reconciling the world to himself'?

Judaeo-Christian revelation locates God's action in *this* world. It is inescapably historical, which means that it is inescapably interpretative. It operates within the limits of memory, sight, and expectation. In cosmological terms it occurs upon the third planet of a medium-sized star in one of a host of galaxies all of which belong to God's creation. It has nothing to say about what God might be doing in other parts of the universe, or in other universes, concomitant or successive. Augustine thought it otiose to enquire what God was doing before he created our universe, since before the creation of our universe there was no time. It would appear that today's cosmologists would approve both the logic and the implicit physics of Augustine's view, whatever they might think about his theology.

The point is important, and it is closely linked to the

31

question of the 'limitations' imposed on God by what is known about our universe. What God does, could do, or might have done elsewhere are speculative questions. Creation and salvation, as treated in Judaeo-Christian theology, are enacted in *this* universe, on *this* planet, Earth. The fact that the authors of our sacred books knew little or nothing about what contemporary science has discovered about our universe does not invalidate their teaching. They were not teaching as scientists but as receivers and interpreters of God's self-disclosure. We should not, however, use this circumstance as an argument against the religious and theological relevance of what contemporary science can tell us about our universe and about the processes by which it has evolved, with the consequent forming of our planet and its inhabitants. Salvation is a concrete, historical phenomenon in its beginnings. It is there to be seen, felt, enjoyed, and ministered to one another. Since it takes place in the real physical world in which we live, it has to be related to that world with all its processes, natural as well as cultural. We have no business relegating it totally to eternity. Eschatology is not an alternative to history or science. Rather, it treats of their completion and ultimate fulfilment.

We are the product of natural forces which are in fact or principle open to empirical inspection. God creates us as the culmination of a long and complex process. Being the culmination of that process does not mean that we are the exclusive focus of God's attention. The sun flames for God as well as for us. The trees grow and the flowers bloom for God as well as for us. God's loving attention to a flight of birds is not diverted by the spectacle of *homo sapiens* commuting between London and New York in Concorde. When we know ourselves to be addressed by God, it is the universe which knows in us. That knowledge allows us to appreciate Paul's vision of *all* creation groaning for salvation. This is the indispensable theological background to the ecological problems which face us today as never before.

With the arrival of man, nature evolves into culture. It is at once a marvellous and an appallingly dangerous development. There is no need to dwell on what has happened. The atomic mushroom has already become the symbol of what culture can do to nature. We now have the power to respond to God's 'let there be light' with our own 'let there be darkness'. That sickening mushroom embodies many of our counter-creative proclivities. Not merely can we reduce our habitat to cinders; we can count it as patriotism, and therefore as virtue, to be ready to do so. Moral cripples, we have embarked on a marathon race which will either finish us off or finally teach us the lesson of interdependence and mutual caring. We have a power not granted to galaxies: We can say yes or no to God's creative invitation. That awesome power is what makes salvation necessary. Emergence into freedom is emergence into a condition which the New Testament teaches us to call the new creation. Natural laws no longer suffice to bring about God's purposes. Something radically different becomes necessary when creation reaches intelligence and freedom. The garden of paradise now has its antitype, the hell of Auschwitz and all it symbolises.

With all this in mind we ponder the creative purposes of the God who made us together with the universe within which we have come to being. The pilgrimage of *homo sapiens* is a divine as well as a human adventure. One does not have to be a card-carrying Process theologian in order to recognise that God has freely accepted limitations on his absolute power when he creates our universe. And since there is biblical warrant for doing so, we can go further and claim that in willing the universe of which we are a part, God risks failure, at least in the short run. Whether it might have been different is not within our competence to say. In questions of freedom and necessity we are intellectual pygmies. We do, however, have one invaluable clue. We call God love, daring to borrow from our own human experience a quality which we know intuitively to be the most important feature of the universe and one which, because of its conceptual purity, can be applied to God with virtual univocacy. From our limited, compromised, and compromising experience we know that there is no love without risk. There seems no compelling theological reason for supposing that divine love is different in this respect at least. Creation is a divine adventure attended by risk and prompted by love.

2

Creation and Humanity

WE have already seen how and why Process theologians postulate a closer and more dynamic relationship between God and creation than classical theism was prepared to allow. We have also taken note of John Macquarrie's measured thesis of 'dialectical theism' which affirms certain limitations on God's absolute power to do whatever he wills in the world but which ascribes these limitations to a deliberate act of self-surrender and abnegation on God's part. Finally we have considered briefly the world revealed to us by science — a world with chance and unpredictability built into its processes.

Contemporary theologies have no difficulty in accepting that God's relationship with creation can be discussed only obliquely and through models. The most common model has been the artist and the work of art he or she produces. This model is open to further differentiation. The world can be seen as a painting or a piece of sculpture or a great building. There is something too plastic, too static, in this model. It appears to suggest the God of eighteenth-century Deism who produces his work of art and then goes on a holiday. The world as literary text has some possibilities, notably the fact that a text takes on a life which is independent of its author, so that the inter-pretative process at the receiver's end makes a real contri-bution to the whole communicative enterprise. There are, however, serious defects in this model too. As in the preceding case, it lends itself to deistic interpretation: an absent author hands over his text to readers who have no need of the author in order to read the text. Writing, then, is an act of alienation on the part of the author. According to Bergson it destroys immediacy, vitality, and feeling. In addition, the model of a written text lends itself to deterministic interpretation. 'It's all in the book, we only turn the pages', as a romantic novelist has put it.

The performing arts offer better possibilities. The theatre comes immediately to mind as a classic metaphor for life: 'All the world's a stage...' Actors work from a script, but they have considerable liberty of interpretation, so that it can be reasonably claimed that the script of a playwright suggests less determinism than the text of a novel. The playwright, however, does not have to be present at rehearsals or performances. This leaves the director—not perhaps the most promising model for a self-emptying God!

Were it not for the disciplined restrictions of choreography, dance would have impressive possibilities as a model for creation. Moltmann instances the Hindu myth of Shiva as cosmic dancer.[1] Dance has the advantage of suggesting movement, play, and spontaneity (at least when not heavily choreographed), all of which, when applied to God, constitute a valuable corrective to the rigidities so easily associated with classical theism. Moltmann adds a refinement: 'The special thing about this dance metaphor is the link between space and time forged by rhythm. In the rhythmic vibrances and movements of the dance-steps, space is measured in terms of time, and time in terms of space.[2] Moltmann goes on to note the appropriateness of this image when applied to 'the mystery of structures of matter'. Whatever the limitations of these literary and artistic models, one thing seems clear: the world of art provides a better model for divine creation than most other spheres of activity. Let us explore it further.

Some eighty years ago, George Tyrrell, an Irish theologian of originality and courage, gave a lecture entitled 'Divine Fecundity'.[3] The occasion of the lecture was the response of the religious press of Italy to the dreadful earthquake which occurred in southern Calabria and eastern Sicily in December, 1908, and which killed an estimated 150,000 people. Tyrrell quotes from several papers including the *Osservatore Romano* and the *Unità Cattolica*. In the latter these words occur:

Faith, Earthquakes, and Tidal waves assure us sufficiently that God exists and makes himself felt. And, if He punishes the innocent with the guilty, He does not on that account cease to be a most loving Father; for Faith tells us that the wicked are justly punished, while at the same time the innocent are rewarded. It tells us, moreover, that God punishes men that they may repent.[4]

We shall return to the mystery of suffering in Chapter 8 but the really fascinating feature of Tyrrell's response both to the Messina earthquake and to the appalling comments of papers like the *Unità Cattolica* is that he is less concerned to provide an exercise in theodicy than to reflect on the mystery of creation. There is a sombreness about his lecture which reflects the melancholy of Tennyson and Arnold but which goes much further than either in a positive direction. When Tyrrell delivered the lecture, he was suffering from Bright's disease, which was to kill him in a few months' time. He had been reading Henri Bergson, and this prompted him to give his reflections an evolutionary flavour.

Tyrrell disliked Deism intensely: an absent God seemed to him to leave a vacuum which is all too easily filled by idols, or by those who claim to speak for God and with his authority. Tyrrell makes it clear that he is presupposing a God who is 'immanent in and coincident with Nature, and not as supernatural and transcendent'.[5] (No wonder some have found in this lecture an anticipation of the dipolar God of Process thought.) 'The fly and the mouse perish that the spider and the cat may live. Yet Nature is on both sides at once.'[6] With Tennyson Tyrrell notes the wastefulness of nature: fifty thousand seeds are flung abroad where only one takes root. He notes too 'the boundless ocean of chaotic potentialities'[7]—a phrase which beautifully describes the world of sub-atomic particles most of which were undiscovered in his time.

Look at the stars: are they not the product of 'a competition between brute masses and brute forces?'[8] Organic nature, 'when forced by external pressure to develop', does so in an unpredictable manner. 'nature is not working to one end, but has just as many ends as there are living individuals'. The universe is not aimless and meaningless. 'Rather it teems with aims and meanings, although it has no *one* aim or meaning.'[9]

Tyrrell then springs a surprise by coolly reversing Tennyson's 'so careful of the type she seems,/so careless of the

36

single life'. 'As far, then, as God in Nature seems at all to care or provide, it is not for the type but for the single life...' Tyrrell is not simply proclaiming the values of individualism. Rather he is rejecting the note of calculation which seems to be implicit in the sort of masterplan which is ready to sacrifice the individual to the type. All created beings matter, and matter to God, in their own right, and not simply as steps to a future goal. They do not have to be going somewhere; they simply have to be. This 'wasteful luxuriance' strikes us as strange because of our parsimonious and calculating ways.

At this point in the lecture there occurs one of the most stimulating insights to be found anywhere in Tyrrell's writings.

> We have made our God in the image, not of the artist, but of the artisan or the man of affairs. 'What is He going to make out of it all?' Perhaps nothing; perhaps the universe is but His eternal keyboard, His eternal canvas. Perhaps each melody, each picture, may have a worth in itself apart from all the rest. Lost stars, lost species, lost civilisations, lost religions—lost as far as any influence on our own is concerned—may have justified their existence, though they have led to nothing further.[10]

Like Dostoyevsky and Horkheimer Tyrrell protests against a teleology, religious or secular, which makes earlier and more primitive forms of life mere steps to later and higher forms. 'The good of posterity is the result, not the end, of our living as well and as fully as we can.'

Catastrophes like the Messina earthquake are not sent for any purpose. They occur precisely because nature does not organise for a definite purpose. It is man who speaks of progress. (We must remember that Tyrrell is speaking at the end of a golden age before the First World War changed everything.)

> Men come to care more for 'causes' than for the persons in whose behalf they are taken up; more for the Sabbath than for man, more for the temple than for Him who dwells in it. Humanitarians may be very inhuman, and Churchmen often put the Church before Christ.[11]

Human beings must never be seen as means to a future end. We serve posterity best by making the best of the present.

Tyrrell does not see the parts subordinating themselves to the good of the whole; he sees the whole expressing itself through the parts. 'There is no arrangement of the garden, only a wilderness of glorious stars, each a world in itself.'[12] God produces an abundance of things in a burst of creative abandon. He delights in them for their own sake and not for some hypothetical contribution they may be making to some eventually ordered and culminating whole.

> On this hypothesis He cares, and cares supremely, for each individual thing as though it were a world apart. He equips it for the struggle; lives, fights, feels, devises, plans with it.... He does not will, but He cannot help, the conflict and agony. His will is plainly to minimise and abolish it if it were possible.[13]

Tyrrell in effect sees creation as an act of utter prodigality on God's part. God is infinitely fecund and this fecundity leads to inevitable problems. These he seeks to resolve or minimise, most of all the problem of suffering. He bears our griefs and carries our sufferings. Tyrrell was a sworn enemy of liberal optimism and of what he calls 'a cheap eschatology'. He was 'suspicious of prosperity and the insolence it fosters'.[14] When he proclaims the value of the individual, it is in protest against the notion of a carefully calculated plan in which the destruction of the lower is necessary for the growth of the higher. The lower has its value in itself. God loves and enjoys it for itself, not for whatever contribution it may be making to 'progress'. The dinosaurs led finally nowhere in the evolutionary scheme of things, but on Tyrrell's principles, God enjoyed them and was glorified in their truncated existence on earth.

There is a grandeur not untouched by the tragic in this view of the universe and especially of man's place in it. Man has achieved the knowledge of death which is concomitant with his calling to co-operate freely with the Creator. It is God who gives all things their value and man is called to be at one with God's will, 'to enter into and co-operate with God's struggle in the battle of life'.[15] Thus we share in God's fecundity and in all the problems it raises.

To believe that every moral and social problem admits of ultimate solution may be merely a necessary illusion to protect [man] from the apathy of despair, until such time as religion has taught him the duty of fighting for victory in the face of certain eventual defeat, and for no other reward than that of eternal life, through union with the Eternal Life.[16]

It is clear that if Tyrrell had lived longer—he died at the age of forty-eight—he would have developed some of the themes he deploys here. He actually appends a number of short points to the published lecture which he recognises as being incomplete. He would, he tells us, like to develop further an 'exoneration of God from the charge of willing, even permissively, the hurt or destruction of any individual life'. He would particularly like to attack more effectively the 'Gospel of Progress', especially when that progress is thought to reside in a collectivity. He has prescribed a 'provisional pessimism'; he would like to complement it with a study of hope. That provisional pessimism would have given his theology of hope an added dimension.

I have dwelt on this neglected essay of George Tyrrell because even today it has a freshness and relevance about it which is quite striking. It has its defects, of course. Many today would find it rather too individualistic and insufficiently political or social in its concerns. (It might, however, serve as a corrective to the totalitarian tendencies of some political theologies.) Tyrrell was deeply antipathetic to utopias. The quest for them seemed to him to threaten rightful autonomies and the smaller freedoms which give life its meaning. His theology is, in point of fact, holistic in its approach to nature and anti-teleological where teleology appears willing to sacrifice individuals and species to the alleged demands of a grand design. Tyrrell's God is a generous not a calculating God, delighting in the profusion of things which he brings into being. Tyrrell wastes no time on the God of the religious press of his time—a God who, on the evidence of the religious press's response to the Messina earthquake, is mean, spiteful and vindictive. Instead Tyrrell is prepared to find a tragic nobility about the condition which results from the very fecundity of God's creative energies.

God, then, should be thought of as an artist rather than as a technician or a manager. Tyrrell sees the Creator standing before the canvas or seated at the keyboard. It is the latter image which lends itself to more fruitful development. As David Jasper suggested in a recent lecture, the images promoted by the models of artist/work of art, or author/text are open to attack from deconstructionists who wish to free the text from its origins so that it may live its own life in constantly renewed freedom from its authorial origins. This degree of semantic autonomy constitutes an assault on causality and would, if true, render both literary and artistic models useless as a means of portraying creation. What we need is a model which *both* respects the autonomy of the text or work of art *and* recognises the indispensable *and continuing* role played by the author or artist. I think that such a model can be found in the second of Tyrrell's images, namely, the musician at the keyboard. Tyrrell was not musically inclined or endowed, and so he leaves his image undeveloped. Let us therefore develop it a little.

Suppose we envisage an organist, not performing a finished piece, but extemporising on a theme. The theme is the *given*, the principle of continuity and identity, the *telos* which gives overall coherence together with considerable freedom in the attaining of it. The continuing act of extemporisation is the principle of development, novelty, unpredictability. The organist keeps the theme before her but does not *foresee* where the extemporising spirit will lead her. Each moment, each stage in the extemporising process, offers new possibilities which were originally unforeseen; a new delight is born with each realised possibility. God seated at the organ of the universe is the supreme musical genius who is in final 'control' of the whole enterprise but whose skill and artistry are engaged, not at the beginning only, like the composer who gives the performer a completed score (with limited freedom of inter-pretation), but rather also at the challenge of each moment, when, for example, a new development suggests a modulation in key and perhaps a fresh counter-melody or registration, or any of the many devices open to a truly great musician. A gifted extemporiser is not afraid of false turns or initiatives which in the event lead nowhere. She or he delights in them momentarily before returning to the exigencies of the original theme.

Of course the analogy has its limitations. It is designed to express the Creator's rather than the creature's freedom of action. But it does suggest a mode of action which has purpose but which respects freedom and allows for deviation. It recognises the causal link between God and the world, but it also goes some way to meeting Moltmann's objection against invoking the concept of causality in connection with creation. Moltmann holds that 'the causality approach allows us to conceive only of the transcendence of the divine *causa prima* which, since it is divine, must also be *causa sui*'.[17] Leaving aside the logical problems inherent in the concept of *causa sui*, one notes Moltmann's claim that 'creating the world is something different from causing it'. Moltmann appears to believe that the invocation of causality inevitably suggests a deistic relationship between God and world and moreover appears to start from 'an antithesis between God and world'. 'Causality' in this way of looking at things, is a 'one-sided' word matched by the equally one-sided word 'transcendence'. 'Creation', on the other hand, is for Moltmann a word suggesting mutuality matched by the equally warm word 'immanence', which speaks of concerned involvement. However arbitrary this usage may seem, it has the merit of drawing attention to the truth that God not merely makes the world, he is present in it. Tyrrell's analogy of the cosmic organist preserves more of the concept of causality than Moltmann might approve, but it at least avoids the cold detachment of of the cosmic policeman, to say nothing of the sadistic schoolmaster as presented by the *Unità Cattolica*. We need a number of models and images to represent divine action to ourselves, and each has its limitations as well as its possibilities.

Moltmann's wish 'to eliminate the causality from the doctrine of creation' is hardly feasible; but his warning that undue emphasis on divine transcendence damages the doctrine of creation is important, especially when we are seeking to discover firm theological roots for the exercise of ecological responsibility.

Judaeo-Christianity has its roots in a prophetically inspired reaction against nature religions which discerned the divine in natural processes such as the growth of crops and which worshipped the divine through fertility cults. Israel with difficulty achieved faith in a God who is distinct from his creation. Eventually, however, it could afford to mock other peoples who worshipped idols, *baalim*, and false gods. Israel's God is invisible, majestic, and utterly distinct from the work of his hands. Christianity inherited this austere and chaste image of God. A price, however, has had to be paid for a dialectically unmodified doctrine of divine transcendence. Nature was cut adrift from the sacred scheme of things and thus, through being radically secularised, natural processes ceased to suggest the numinous and the mysterious, unless of course they were spectacular and could be interpreted as a divine warning or punishment. God's presence was now to be found in history rather than in nature; in temple, church, word and sacrament, rather than in trees, brooks, seasonal rhythms, and high places. Israel's theology was centred upon a God who accredited himself to a people rather than to a land. Indeed the land was given to the people to be subdued. For centuries to come this attitude would have few ecological repercussions. If a field ceased to produce crops, it was, *faute de mieux*, left fallow until it recovered its fertility. Man co-operated with nature, not out of ecological virtue, but because there was no alternative available to him.

The rise of science and technology, made possible by the secularisation of nature, brought about a new situation which in a sense politicised knowledge. This is reflected in Francis Bacon's remark that knowledge is power and in his disturbingly violent language about how man should dominate nature. Science in its early years had to operate with a primitive technology, but this situation changed when the Industrial Revolution enhanced the role of capital in social relationships. From this point on evolution initiated another of its periodical leaps, only this time the leap was cultural rather than natural. Rivers were supplemented by canals. Railways carved their way into the countryside. Tools became ever more sophisticated; and since tools are merely extensions of their human users, they quickly became instruments for the production of capital, often, in the process, adulterating nature and dehumanising their users.

When evolution occurs in culture rather than in nature, an entirely new set of problems arises. It is inevitable that we should want to progress from primitive tools to ever more efficient machines, just as millions of years ago our ancestors left the forests, learned to stand up, lost their hairy bodies and began to communicate through language. Language endowed our ancestors with a new and disturbing autonomy. Natural evolution is not planned by the creatures who are affected by it. It simply happens; and its happening is the immediate product of random forces. Human beings, however, are in charge of their own cultural evolution and they do not exercise nature's long-scale and unhurrying approach to change. Nature is immune to the profit motive which dictates that if one machine can match the output of ten men or women, then you opt for the machine.

Nature meets her challenges and solves her evolutionary problems in her own good time. If you leave the water for dry land, you will need legs instead of fins; and, as long as you survive and are prepared to wait a few million years, you will get them. A nineteenth-century coal baron does not have that sort of patience. Cultural evolution, in short, has to reckon with spiritual problems unknown to natural evolution; and it is human values which make the difference. If these human values are corrupted by greed and lust for power, culture, instead of being an extension of nature, will take on a life of its own divorced from its natural matrix. In theological language sin enters creation through culture. Nature becomes the victim of culture when man, divided within himself, imposes his divisive and domineering proclivities upon nature at large. This, however, is to anticipate the subject-matter of later chapters.

Let us return to a consideration of the theological foundations for a sound approach to ecology. Moltmann's prescription is straightforward. 'Interpreting the world as God's creation means precisely *not* viewing it as the world of human beings, and taking possession of it accordingly.'[18] One immediately appreciates and applauds what he intends to say: Man has to learn again how to live in harmony with nature because (a) man is part of nature; (b) God has given men and women the world as a trust; and (c) abusing nature offends against God's sovereign intentions and ultimately damages men and women themselves. Where Moltmann may be challenged, however, is on his stratagem of opposing anthropocentrism to theocentrism. He states bluntly that the view that 'the human being is the crown of creation' is not, as is often claimed, a biblical doctrine. Now, it is perfectly true that 'Even without human beings, the heavens declare the glory of God', but the point of the declaration is surely that there should be someone there to perceive and worship that glory. To the best of our knowledge, at least at present, it is only in men and women that the universe becomes aware that its existence shows forth the glory of God. If by anthropocentrism is meant looking at the universe from a human perspective, then it is not something we choose; it is imposed on us by our condition. Only when anthropocentrism leads to exclusivism and abuse or neglect of other species, together with their and our physical environment, does it become an evil.

A sound response to the ecological problems of today does not entail a devaluation of what it means to be human. On the contrary it entails a deeper appreciation of values which are truly human. Among those values is, or ought to be, a regard for the autonomy of non-human creation and a readiness to respect its mysterious processes, especially its systemic relationships. Genuine ecological concern is a *spiritual* condition and is not to be confused with cunning self-interest of the kind that recognises the diminishing returns, say, of over-fishing the seas or of chemically dependent farming. In Ireland we are often told that if we pollute our rivers, plunder our bogs, and generally fail to care for the environment, tourists will fail to come and the loss to the economy will be heavy. This is undoubtedly true, but it is not a spiritual motive for care of the environment. Enlightened self-interest recognises that in many instances ecological prudence is also economic prudence. Such self-interest is not to be spurned, but neither is it to be counted as high virtue. Something deeper is needed. Reductionism, endemic in post-Cartesian science, has to give way to holistic attitudes which are concerned not so much with individual entities or elements as with the *whole* to which they belong. Nature studied macroscopically reveals networks of relationships in which what happens to one element or species intimately affects other elements or species, so much so that, as Fritjov Capra remarks, when a system breaks down it hardly matters which element was the original cause of the breakdown.[19] Capra goes on to observe that 'Even predator-prey relationships that are destructive for the immediate prey are generally beneficient for both species.'[20] Thus does God hunt with the hound and run with the hare. Ecological wisdom often depends on willingness to take the long view and not to seek the quick profit. In this it may be fruitfully seen as a reflection of God's self-emptying in the creative process itself. Men and women are called to share with God in creation (since creation is now cultural as well as natural); but just as God makes certain renunciations in deciding to create, so must men and women in deciding to co-operate. We are coming to realise that ecological care costs, and that willingness to pay the price is part of the business of being human in the fullest sense.

Holistic or systemic thinking can point us in the direction of justice and human rights. It has always been Christian doctrine that we are members one of another (1 Cor. 12:12-13). Today, however, the world-wide implications of that doctrine are impossible to ignore with spiritual or moral impunity. Much has been, and is being, written on this, and I shall not add to it here except to observe that every phase of creation, from sub-atomic particle to human politics and economics, is systemic and holistic in its implications if not in its actual make-up. When Jesus called love his pre-emptive commandment, he was not simply imposing a moral imperative more or less arbitrarily; he was reflecting the very structure of creation. Spiritual health, no less than bodily health, is holistic, and it is more than co-incidental that 'holism' and 'holiness' are etymo-logically related.

Most of our spiritual and moral failures are the product of our unwillingness to appreciate and live up to the glory of being human, that is, to the glory of having evolved within nature to a point where we can hear and respond to God's address and declaration of love. This response is possible only to beings who have reached a certain pitch of intelligence characterised by self-awareness, freedom, and the power to love. As Augustine pointed out, we are lovable because we are loved. In *homo sapiens* God has created a being who is free to say yes or no. This awesome freedom is not shared by the other inhabitants of our planet, and from it flow our responsibilities towards God, our fellows, and the rest of creation. For better or for worse we control our planet, with the result that other living species are at our mercy. Our ecological responsibilities stem from our humanity, and so it might be appropriate to make *noblesse oblige* the motto of the ecological movement.

Precisely because we possess an autonomy not granted to other species on our planet, we need to exercise a proper humility not merely towards God but also towards the products of other and earlier evolutionary strains. Nothing is gained by the false humility of pretending that we are no more than just another species upon the face of the earth. We are where we are in the evolutionary scale, and it is our duty to use the power which God, through evolution, has bestowed upon us as a species for the good of all nature, animate and inanimate. We can reflect profitably on the sheer contingency of the circumstances which have led to our presence on the third planet of an unremarkable star in an ordinary galaxy. From the first microsecond of the Big Bang down to the beginnings of human history, if matters had taken only a slightly different course, we should not be here. This is a salutary reflection and one which we should not try to make bearable by the thought that God has secured it all in advance. Whatever theory of divine providence we may hold, we ought not to appeal to it as a way of evading the *angst* inspired by the spectre of non-being. Such *angst* is an important element in cosmic humility, just as it is a prerequisite for religious faith. Whatever means God may use to govern the physical world, his governance cannot be legitimately invoked as an *a priori* argument against the presence in nature of chance and contingency.

The 'anthropic principle' in contemporary cosmology considers the relationship between the evolving universe and the emergence of *homo sapiens*. The theories advanced by cosmologists are highly technical, involving as they do a knowledge of advanced mathematics and an appreciation of quantum theory and the new physics. A non-scientist, and especially a non-mathematician, approaches them at his peril.

46

Yet they belong to the actuality within which Christian faith must be lived and thought about. The principle is stated by one of its original articulators, Brandon Carter: 'The universe must be such as to admit conscious beings in it at some stage'.[21] The anthropic principle has different forms, but common to all of them is the observation that the emergence of life on earth depended on finely tuned processes extending back to the Big Bang itself.

If the universe were expanding at a greater or less speed than it actually is, the conditions for life would not have come about. Can we therefore conclude that the universe has been designed *so that* intelligent life would be not merely possible but would actually occur? Theologians can be expected to reply affirmatively, but in doing so they need to recognise the *frisson* that such a suggestion can cause in the scientific breast. (It might be compared to that caused in the believer's breast by any suggestion of blasphemy.) To make man the measure of cosmic evolution is to raise the question of teleology, i.e. the notion that there is finality and purpose behind natural processes, and thus to import into scientific thinking the suggestion of a supra-natural influence (the scientific equivalent of blasphemy). The need to avoid such an hypothesis has led to some fascinating speculations which ought to interest the theologian, if only because they may act as a warning against any facile appeal to the new physics for help in constructing a new religious apologetics. Take, for example, the Big Bang theory which now commands the near unanimous support of cosmologists. There may be a temptation for theologians to identify the Big Bang with the initial creative moment of the Genesis myth. Such an identification would, however, be a great theological and tactical mistake, induced mainly by the ambiguity which now attaches to the word 'creation'. The theological reference of the word 'creation' is semantically different from the scientific reference. The theological reference is about the relationship between God and all that is not God. The scientific reference is about the beginning of the physical universe in which we live. The *theological* doctrine of creation, when properly understood, does not depend on any *physical* theory of the universe.

Theologians should, however, note that some

contemporary cosmologists are prepared to speculate on the possible existence of parallel and/or successive universes, possibly infinite in number and with physical laws different from ours. They consider it an open question whether there is life elsewhere in our actual universe. It would be as theologically inadvisable to dismiss these theories as 'only theories' (a foolish phrase at the best of times), or, worse, as 'science fiction', as it would be to try to annexe any of them for apologetical purposes.

Take, for example, the possibility of intelligent life elsewhere in the universe, or for that matter in any other universe, parallel or successive. It is a perfectly valid theological exercise to ask how the discovery of such extra-terrestrial life would affect one's Christian beliefs. A christology or soteriology which could not survive such an exercise—and most kinds of biblical or ecclesiastical fundamentalism probably could not—would be seriously defective. Judaeo-Christian teaching on revelation does not, and in its formative stage could not, deal with the speculative hypotheses thrown up by relativity and quantum theory. The formative documents of Judaeo-Christian theology did not, and could not, deal with the Copernican and Newtonian, not to speak of Einsteinian and quantum, paradigms for understanding the world. To take stock of this is merely to recognise that religious doctrine, even the most central and normative, is always culturally controlled and limited.

It is perfectly legitimate to ponder the theological implications of intelligent life elsewhere in our universe or in some other undisclosed or undiscoverable universe. Such life is at least possible in principle. What would its demonstrated existence mean for a christology and soteriology forged in an age which never dreamed of such a possibility but which had no difficulty envisaging angels and devils? There are those who would impatiently dismiss this kind of question as inept or frivolous. Such dismissal may be evidence less of hard-nosed realism than of a seriously impaired ability to employ the imagination in the service of theological exploration. The sort of universe now being shown to us by cosmologists demands an imaginatively flexible response from theologians. In point of fact it raises important anthropological questions, and these questions in turn have a significant bearing on the theology of creation and salvation. The Psalmist has asked 'What is man that you are mindful of him? (Ps. 8:4) The question, addressed to God, need not and should not be taken as exclusively anthropocentric. Jesus himself spoke of God's care for all of creation, including the lilies of the field and the birds of the air (Mt. 6:26-33). Any sound contemporary theology of creation needs to consider man's place in nature even, and especially, when it operates from a strong anthropocentric base. The theologian clearly has to give close and frequent attention to the question, What does it mean to be human? I do not believe that the question can be comprehensively answered by use only of the transcendental method, which pays little if any attention to the biological features of our evolved humanity.

Karl Rahner is a master of the transcendental approach to God, but he is startlingly insouciant about what Theodosius Dobzhansky has called 'the biology of ultimate concern'. Rahner, in his *Foundations of Christian Faith*, draws some stark conclusions from his reflections on divine transcendence.

> Insofar as the world, established by God in his freedom, does indeed have its origin in him, but not in the way in which God possesses himself, it really is not God.

From this unexceptionable premise Rahner goes on to draw conclusions which cry out for, but do not receive, any further qualification.

> It is seen correctly, therefore, not as 'holy nature', but as the material for the creative power of man. Man experiences his creatureliness and encounters God in it, not so much in nature, in its stolid and unfeeling finiteness, but in himself and in the world only as known by him and as freely administered in the unlimited openness of his own spirit.[22]

Rahner goes on to concede that 'This observation, of course, does not give a complete description of the proper relationship between man and "nature" as his environment', but he refuses to take the matter further. This refusal does a disservice to the magnificent transcendental vision which Rahner opens out before his readers.

We are called to a higher form of life through the instrumentality of our intelligence and freedom. In this respect we are indeed different from our animal forebears. But we also have much in common with them. The DNA structure of the higher primates is remarkably similar to that of *homo sapiens*. The physical similarities between them and us are obvious to any observer who is not afraid to make the comparison. The difference is equally obvious to any observer who is not intent on reducing human spirituality to a purely chemical development. Something happened over a long space of time which led to the emergence of a new species. That something is in principle open to scientific investigation and explanation—but not in its totality. Something enormously significant also happened which escapes purely scientific detection and which is properly the object of Rahnerian transcendental analysis. It is a wise man or woman who recognises that the empirically observable and the spiritually significant are not two mutually exclusive processes. The believer who denies or dismisses as irrelevant the physical processes which made us humans what we are is as crass as the positivist who refuses to recognise their spiritual implications.

Christian theology has traditionally treated of those implications in terms of soul and body. The doctrine of the human soul is a symbolic representation of human spirituality. In academic terms it owes a great deal to Greek, and especially to Platonist, philosophy. *Some* language was needed for the purpose of designating the spiritual principle in men and women. It so happened that many of the Christian Church's earliest theologians were strongly influenced by Greek philosophy, and they drew on that philosophy in order to articulate their beliefs about what it means to be a human and, precisely as human, to be addressed by God. The trouble is that they were so impressed by the phenomenon of human spirituality that they almost inevitably tended to undervalue the physical matrix of that spirituality. They seized on the doctrine of the spiritual soul and discovered in it the principle which seemed to them to make men and women Godlike. From this point on it was the soul which became the principle of spirituality, the instrument and object of salvation, and the repository of God's self-disclosure. Thus the dualism of soul and body became endemic in Christian self-understanding. In its more extreme form this dualism developed into a positive hostility towards both the body and physicality in general. It made it possible to envisage a disembodied soul—a sort of reification of the human spiritual principle which was torn away from its physical and corporeal matrix. One spoke of 'saving one's soul'. A symbol had become an autonomous object in its own right, and a spirituality was developed to cater for the needs of this object. It became impossible to discuss spirituality except in terms of the soul.

Significant social consequences followed from an exaggerated dualism of soul and body. The spiritual doctrine of *fuga mundi*, flight from the world, was a natural consequence of playing down the God-given realities of bodily existence. The dangers of this dualism were, however, appreciated by the early teachers of Christian belief. Gnostic dualism threatened the doctrine of Christ's human nature. In its most extreme form, called docetism, the idea was propagated that Jesus did not have a real human body but only *appeared* to do so. The early manifestation of this perverse christology alerted Christian thinkers to the dangers of exaggerated spiritualism in general. Human existence is embodied existence. Something like an uneasy truce was therefore struck between the demands of corporeal and spiritual existence. Christian Neoplatonism continued to regard the body as an encumbrance, but nonetheless a God-willed encumbrance within which salvation was to be attained.

We probably underestimate the continuing effects of this body/soul dualism. The term 'soul' is still employed as a description of the higher, religiously orientated, dimension of being human. There has, to be sure, been a reaction against it in much contemporary Christian theology and spirituality; but old habits of thought die hard. It is not so long since Catholic theology taught that one might speak of the evolution of the body but not of the evolution of the soul. It is instructive to examine this stratagem for reconciling traditional Christian doctrine with the accepted findings of science. It is almost as if Christian theologians were saying to the scientific anthropologist 'You can have the body; we'll hold on to the soul'. This attitude is a throwback to the old hellenistic dualism. In effect it refuses to recognise the potential spirituality of physical evolution. It likes to represent the parents of a child as providing its body while God intervenes to infuse a soul not merely at the supposed moment of hominisation but also at the moment of conception of all subsequent human beings. The image of a kind of divinely operated assembly-line does little justice or respect to the dignity of a Creator who has called his creatures to co-operation with him in the work of continuing creation.

Body/soul language is one way of expressing the irreducibly spiritual principle in man. It is, however, so open to distortion and so vulnerable to parody (e.g. Gilbert Ryle's description of the soul as the 'ghost in the machine') that a good case can be made for avoiding it altogether today.

Ryle's parody is aimed at Descartes rather than at Plato. René Descartes, having cleared the epistemological screen of all inherited ideas, and using a type of philosophical investigation based on methodical doubt and the indisputable attainment of indisputable certainties, arrived at some basic and, he claimed, indisputable truths. These were (a) the existence of God; (b) the existence of mind and body as distinct substances and (c) the definition of matter as extension. When Descartes proclaimed the most basic investigative principle as *cogito ergo sum* ('I think therefore I am') he understood the 'I' to be his soul, which he sharply distinguished from his body: 'I am in very truth different from my body and can exist without it'. He never devised a convincing explanation of how soul and body interacted with one another (he advanced the idea that the pineal gland was the connecting link). This hard and fast segregation of mind from extension, by someone for whom mathematics was the paradigm of organised mental activity, reinforced the tendency already strongly present in Christian thought to underrate the sheer bodiliness of human existence. With Descartes, however, the body becomes a machine inhabited by a soul (he favoured the analogy of the clock). In this unequal partnership the soul is the principle of subjectivity and the body becomes the means by which the conscious subject makes contact with the 'objective' world. As Jürgen Moltmann puts it, Descartes 'translates the old body-soul dualism into the modern subject-object dichotomy'.[23] In so far as Cartesianism underwrote the disposition, already present in Christian thought, to attribute 'spirituality' to the disembodied soul, it also underwrote the doctrine that the human soul was the object of a *special* act of divine creation.

The doctrine of 'the particular creation of the human soul' can, however, be fully safeguarded by a different model and a different form of words. What has to be safeguarded is the doctrine that something altogether special happens when evolution issues in *homo sapiens* (perhaps it *begins* to happen even earlier in *homo erectus* and *homo habilis*). God relates himself to creation in a different way when man appears on the scene, and this new relationship is one in which men and women are called to be conscious collaborators with God. Something radically new happens to nature with the arrival of *homo sapiens*. One can call this 'the special creation of the human soul'. and this was in fact the mode of speech used by, for example, Pope Pius XII in his encyclical *Humani Generis* (1950): 'The Catholic faith obliges us to hold firmly that souls are immediately created by God'.[24] This doctrine is commonly called 'creationism' to distinguish it from 'generationism', i.e., the notion that the soul is inherited directly from one's parents. The doctrine of 'creationism' was never defined; and there is no intrinsically compelling reason for holding that it is an indispensable model for treating of human creation.[25]

By way of conclusion it may be helpful to list some points which summarise the main elements in the Christian doctrine and theology of creation. The doctrine took shape against certain contexts, and this limitation should be kept constantly in mind, especially if one is appealing to specific Church documents:

(1) Everything which is not God owes its existence to God. This includes all that is known to us actually or in principle, i.e., the universe in which we live. It may also include other realms of being unknown to us or known only in mythological form. Angelology and demonology would be a case in point.

(2) Created beings are *distinct* from God, though they may be, and in man have been, given a destiny which makes them more God-like. The Christian mystical tradition allows one to speak of 'sharing in God's being' or of 'deification'. Later

53

theologians speak of 'panentheism'—an indwelling of God in men and women and they in him. Both these mystical doctrines, when properly understood and deployed, safeguard divine transcendence, i.e. God's ontological distinctness from created being.

(3) All creation is good. This is stated (a) in opposition to gnostic dualism in which spirit (or soul) is seen as good and matter (including the body) is seen as evil; and (b) in spite of the manifest existence of evil, moral and physical, in the created world.

(4) The doctrine of creation implies no specific cosmological theory such as the Big Bang. Our universe is created, but not necessarily uniquely so. Christian revelation is concerned with the world we actually know and live in.

(5) Creation refers not merely to an *initial* moment but to a continuing relationship. It *may* be conceptually distinguished from (a) preservative action (ontological) and (b) providential governance (grace and the supernatural), but these distinctions should not be allowed to obscure the overall unity of divine presence and action in the world.

(6) The theological designation of creatureliness is primarily a statement about nature's relationship to God. In man it entails the privilege and duty of worship, adoration, gratitude, and that willing and loving acceptance of obligation (especially to the neighbour) which is the hall-mark of true morality.

(7) Although nature (in its ontological reference) is to be distinguished from grace, the distinction should be deployed in such a way as to avoid the kind of supernaturalism which sunders grace from its proper setting in nature and history. Although grace may be treated as a conceptual abstraction, it is concretely encountered in graced persons, events, and things. Sound sacramental theology depends on a recognition of graced creation. One effective and biblically sanctioned way of keeping nature and grace in fruitful interrelationship is the model of primordial and new creation.

(8) The doctrines of creation and redemption should be developed *together* and in a way which recognises the feedback of one into the other. Salvation is not an afterthought: it is implicit in the creation of a truly free being. When the created universe arrives at hominisation, it becomes an arena for salvation.

(9) The doctrine of creation, when considered historically, is both a negation of doctrines such as Gnosticism and pantheism, on the one hand, and, on the other, the expression of 'an awe that is appropriate to grace, to that which is given for the well-being of the recipient and is neither earned by the recipient nor compelled by the circumstances of the giver'.[26]

Matter, Spirit and Creation

MOST religions, and all historically based ones, concern themselves with spirit and matter and particularly with the
relationship between them. All religions can be expected to
give primacy to the spiritual, but they may differ on how they
understand and define the spiritual. Some will define it in such
a way as to play it off against tangible and mundane reality. In
this way of thinking, the physical world revealed by the senses
will be an inferior, if not actually an evil, world. It will be a
world from which one prays and strives to be rescued. Religion
of this kind will have little time for a theology of creation.
Having proclaimed that God has made us for himself, it will
inspire us to sigh to be released from 'this vale of tears' in order
to be with him and thus achieve our spiritual destiny.

I am far from ridiculing or rejecting this attitude out of
hand. It has sustained generations of victims for whom this
world was rendered insupportable by political and social oppression. Even in more conventional and pietistic form it has
comforted the distressed, and drawn from John Sebastian Bach
some of his finest music. Nevertheless it has its dangers, not
least of which are artificiality and unintended insincerity.
There is something unreal about a rudely healthy and well-fed
congregation singing 'Come sweet death', even to the music of
Bach. From the perspective suggested by these sentiments,
planet earth will inevitably appear as a penal colony unworthy
of more than glancing, and usually oppressively moralistic,
attention. The resulting theology of creation will be cursory
and totally overshadowed by the theology of salvation.

There is in orthodox Christian tradition a persistent seam of
distaste for material reality. 'Materialism' is a word that falls
easily and frequently from the lips of some preachers. It is a

weasel-word, which lends itself to conventional and often superficial moralising. What the preacher presumably wishes to condemn, when he uses the word 'materialism', is the lack of a spiritual dimension, a selfish preoccupation with one's own comfort, and an unwillingness to put oneself out in any way for the sake of others. Of course material things can absorb our attention to the detriment of spiritual well-being. No Christian remembering the gloss placed by the early Church on Jesus' parable of ths sower could plausibly deny that the cares of the world can choke the life of the spirit. It is not the materiality of material things which makes them a threat to the life of the spirit; it is the dispositions of the person who uses them, who is preoccupied with them, and who makes of them an extension of his or her own self-absorption. 'Materialism' is on the whole a misguided word to describe all this, because it easily conveys the impression that matter, as opposed to spirit, is itself bad.

I make these brief comments from the outset because it is a basic contention of this book that a sound Christian theology and spirituality must accept without reserve the God-given reality of physical and historical existence as the theatre within which we human beings are called upon to respond to God's gracious invitation to us to share in his life and to cooperate in the purposes which underlie his creation, of which we are part. It is human beings who sin, not the material world. We can, however, leave sin for later discussion and turn here to some attitudes which have shaped, or have attempted to shape, Christian consciousness in regard to creation.

Early Christianity had to contend with a powerful school of spirituality which proved attractive to many and which was opposed by several of the early Church Fathers such as Irenaeus and Ignatius of Antioch. This was Gnosticism. The term comes from the Greek word, *gnosis*, meaning knowledge. It was, however, used in a specialised sense by the Gnostics. They intended it to refer to the knowledge acquired and cultivated by the religious *cognoscenti*, i.e. those 'in the know' about what was happening in the universe and about how salvation was to be sought therefrom. It is important in our present context to notice that Gnosticism was a religion greatly taken up with man's sense of alienation in the universe and with his efforts to escape from the dark forces which he feels are oppressing him. The Gnostics expressed their theology of creation and redemption in a variety of strange, even bizarre, myths.

These myths shared a common pool of basic convictions which may be listed as follows: (1) a profound dualism between the material world (darkness) and the spiritual world (light); (2) a sharp distinction between the real, true, and transcendent God, on the one hand, and, on the other, an inferior deity who was responsible for the creation of the material universe and who was commonly identified with the God of the Old Testament; (3) the conviction that man has within him a spiritual core, a spark of heavenly light which makes him yearn for salvation and therefore for escape from a radically evil material creation; (4) a persuasion that the salvific process by which man ascends to his origin in the realm of the true God is *gnosis*, the privileged knowledge that makes him aware of his fallen state; and (5) the general awareness of a saviour, or saviours, descending from the realm of light down through layers of increasing materiality until they reach, and seek to help, man who is trapped in the created world.

Gnosticism employed the mythical imagery of warfare. The supreme God is a figure of light and is at war with the inferior god (or Demiurge) who through material creation has brought about a realm of darkness. Primal man, originally a spirit of light, fell under the power of the realm of darkness, but he preserved within himself certain vestiges of the light which marked his original condition. God sends his 'image', his son, as a redeemer whose task it is to awaken man to his condition and to inspire him to cultivate *gnosis* and thereby to ascend to his heavenly home.

There is now general consensus among scholars that Gnosticism was not simply an aberration within Christianity but had origins which were separate from those of Christianity, though in the course of time each religion influenced the other. Christians like Clement of Alexandria and Origen were quite willing to describe themselves as 'Gnostics', by which they implied that Gnosticism could be expressed in a form which was in keeping with Christian orthodoxy. As Werner Jaeger has pointed out, pagan

Gnosticism was a 'dangerous rival of Christianity'.[1] Clement and Origen were well aware of the Gnostic threat to Christian orthodoxy, but they also appreciated what it was that made 'gnosis' so attractive to the educated classes with a leaning towards the mystical properties of a knowledge which promised salvation from the oppressive forces at work in the material world. Both Origen and Clement claimed to find their Christian version of gnosis in the Scriptures. Theirs was an exercise in interpretation designed to commend Christianity to those whom Friedrich Schleiermacher was later to describe as its 'cultured despisers'. Origen's commentary on John's Gospel certainly had this aim and contains 'some speculative flights, no doubt designed to show... that orthodoxy is not duller than heresy'.[2]

The modern reader may wonder about the relevance of all this to contemporary Christian life. Has not the world of apocalyptic speculations and the secret rituals of the mystery religions passed into history? Maybe; maybe not. There are some elements in eccentric religious thought and practice which never finally die and which make surprising reappearances in different forms. Taking the word 'gnostic' in its broadest sense, we may single out certain characteristics which have continuing relevance and against which the Christian Church has set its face. It may help to identify them:

(1) Christian history provides numerous examples of the sort of élitism which was characteristic of classical Gnosticism and which sees the ways of salvation as essentially secret and known only to a chosen few. Christian orthodoxy has responded to the élitism with its doctrine of salvation effected and offered for *all* men and women by Jesus Christ. The Christian faith can never with impunity allow itself to be reduced to the status of a clique of those to whom God has revealed the secrets of salvation. Salvation is universal in its scope and intent, and it is the duty and vocation of the Church to make this known to all humankind.

(2) The Gnostics saw salvation as primarily a matter of knowledge. The Church responded with the biblical doctrine that salvation is a matter of faith issuing in loving action performed under the influence of grace.

(3) The Gnostics regarded material existence as radically evil.

59

The Church replied with an affirmation of the essential good-ness of creation in spite of the distortions and disorientation brought about by sin. Echoes of Gnostic dualism can be heard at various times in the history of Christian theology and spirituality. Any condemnation of the body or of bodily exis-tence can be fairly described as gnostic (in the broad sense of the word).

(4) By designating physical creation as the work of a demonic principle, the Gnostics ruled out all possibility either of a theology of creation or of a soteriology which would be related to the physical world. Salvation begins and ends in the mind, though the Manichees in the fourth and fifth centuries would prescribe an ascetic life for those who took the oath which made them inner members of the sect.

(5) The Gnostics withdrew the whole enterprise of salvation from the realms of physical nature and human history. The Church responded with a doctrine of salvation history. Redemption is effected within the empirically observable events of human history, specifically and finally by the Word of God who became a man in order to effect it. There is much dis-cussion today about the relationship between salvation history and universal (secular) history, but there is extensive agree-ment that salvation cannot be properly understood apart from historical events. To seek to escape history is to seek to escape the divinely willed means of salvation. Oscar Cullmann, stung by Rudolf Bultmann's attack on him for so tying salvation to history that, according to Bultmann, he was placing the wrong stumbling-block before believers and would-be believers, retorted:

> It is not by accident that Docetism [the heresy which stated that Christ only appeared to have a human body] is the primal heresy of ancient Christianity, the only one which we can distinctly see to be attacked by the New Testament. Up to the present day it emerges again and again wherever the event is underestimated in favour of the *kerygma*.[3]

Cullmann may have been less than fair to Bultmann here, but he was affirming in very firm language what Gerhard Kittel had called 'the scandalous particularity' of Christian faith.

It is undoubtedly true that many philosophically educated Christians in the early Church found it exceedingly difficult to come to terms with the intellectual offence of a doctrine of salvation which was rooted in the (for them) limiting circumstances of time and place. It is the sheer particularity of Christian faith which has left it open to so much intellectual challenge since the Enlightenment. An updated version of classical Gnosticism can seem attractive to any believer who wishes to avoid any engagement of faith with science. Friedrich Schleiermacher said that his purpose in writing his great *Doctrine of Faith* was to show 'that every dogma truly representing an element of our Christian awareness can also be formulated in such a way that it leaves us uninvolved with science'.[4] I am not implying that Schleiermacher had taken refuge from the modern world by flight to a latter-day gnosticism, only that he had wished to frame the tenets of his faith in a way which would not leave them gratuitously open to scientific attack. Considering the way some Christians had tangled arrogantly and foolishly with science (for example in the Galileo affair), Schleiermacher might seem to have been acting prudently in an age when science was well on the way to intellectual primacy in the modern world. Later liberal theologians, while not sharing Schleiermacher's theology of religious feeling, would nevertheless adopt his attitude to science, so that they could continue to commend their Christian faith to the modern world. Although Karl Barth called a dramatic halt to the concessionary techniques which liberal Protestantism had devised for dealing with the advances made in modern scientific and critical thought, Rudolf Bultmann, who had initially joined him in forging a theology of the Word, made use of Heideggerian existentialism to shape a theology of faith which could go on its way without depending on what the Jesus of history might have said or done. It may not have been gnostic in intent, but it seemed to be so in effect.

One may think it to have been no accident that Gnosticism was the first great heresy to affect the Christian Church. It contained within it currents of thought which if successfully propagated would have destroyed the heart of Christian faith. Long after the demise of classical Gnosticism, however, there remain modified versions of some of its tenets. One of those tenets is the radical dualism of matter and spirit. Since this dichotomy has profoundly important implications for the doctrine of creation, we ought perhaps to clarify what we are talking about.

'Dualism' is a useful but treacherous word. Today's theological student will constantly meet it employed in different, though usually related, senses. Like the word 'mysticism' it can be used with precision by specialists in certain fields of research, or it can indicate a general area of reference. Often one infers from the way an author or speaker uses it that he or she disapproves of it. Thus for example the phrases 'Platonic dualism' or 'Cartesian dualism' tend to be used not simply descriptively but pejoratively. Perhaps, then, the first thing that ought to be determined about the word 'dualism' is whether it is being used neutrally or pejoratively. In its pejorative sense it refers to the sort of division which breaks up a unit or a unified set of relationships, causing an opposition where none should exist, or even forcing a choice where none should have to be made. Cartesian dualism, for example, forces a division between mind and body which does not allow one to discern spirituality in bodily life or materiality in mental activity. That which has extension is mindless, while mental acts are totally without material references. Psychosomatic medicine can demonstrate the ineptitude of too firm a partition between mind and body. Philosophical investigation into the relationship between mental acts and neurophysiological events has revealed a logical minefield lying in wait for the incautious.

In theological usage the word 'dualism' can have an ontological or a moral reference, and more often than not it has a reference which is an amalgam of both. As we have seen, Gnosticism adopted an ontologico-moral dualism in its view of God. The supreme and true God did not, indeed could not create material beings, therefore another deity (albeit an inferior one) must be postulated to account not merely for material creation but also for evil, which is, for the Gnostic, metaphysically to be identified with material creation. Dualism, as applied in a pejorative sense to the doctrine of God, has a connotation which is inescapably moral and inescapably metaphysical. Its theological attraction has often lain in its apparent ability to offer a comprehensive resolution of the problem of evil. St Augustine found Manichean dualism attractive precisely because it appeared to answer the question which never ceased to haunt him: *unde malum?* (where does evil come from?). Manicheism, by reducing evil to its material manifestations, in effect bypassed its spiritual character together with the challenge it posed to the theology of divine omnipotence on the one hand and human freedom on the other. The Manichees could afford to pity and patronise all those for whom the existence of evil posed an insoluble problem of theodicy. Christian orthodoxy, by refusing the seductive charms of theistic dualism, necessarily opts for the long and arduous task of accounting for the existence of evil while justifying the omnipotence of a good and provident God.

Today there is, in secular as well as religious thought, a reaction against Cartesian dualism. It is of interest to see why this should be so. In many respects Descartes's rigid dichotomy between extension and mind (matter and spirit), allied to Newtonian physics, underwrote what was happening in science. The model was straightforward, uncomplicated, and easy to use. Nature with its fixed laws was a world apart, a huge laboratory specimen, apt and ready to be studied by detached observers who, as long as they were prepared to abandon dogmatism and espouse the 'objective' principles of scientific investigation, would be able to discover how things really are in the physical world. Subjects were subjects, and objects were objects. Subjects were of course liable to all sorts of dogmatic prejudices but were nonetheless capable of surmounting them to arrive at the summit of human intellectual achievement, i.e. dispassionate scientific observation and measurement. Objects were there to be broken down into ever smaller component parts, with the analysis of each one yielding fuller information about the composition of the physical universe. The model of subject/object opposition worked extremely well. It continued to deliver a stream of exhilarating results. Few scientists were interested in the naïve philosophical theory which lay behind it. Science is, after all, a pragmatic discipline whose theories must be open, at least in principle, to empirical verification or falsification.

Quantum theory came as a rude shock to this orderly and

cosy enclave. With the new physics the laboratory became a glass bowl and the observer became the observed. The god-like scientist was now forced to recognise that he was part of his own experiment. More than that, the descriptive powers of language were being seen to be seriously inadequate to cope with the atomic and sub-atomic world. 'We cannot speak about atoms in ordinary language', said Werner Heisenberg.[5] Scientists had since the early twentieth century become increasingly aware that everyday language was seriously deficient in its ability to describe the new world of particles which was opening up before the scientific investigator. Worse was to come when logic itself began to break down under the strain imposed by attempts to describe what happens in the nuclear world. Scientists found themselves face to face with paradox—a condition which many of them would have considered more appropriate to departments of literature or theology than to laboratories like the Cavendish. Heisenberg was forced to ask 'Can nature possibly be so absurd as it seemed [to himself and Niels Bohr] in these atomic experiments?'[6] The search for the ultimate components of matter was actually dissolving the solid framework which supported Newtonian physics. The billiard-ball atom, with a history stretching back to Democritus, was now revealed to be a composite of nucleus and electrons and the nucleus itself a composite of protons and neutrons. In the age which has followed there has been what one book calls a 'particle explosion', as physicists observed or postulated the existence of hitherto unknown particles. How could all this be described by the soberly descriptive language which science had traditionally seen as its own particular characteristic? Logic and commonsense seemed to be the first casualties of this strange and startling world. The great Einstein himself experienced the intellectual scandal of a universe whose most basic components are a bundle of energies behaving in an unpredictable fashion, colliding with each other, appearing and disappearing in a riot of ceaseless movement. 'God does not play dice' was Einstein's famous and defensive reaction to what was being revealed by Bohr and Heisenberg.

Admittedly Einstein's 'God' was here intended to symbolise the over-arching and ultimate unity of things and must not be immediately identified with the God of Judaeo-Christian revelation. By a process of imaginative interpretation the Judaeo-Christian theologian can, indeed must, seek to relate Einstein's God to the God of revelation. The process is a delicate one, which must foreswear any trace of religious imperialism. If Einstein's God does not play dice with the universe, the Judaeo-Christian God has been normally construed to be in even firmer charge. What then are we to make of a creation which is *demonstrably* composed of particles that behave in an unpredictable fashion? This, after all, is the nature which Moltmann enjoins on Christians to interpret as creation. A theology of creation simply has to reckon with randomness and unpredictability. Yet Christian theology has been traditionally schooled to see creation as an ordered body of substances existing and functioning in obedience to an omnipotent Designer. Indeed the argument from design had, from the eighteenth century on, become the most immediate and effective of the arguments for God's existence. Newtonian physics only served to increase the perceived efficiency of the design argument. God was now seen as the supreme geometer, giving the world its foundational order and allowing scientists to measure the manifestations of that order. Hume and Kant might attack the logic and epistemology underlying the proofs for God's existence based on causality as a metaphysical principle, but the argument from design continued to exercise an influence over ordinary people. It probably always will, and with good reason. At the macroscopic level we see the seasons, the crops, the sky at night, migrating birds and a host of phenomena which continue to speak to many men and women of a provident God who orders creation in a beneficent and wonderful manner. The conviction is intuitive rather than discursive.

At the microscopic level, however, design is more difficult to discern amid the riot of dancing particles and molecular unpredictability. Here one must reckon with chance and random happenings. The Cartesian world, based on a firm dichotomy between mind and matter, quite simply breaks down not merely under philosophical attack but even more under the revolution launched by quantum physics. We do not have to remain at the level of microscopic particles in order to discover a fascinating interplay between order and chance. In 1969 the French biologist and Nobel prizewinner, Jaques Monod, delivered the Robbins Lectures at Pomona College in California. These Lectures were the basis of a book published in France in 1970 and translated into English under the title *Chance and Necessity*.[7] Monod pointed out that the molecular processes by which living organisms replicate themselves are subject to random accidental mutations. It is these mutations which allow evolution to operate. If mere replication were all that took place, there would be no problem: the process would be seen to operate on fixed laws; but within such a process no change could take place. It is the mutations which make evolution possible; and these mutations are, according to Monod, entirely unpredictable. The mutations which occur in the genetic code bear no causal relationship to the biological needs of the organism of which they are a part. Monod's conclusion is confident, not to say dogmatic: There can therefore be no question of design or purpose governing the processes which have led to life. Life appeared as a cosmic accident, the product of pure chance.

> The universe was not pregnant with life nor the biosphere with man. Our number came up in the Monte Carlo game. Is it surprising that, like the person who has just made a million at the casino, we should feel strange and a little unreal?[8]

Chance is Monod's Demiurge. He assumes that anyone who knows that he or she is the product of pure chance will be oppressed by a sense of the absurd. Why he should assume this is not entirely clear. One remembers that Monod is a fellow countryman of Sartre and Camus. He has nothing but pity for those who search for finality and meaning in human existence.

> We would like to think ourselves necessary, inevitable, ordained from all eternity. All religions, nearly all philosophies, and even a part of science testify to the unwearying, heroic effort of mankind desperately denying its own contingency.[9]

Monod on molecular biology speaks, at least to the non-biologist, with the authority of the expert. Monod the philosopher of the absurd, however, need not be treated so respect-fully. The fact is that many theologians and spiritual masters have not merely not denied the contingency of mankind, they have gloried in it and made it the springboard for an ascent to God. The 'sting of contingency' is how Friedrich von Hügel used to describe it, and he found in that sting the very essence of creaturehood and a condition predisposing to holiness.[10] There are, however, also Christians, it must be admitted, who do fit Monod's description of those who feel constrained to think of themselves as 'necessary, inevitable and ordained from all eternity'. It is a viewpoint with which any theology of creation has to reckon.

Monod himself concedes that there is a certain type of religious faith which will be impervious to his thesis. He is of course referring to faith-inspired determinism. According to this type of faith God is in direct and immediate physical control of all that takes place in the universe, down to the evanescent life of the most fleeting of particles. 'Chance' is therefore, in this way of thinking, merely a human device for describing how certain of God's acts appear to us. God's ways are not our ways. This view of God's dealings with his creation is logically impregnable. Protesting and agnostic scientists are simply construed as a mysterious part of a God-willed world. It is a kind of sublime imperialism, impervious to criticism or intellectual contempt.

For many believers, however, this comfortable position is strongly akin to gnosticism. It refuses an encounter with the world as it actually is. They see the refusal as a kind of fideism which considers itself absolved from any obligation towards reason or scientific findings. Christian faith, in their view has no choice but to face the often abrasive challenges of both history and natural science. In this spirit it is worth considering how one might respond to Monod and in general to the theological challenge of chance and randomness in the pro-cesses of nature at both micro and macro levels.

Cartesian epistemology and Newtonian physics supported the argument from design which played such an important part in eighteenth- and nineteenth-century Christian apologetics. God was the supreme geometer and mechanical designer. Newton was even disposed to discern a divine intervention whenever a physical process appears to break down—the now notorious 'god of the gaps'. This was the great age of natural theology, i.e. of the kind of philosophical reflection on God which ostensibly owed nothing to revelation as a supernatural source of knowledge about God. The carefully secluded God of eighteenth-century Deism was needed only to account for the existence of the universe as a piece of magnificently ordered machinery which, once started, continued to operate under the laws then being discovered and formulated in physics. Those who still subscribed to Christian revelation were forced to rely on miracle as the main apologetical argument for the truth and authenticity of Christian faith. The very concept of miracle in this apologetical sense depends upon the universal validity of Newtonian physics. Unless there are fixed and universal laws, there is little point in referring to an event as miraculous in the apologetical sense of the word. The more one respected the determinism of physical laws, the more one was prepared to accord to miracles the apologetical value which gave rational underpinning to Christian faith. In this best of all possible worlds whatever was was right. Basil Willey refers to this comfortable view as 'Cosmic Toryism'.[11] For a brief period it served as a seemingly relevant apologetic for Christianity, but it laid itself open to the devastating critiques, first of David Hume, then of Immanuel Kant, and finally of scientific biblical criticism in the nineteenth century. John Dillenberger tartly remarks

> If theologians and scientists had been less interested in writing apologetics for each other, their relationship might have been more creative in the long run. They might have been able to distinguish and then relate their concerns. As it was, they met on grounds detrimental to both.[12]

Hume's attack on causality as an ontological principle and Kant's critique of any metaphysical system which claims to transcend the world of phenomena left natural theology crippled and disheartened. German liberal Protestantism turned the attention of believers inwards to their own religious experience and made a virtue of necessity by construing apologetics as a kind of unfaith. There was therefore in the nineteenth century little theological as distinct from poetic stimulus to seek God's presence and action in the world of nature. Even before Darwin's *Origin of Species*, 'the spectre of a Nature ringing its changes of chance and death regardless of human welfare and aspirations' through a timescale that seemed to be lengthening with each new geological discovery put a question-mark over all the old certainties.[13]

It can come as a surprise to realise that Tennyson wrote his *In Memoriam* before Darwin published the *Origin of Species*.

> Are God and Nature then at strife,
>   That Nature lends such evil dreams?
>   So careful of the type she seems,
> So careless of the single life;
>
> That I, considering everywhere
>   Her secret meaning in her deeds
>   And finding that of fifty seeds
> She often brings but one to bear
>
> I falter where I firmly trod,
>   And falling with my weight of cares
>   Upon the great world's altar-stairs
> That slope through darkness up to God.
>
> I stretch lame hands of faith, and grope
>   And gather dust and chaff, and call
>   To what I feel is Lord of all,
> And faintly trust the larger hope.

In this vision Nature was not merely capricious and wasteful, but also 'red in tooth and claw'. Darwin's masterpiece, when it appeared in 1859, served only to intensify the agony and provoke Christian apologists into another futile and ignorant battle with science. 'Extinguished theologians lie about the cradle of every science as the strangled snakes beside that of Hercules', jibed T.H. Huxley.[14] A.R. Peacocke, who quotes both Tennyson and Huxley, goes on: 'Clearly to attribute the processes of the universe to "chance" can trigger off in sensitive men a profound sense of despair at the meaninglessness of all life, and of human life in particular'.[15]

Chance, that 'emotive word', as Peacocke calls it, has

returned with reinforced vigour in quantum physics and molecular biology. Yet somehow Christian faith today need not, and on the whole does not, react with Tennysonian melancholy. Matthew Arnold also indulged in the gloom of regret for a faith which with 'Its melancholy, long, withdrawing roar' seemed to him to be receding from the shores where once it 'Lay like the folds of a bright girdle furl'd'. Arnold, however, sensed a future rebirth. He knew himself to be

> Standing between two worlds, one dead,
> The other powerless to be born.

But he also believed 'that Christianity will survive because of its natural truth. Those who fancied that they had done with it, those who had thrown it aside because what was presented to them under its name was so unreceivable, will have to return to it again, and to learn it better.'[16]

Victorian religious pessimism to some extent stemmed from a conviction that one had to choose between God and Chance. Today we are coming to see here less a dilemma than a healthy summons to faith to snap out of its self-pitying reverie and start to look for God in the dance of tiny particles and in the jungle of evolutionary biology. It may very well be that Arnold's limbo has ended with the New Physics. At any rate that would seem to be the spirit in which some scientists are prepared to approach the phenomenon of chance. Their message is not God *or* chance but God *and* chance. Just as we have learned to see creation expressed in the mode of evolution, so we must come to appreciate how God can work through the unpredictable behaviour of particles and through the hazards of genetic process.

Arthur Peacocke points out that the word 'chance' can have two meanings. (1) If you toss a coin there is an even chance that it will come down heads or tails. In principle, however, if one knew all the parameters involved, it would be possible to predict which way the coin would fall. (2) If you come out of a building and a painter working on the roof accidentally drops a hammer on your head, the accident can be rightly ascribed to pure chance, because there are *two* causal chains involved: your progress from the building and the painter's carelessness with his tools.[17]

Monod's thesis is that evolution depends on chance in the second sense. The DNA code constitutes one causal chain which is totally distinct from and unaffected by the biological needs of the organism. Mutations which produce biological change are therefore completely adventitious. This fact, according to Monod, commits us to seeing the universe as a gigantic Monte Carlo gaming room. Ergo, there is no purpose or design in the universe.

Peacocke gently but firmly responds, first, that there is no warrant for raising randomness to the status of a metaphysical principle (i.e. 'Chance' with a capital 'C'). Second, the fact is that microscopic forces, however random, when combined with other microscopic forces into a macroscopic phenomenon, achieve a regularity sufficient to allow one to speak of 'Laws'. Third, randomness at the microscopic level is actually necessary for progress at the macroscopic level, since it provides the materials for choice. Fourth, the fact is that 'the original primeval cloud of fundamental particles must have had the potentiality of being able to develop into the complex molecular forms we call modern biological life'.[18] Randomness was and is simply a feature which allows all these potentialities to be fully explored. It does not exclude a long-term causality. Design and chance are not necessarily mutually exclusive. Drawing on the work of Ilya Prigogine and Manfred Eigen, who have studied the subtle interplay between chance and law in biological processes, Peacocke concludes

> These studies demonstrate that the mutual interplay of chance and law is in fact creative, for it is the combination of the two which allows new forms to emerge and evolve.[19]

Since we shall later have to reflect on the use and abuse of human freedom, there is no need to dwell on the matter here. We should, however, note in the present context the striking analogy which exists between both randomness in molecular, atomic and sub-atomic nature and freedom as a defining feature of human nature. Physical randomness prepares the way for human freedom. God is indeed in charge, but in such a way that our freedom, including our freedom to resist his intentions, forms part of the Creator's master-plan. D. J.

71

Bartholomew, Professor of Statistical and Mathematical Science at the London School of Economics, puts the matter thus in his book, *God of Chance:*

> ... only in a world with a sufficient degree of randomness is there enough flexibility to combine a broadly determined line of development with adequate room for the exercise of real freedom on the part of individuals.[20]

Later in his book he adds that the world-view he is adopting 'allows us to maintain at one and the same time that God determines the end and the lawfulness of the macro-universe and that there is indeterminism on the micro-scale.'[21]

What relevance has all this for theologians? There are some who would say none at all. For them theology begins with humanity and is restricted to humanity. Such a view states, or simply assumes, the discontinuity between *homo sapiens* and the pre-human species from which human beings evolved. I do not believe that this view can be credibly adopted today. Man's place in the universe, including his/her evolution from the Big Bang down to the present moment, is profoundly relevant to a study of what God is saying and doing in the universe. Lack of scientific knowledge, coupled with a philosophical system rooted in substances, enabled earlier theologians to construct their theology on essentialist and even existentialist lines without reference to the empirical foundations of the universe. Many of them made a virtue of disregarding the material world. When the time came for changing the paradigms of Christian theology, the journey lay from substance-orientated thinking to historically orientated thinking. This did not simply mean that essentialist thinking had had its day and was now to be replaced by historical and, later, existentialist modes of thought. There was, in fact, a growing recognition that no one mode, essentialist, historical, or existentialist, can exhaust the possible approaches to God. Human culture has become inescapably pluralist. Diversity of theological models is an enrichment rather than a flight from order and clarity.

I wish to argue that modern science has revealed phenomena which the theologian is not free simply to ignore. There is a long Judaeo-Christian traditional conviction that God discloses himself through nature as well as through history.

Theological treatment of nature, to be sure, often amounted to little more than conventional aesthetic reflection on its beauty and its order. Its disorder and its frequent cruelty were either glossed over or consigned without much logic or consistency to the realm of sin. We are now, it seems to me, being called upon to cash the cheque which our theological ancestors issued when they spoke about 'natural revelation'. If God is disclosed in nature, then what scientists are discovering about nature matters in any intelligent reflection on faith as it must be lived in today's world. More than that, I shall argue that the well-springs of morality signalised by the birth of conscience are to be found in the processes by which our species came to being. There is in our human makeup a subtle interaction between continuity and discontinuity with the previous states of our evolution. Getting the balance right in our estimation of that continuity and discontinuity is essential to a proper reading of our human constitution and function. We have to chart our course between reductionism and supernaturalism.

Reductionism is the attempt to explain all phenomena by resolving them analytically into their simplest and lowest component parts. Reductionism becomes an ideology, and one which is totally inimical to religious belief, only when it becomes the controlling element in an analytical system which operates on the assumption that a phenomenon can be exhaustively explained only by breaking it down into its component parts. It is perfectly proper to point out that we are composed of innumerable particles, that at the molecular level we are genetically programmed, and that at the biological level we are descended from a long line of animal ancestors. We are, however, only partially defined by all this. It is only the claim that men and women are *nothing but* an assembly of particles, a system of molecular codes, a genetically constructed machine, a being of instincts and drives, and so on, which constitutes reductionism as an ideology. Reductionism goes to extreme lengths to affirm the continuity between simpler and more complex states, but it does so in such a way as to deny the discontinuity between these states. Any adequate response to reductionism must take the form of a strong affirmation that the higher cannot be exhaustively explained by reference to the lower.

There is no need for most Christians to dwell on the defects of reductionism. They are far more likely to offend in the opposite direction by ignoring our continuity with the elements which go to make us up physically and biologically. 'Supernaturalism' is a graver temptation for believers. It was horror at having to recognise kinship with the apes that shocked some of Darwin's pious opponents quite as much as the offence to their conviction that the theory of evolution was an assault on the inerrancy of Scripture. Forgetting one's social origins is a feature of one kind of snobbery. There is also a kind of supernaturalist snobbery which likes to dwell on the thought that man has been made little less than a god (Ps. 8:5), but not on the thought that man has come from the slime of the earth via some fascinating species similar to those that can be seen in zoos and museums.

4

The Way and the Cosmos

ANY Christian theology is committed to discerning in the life of Jesus of Nazareth a focal and controlling point of reference. This is not as simple a task as might appear at first sight. If God is present everywhere, how can his presence in a particular being be uniquely significant? If God has created time, how can the three-decade span of one man's life be central to all of history? The educated hellenistic mind found these questions disturbing when it was confronted with the good news of Jesus the Christ. This particularity continues to disturb minds shaped no longer by Greek philosophy but by the intellectual currents of modern cultural pluralism. Particularity suggests élitism, and élitism is hard to square with a salvific ambience which instinctively we feel must extend to the whole human race. It is also hard to reconcile with the existence of billions of people, past, present, and to come, who have either never heard of Jesus of Nazareth or do not profess his lordship over history. Karl Rahner's brave attempt to describe them as 'anonymous Christians' witnesses to the intractability of the problem.

If Jesus is Lord of history can he also be called Lord of nature? There are several Christian texts, together with Christian interpretations of Jewish Wisdom texts, which do indeed make the Christ Lord of the cosmos. These texts are easily read as devotional hyperbole, the sort of exaggeration which stems from worship and its demands. If the Word was with, and was, God from the beginning, the Word was present at, and shared in, the work of creation. But what of Jesus of Nazareth? Could everything that was said of the Word of God be said of Jesus? To answer this question many subtleties of thought were needed, including the crucial distinction

75

between the divine and human natures of Jesus. By the time the great Christian theologians of the first centuries of the Church had completed their work (insofar as this sort of work could ever be completed!), the Christian doctrine of Christ had become a complex, abstruse, and intimidating set of formulas designed to protect the Church from error about God and his dealings with his people.

The early Christian intellectuals were faced with a daunting problem: how were they to speak in an orthodox manner about God's presence and action in Jesus without entombing him in non-biblical formulas of ever increasing complexity and abstraction? The very earliest Christians described themselves as followers of 'the Way'. Their successors found themselves forced by circumstances to abandon an original simplicity of vision and adopt a plethora of abstract beliefs which, to some at least, appeared as a harmful diversion from the original vision. This situation was not chosen for its own sake. It had become necessary because no faith which accepts its responsibilities to rationality can avoid the legitimate questions about doctrinal beliefs which are raised by philosophical minds. The tension between reality and the formulas chosen to express it is an ever-present feature of healthy Church life. One cannot practise faith in a linguistic vacuum. One cannot plausibly say 'I believe' without specifying what one believes in. When a philosopher, however, says what he or she believes in, this expression is necessarily technical, especially when it has to be measured against opposing statements which are perceived to be wrong.

Some early Christians appreciated this. Others, like Tertullian, saw the danger. He put his case in very strong language. *Quid Athenae Hierosolymis?* ('What has Athens to do with Jerusalem?'). It turned out to be a minority view. Jerusalem needed Athens if it was to penetrate the non-Jewish world and also if it was to avoid the trap of fideism, i.e. the kind of faith which considers itself absolved from all responsibility to reason. Tertullian had sounded a note of warning which was often to be echoed by later Christians who felt that the vision of Christ as the Way was being sacrificed to the need for complex doctrinal statements which seemed to aim at the condition of eternal and disembodied validity without reference to either nature or history.

The Fathers liked to dwell on Christ as the Second Adam, showing what the first would have been like had he not fallen. The comparison easily becomes conventional. Irenaeus, however, anxious to combat Gnosticism, avoids conventionally pious metaphor:

> Man is created in the image of God, and the image of God is the Son, in whose image man was created. For this reason the Son also appeared in the fullness of time to show how the copy resembles him.[1]

Jesus the image of God is also 'the first-born of all creation' (Col. 1:15), and in his earthly life is the exemplar of human perfection. It is Tertullian, of all people, who gives us perhaps the clearest and most graceful statement of how Christ is related to creation.

> Think of God utterly taken up with, and given over to, the task [of creation], with hand, sense, industry, forethought, wisdom, providence, and, above all, with that loving care which was determining the features. For the image of Christ, the man who was to be, was influencing every stage in the moulding of the clay; because what was at that moment happening to the earth's clay would happen again when the Word became flesh.[2]

For those splendid words one can forgive Tertullian much of his puritanical élitism and tetchy moralising.

Significantly, perhaps, it was not a theologian but a mystically minded scientist, Pierre Teilhard de Chardin, who proposed to make Christ central to evolution. The evolving cosmos, through the functioning of a 'law of complexity consciousness', folds in on itself until it reaches its culminating point. This Teilhard calls 'Omega Point', the last term in the series which began with the birth of the cosmos. Omega Point, however, is not merely the last term in the series. 'While being the last term of its series, it is also *outside all series*. Not only does it crown, but it closes.'[3] Omega embraces physics, chemistry, biology, anthropology, history, and eschatology. Teilhard quite simply identifies it with Jesus Christ.

> To be alpha and omega, Christ must, without losing his
> precise humanity, become co-extensive with the physical
> expanse of time and space.[4]

This is Tertullian's scenario mounted in modern evolutionary terms: Christ is the focal point of cosmic evolution. It was a magnificent vision; but was it either science or orthodox theology? Teilhard outraged the susceptibilities of both the scientific establishment and the ecclesiastical establishment. The former objected to his introduction of teleology and mysticism into science; the latter objected to what they called his 'concordism', that is, the allegedly promiscuous mingling of nature and supernature.

Today it is possible to express theological reservations about some of Teilhard's views while recognising the far-reaching significance of his attempt to bring together the world revealed to us by science, i.e. the world of evolution, on the one hand, and the world revealed to us by God's word, on the other. In Teilhard's view too many scientists and too many theologians were happy to keep science and religion in hermetic isolation from each other. He refused to declare that his faith in Christ was irrelevant to his scientific convictions. It was a dangerous as well as illuminating stance.

Identification of the cosmic Christ with Omega Point is a feat of combined religious and scientific imagination. It shows the human mind refusing to be contained within the boundaries of one cultural enclave. If the evolutionary journey of the cosmos has culminated in man, as the present state of scientific knowledge suggests, and if the Word of God has become a man, as Christian theology teaches, then in some mysterious way there must be a close and infinitely significant relationship between Christ and the evolving cosmos. This was Teilhard's great insight. Not being himself a professional theologian, Teilhard never worked out a systematic christology. No Christian theologian, however, who takes the human adventure seriously can afford to ignore the christological challenge which Teilhard's vision opens out before us. God the creator and God the redeemer are one and the same God. Redemption comes to us within the created world. It is eschatological, because it points all natural processes to a goal which transcends those processes. It is, however, also historical in that it occurs in history and is made known to us through historical documents; and thereby hangs a problem of daunting complexity.

Identification of the cosmic Christ with Omega Point appears to bypass the crucial problem of the relationship between the Jesus of history and the Christ of faith. The problem may be stated simply enough. Jesus of Nazareth was born into, lived, taught, and died in, a specific culture, that of first-century Palestine. Human cultural evolution, however, has continued to develop since that time. The significance of the life and death of Jesus, together with the Christian experience of his resurrection, transcends the cultural limitations of their historical expression. As the Letter to the Hebrews was to put it, 'Jesus Christ is the same yesterday and today and forever' (Heb 13:8). Exalted to his Father's right hand, Christ continues to intercede for all humankind. The Christ of faith is no longer subject to the forces of cultural evolution. For Christian faith, however, it was the Jesus of history who, by certain specific time-bound and space-bound acts, wrought the redemption of the world. No amount of mystical interpretation after the event could detract from the sheer historicity of Pilate, Caiaphas, and the hill of execution called Golgotha, and least of all the tortured man from Galilee who was nailed to a cross. Later theological reflection would lead to the faith-inspired conviction that 'he died for our sins'. This conviction nevertheless presupposed the plain historical statement that 'he suffered under Pontius Pilate'. Christian theology of redemption is inseparable from the historical event on Calvary.

Since human existence is necessarily historical existence, we should perhaps pause at this point and reflect on what it means to describe a person and his or her acts as 'historical'. The topic has been much canvassed in modern theology. Here I can do no more than single out some characteristics of historicity which have a bearing on the doctrine that Jesus saves us from our sin.

The word 'history' has several meanings. For the sake of clarity I shall reduce these to the two most important. 'History' can refer to *events* which are past, or it can refer to *accounts* of past events. These two senses are distinguishable but inseparable—a fact which tends to give the term 'history' a certain unavoidable ambiguity. To describe a person or event as 'historical' necessarily means that the person actually existed or the event actually happened. We would, however, know nothing about such a person or such an event unless some documentary evidence reached us. From this it follows that though persons and events are, *in themselves,* independent of interpretation, *knowledge* (i.e. 'intelligence' in the diplomatic or military sense) of a past person or event always reaches us through the interpretative eyes of others. Someone had to decide to record some statement or event. This decision then led, consciously or unconsciously, to an interpretative process whereby certain words or acts were selected as significant for the task in hand, while others were not. This simple observation conceals a host of exceedingly difficult philosophical questions, usually subsumed under the title 'hermeneutics' (the science of interpretation). It is not my purpose here to try to enumerate, still less to examine, these questions but merely to alert the reader to their existence. They are highly relevant to our central question, 'What does it mean to say that Jesus Christ died for our salvation?'

All history-as-record, then, is a matter of interpretation, from the moment that somebody decides to commit a record to paper to the moment when somebody, perhaps centuries later, picks up the piece of paper (or a copy of it) and begins to read and ponder what the author wrote. The whole process is mysterious and fascinating once we have ceased to take it for granted and have begun really to look at all that is involved. There is the writer, the text, and the reader, each with his, her, or its own life.

It is, then, no small thing to proclaim that Christianity is a historical faith. It commits one to a two-fold asceticism. On the level of event it commits one to the position that God has expressed himself definitively in a certain place (Palestine) at a certain time (first century AD). This is an embarrassing and uncomfortable claim. It is disturbingly specific and introduces a note of parochialism into what one may instinctively feel should be a cosmic, and therefore universal, drama of timeless proportions. It is all very well for Teilhard de Chardin to identify the culminating point of evolving nature with a mystically interpreted cosmic Christ. Can we, however, say that Omega Point descended into the Jordan to be baptised by John? Mark, who tells us about the baptism, knew nothing about evolutionary nature. He interprets Jesus of Nazareth for us, and his interpretation is a first-century Jewish interpretation.

Here we are faced with the second constriction on faith, namely, the character of the documents which make Jesus known to us. This is not the place to tackle the question of the reliability of the gospels. I wish merely to note the intellectual asceticism required of the thoughtful believer who follows his or her instinct to escape from the later doctrinal or devotional interpretations of the Christ and by means of imagination to draw close to the actual Jesus who lived and taught and healed and inspired others to follow him. I say 'instinct', because when we look more closely at what is involved, we discover that there is no uninterpreted Jesus. There never was. There was a man who went about Palestine doing good but of whom there were many and varied interpretations ranging from the loving to the actively hostile. Mary of Magdala and Caiaphas the High Priest, if they had left memoirs behind them, would have portrayed for us two very different men. The matter is further complicated by the post-resurrection interpretation of Jesus as the One sent by God, the Word, the image of the God we cannot see. History-as-event is simply subsumed into history-as-record. The intentions of the evangelists form an inescapable part of the portraits they give us.

This, in broadest outline and starkest terms, is the problem known to theologians for two centuries as that of the Jesus of history and the Christ of faith. Throughout the nineteenth century, theologians and historians set themselves the task of re-discovering Jesus 'as he really was'. They wanted a Jesus free of the sort of dogmatic interpretation that developed after his life-time. Some of them claimed that St Paul had given us a deeply coloured interpretation of Jesus which owed more to Paul's religious imagination than to the straightforward 'facts' of Jesus' teaching and life. Working from this assumption, they attempted to reconstruct a 'factual' account of Jesus, supposedly free of later doctrinal interpretation. In a word, they acted as if it was possible to have history-as-event without the constricting subjectivity of history-as-record.

In 1906 Albert Schweitzer published a book, *The Quest of the Historical Jesus.*[5] In it he subjected many of the nineteenth-century lives of Jesus to a searching examination which demonstrated the sheer impossibility of the task these biographers had set themselves.

Schweitzer's Germanic thoroughness resulted in a radical conclusion of far-reaching importance. It 'destroyed the portrait of Christ on which liberal Christianity based its appeal'.[6] In general, the liberal view had sought to strip away all the doctrinally inspired interpretations of Jesus that had grown up over the centuries and replace them by a simple ethical figure who had proposed some basic truths and injunctions which would be relevant in any age. Adolf von Harnack, the last of the great liberals, set out to discover the essence of Christianity—that is, a kernel or core which survives every change of culture. He found it to consist in three teachings of extreme simplicity: the Kingdom of God and its coming; the fatherhood of God and the infinite value of the human soul; the higher righteousness and the commandment of love. Harnack's claim to have cleaned the picture and thereby revealed the truth which lay under centuries of accumulated dirt and overpainting rested on a positivistic view of history and a philosophically undernourished confidence in the historian's ability to arrive at uninterpreted 'reality'.

Harnack stood at the end of a movement which had begun with David Strauss's *Life of Jesus* (1834) and had continued in the work of Albrecht Ritschl and his disciples. They had something like an ideological interest in the historian's ability to discover the Jesus of history because they located the object of faith, not in the dogma about Jesus, but in his historically determined God-consciousness. Schweitzer, on the other hand, shared the view of Johannes Weiss that Jesus saw the Kingdom as a phenomenon which lay in the future and which was not at all to be identified with a somewhat bland society subscribing to a broadly-interpreted application of the ethic of love.

Schweitzer showed the impossibility of portraying Jesus 'as he really was'. Every portrait of Jesus, including those provided by the four evangelists, is an interpretation. Historically this is the case; philosophically it has to be the case. History-as-event is inseparable, though distinguishable, from history-as-record. Like it or not, we have to live with the inevitable truth that there is not, and cannot be, any account of the life and work of Jesus which has not passed through the interpretative grid of those who knew him, loved him, preached him, or wrote about him. Schweitzer's great book concludes with some wise and haunting words.

> He comes to us as One unknown, without a name, as of old, by the lake-side, He came to those men who knew him not. He speaks to us the same word: 'Follow thou me!' and sets us to the tasks which He has to fulfil for our time. He commands. And to those who obey Him, whether they be wise or simple, He will reveal Himself in the toils, the conflicts, the sufferings which they shall pass through in His fellowship, and, as an ineffable mystery, they shall learn in their own experience Who He is.[7]

In so far as the gospels allow us to determine the matter, Jesus was killed for politico-religious reasons, and these reasons are germane to any satisfactory theology of salvation, once we have abandoned a pre-critical, 'opening of the gates of heaven', type of soteriology. Redemption is eschatological; but eschatology begins in the events of this world. Sin is expressed in and through historical events and political structures; hence salvation must be expressed in and through historical events and political structures. In short, the Word of God made man has to be Jesus from the town of Nazareth before he can be recognised as the Christ of the kerygma, the cosmic Christ, or the Christ who may be identified as Omega Point. The New Testament writers saw his earthly life in the light of his resurrection. When they portrayed the man from Nazareth, they could not but endow him with the anticipated glory of the risen one. This is especially true of the Fourth Evangelist, whose Christ would escape the pull of history were its author less interested in the symbolic value of historical detail. The Christ of the Fourth Gospel is majestic throughout, though he does not accept the title of king until his sceptre is a reed and his crown one of thorns and there can be no mistake about the nature of his Kingdom. In the other gospels, however, he is shown proclaiming the arrival of God's Kingdom. In fact the proclamation of God's Kingdom is portrayed as the very core of his teaching.

That Jesus preached the coming of God's Kingdom seems a simple enough claim, but it conceals formidable theological questions and difficulties. Did Jesus expect the Kingdom to manifest itself in universal secular history by signs which would be impossible to ignore? If the signs by which it would be known were there for all to see (as some theologians have maintained) what role would faith, which is directed towards things unseen, play in its discernment? Could Jesus have been wrong in his expectation of its arrival? Did he die wondering why it had not arrived? How did this Kingdom relate to the end-time of Jewish prophecy and apocalyptic? How did it relate to Israel? How did it relate to his own death and to the subsequent apostolic and early Christian experience of him as risen?

Liberal theology had more or less identified the Kingdom with a few simple ethical requirements pertinent to the present moment and valid in every age. Because they constituted an 'essence' of Christian faith, these requirements would not change from one age or culture to another. Johannes Weiss and Albert Schweitzer showed that the liberals had totally overlooked the eschatological and apocalyptic character of Jesus' teaching as portrayed by the synoptic evangelists and had thereby strained out an essential element of that teaching. They had created a Jesus in the image of their highest ideals—which were those of the nineteenth not the first century. Their ecclesiology was weak to the point of non-existence.

Alfred Loisy in a lapidary sentence wrote, 'Jesus proclaimed the Kingdom and it was the Church which came.' Through the centuries of Christian history there has been a pronounced tendency to identify the Kingdom with the Church, thus breaking the dialectical tension between Kingdom and Church which many Christian thinkers have held, and continue to hold, to be necessary to the integrity of the Christian message. The Kingdom of God is, in short, a powerful but profoundly ambiguous symbol of God's action in the world. To believe in the reality of that Kingdom is to accept the contingent status of human existence and the historically adventitious character of ecclesiastical institutions.

It is a commonplace of contemporary Christian theology that the Kingdom is eschatological—that is, that it is a divine manifestation of the end-time, the last age, the culminating point of all history. That agreement, however, leaves many problems unsolved. What, for example, are we to make of an end-time which has already persisted for two thousand years? When it became apparent to the first Christians that the coming of the Kingdom did not apparently entail the end of history, a more leisurely reference had to be found for the conviction that 'he will come again'. The intervening time was to be marked by expectation and watchfulness lest the power of his first coming be dissipated in idleness, lapse from faith, discouragement, and apathy.

Many theologians now accept that the tension between present and future cannot be comprehensively resolved in favour of either. Not merely must the ambiguity remain, but it is indispensable to God's creative and redemptive purposes. The future embodies the ideal, and to that extent the present is judged by the future in the sense that what can be and ought to be are always a judgment on what actually is. To speak of the future in this context is to speak of an eschatological and not of a purely temporal future. There is, moreover, a further tensile ambiguity between a future which belongs to time and a future which lies outside time. Hence the theological acceptance of an 'eschatological proviso'—that is, a recognition that no purely this-worldly future can ever meet the demands of the Kingdom. Acceptance of this proviso is particularly important for Christians who emphasise the political dimension of the Kingdom. On the other hand, those who see the Kingdom in predominantly otherworldly terms are in danger of failing to appreciate its implications for political life and institutions here and now. Thus there is an inevitable and healthy dialectical relationship between the struggle for political salvation on the one hand and recognition of the eschatological proviso on the other. Faith commits us to the search for a just and caring world but forbids us to identify that world with God's Kingdom. The political creation of a just and caring world is, however, part of, and indispensable to, the full coming of God's Kingdom.

Jesus lived his life amid the political realities of early first-century Palestine. By preaching a liberating reign of God to his contemporaries, he was making a strong political gesture. While refusing all overt or covert taking of political power when, for example the people wanted to make him king, he nevertheless exercised political influence by his judgment on secular and religious rulers and on the structures, laws, worship, and institutions by which they lived. It could not have been otherwise. He made his judgments in public in the presence of people who were ready to place a fully this-worldly political construction on them. Many of those who listened to him experienced a freedom which could not be restricted to the purely spiritual realm. More than that, they experienced their freedom as coming from God. The problem which faced Jesus was how to preach the reign of God without promoting a theocratic rebellion. He freed men and women by his comprehensive acceptance of them. In the language of a later age, he raised their consciousness, yet without explicitly encouraging them to better their lot in a material sense. The circumstance can pose a problem for us today, especially in the light of the insights of politically sensitive theologies.

It is no accident that today's Liberation theologians stress the Jesus of history over the Christ of faith. Leonardo Boff offers several reasons for this christological emphasis.[8] (1) There is 'a structural similarity between the situations in Jesus' day and those in our own time'. (2) The praxis of liberation, being prophetic, will stir up the same response as it did in Jesus' case. (3) Christians have to follow and imitate Jesus: it is by seeking to transform the world that one comes to know Jesus. (4) It is by conversion and practical change in our own lives, and not by abstract theory, that Jesus becomes for us the way to God. (5) 'The historical Jesus signifies a crisis, not a justification, for the world'.

When Boff goes on to remark that Jesus 'does not proclaim that the kingdom will come in the future', one may feel that, like the nineteenth-century liberals, he is indulging in special pleading and the selective use of New Testament texts. The realised eschatology of Liberation theology is of course vastly different from that of the liberals. Nevertheless it is instructive to note that both are uncomfortable with a christology and

86

soteriology which are finally orientated towards an absolute future, and that both emphasise the ethical (or practical) character of the Kingdom. Nevertheless it is interesting that J. L. Segundo, in, for example, his *Evolution and Guilt*, is profoundly aware of Teilhard's evolutionary approach. Segundo sees the struggle for justice and freedom as belonging to the evolutionary process.[9] He is, however, less concerned with Christ as Omega than with Jesus as Liberator. Segundo dwells on the Johannine presentation of Jesus as the light of the world. In this light much that has been taken for granted as given can now be seen to be sin. Thus Jesus brings about a major step in cultural evolution by provoking a crisis of human conscience. In his light men and women are called upon to reform their lives by re-defining their values.

The political circumstances of first-century Palestine cannot, however, be simply identified with those, for example, of the twentieth-century Third World. The task is a good deal more complicated than that. A complex act of interpretation is called for if we are to discern the mind of Christ as it might fittingly be applied to some of the circumstances in which we find ourselves today. We have first to ask how he approached the circumstances of his own time and place before we can speculate on how he might have wished his followers to act two thousand years later. The scope for error of judgment and for simple self-deception is considerable. It is not easy to discover what was taking place when Jesus spoke to the people, if only because the evangelists exercised a freedom in the management of their sources which would be quite unacceptable today from the standpoint of critical history or biography. Even if, however, we were able to reconstruct events, words, motives, and reactions with a much higher degree of certainty, this would constitute only half our task. The question of the relevance of all this to life as we live it today would remain to be answered. Much of the world goes on its course, seemingly unaffected by the life and work of Jesus.

This matter of the relevance and applicability of the life and death of Jesus to later ages is of crucial importance to any realistic soteriology. As long as it was possible to speak credibly about Jesus' placating an offended and angry God and thereby causing the gates of heaven, shut by reason of the sin of

Adam and Eve, to be reopened, there was no great urge to ask what salvation means, or could mean, for men and women in any age: It meant, in crude terms, securing one's place in the happiness of the world to come. With the breaking of pre-critical myths, however, and an increasing awareness of social and political justice, the question of the meaning of salvation has become crucial to Christian faith. In pursuing this question, we cannot restrict our attention to the Christ in glory, to the Christ proclaimed in the Church's kerygma. We have to ask searching questions about the historical Jesus of Nazareth; who he was, what he preached, and why the religious and civil authorities decreed his destruction. This in turn means facing all the hazards which confront anyone in quest of the Jesus of history. Mystical and cosmic theories can come later, but their credibility will ultimately depend upon their being rooted in certain historically specifiable events which took place in first-century Palestine.

As Friedrich von Hügel observed many years ago, true Christian spirituality operates between two poles, one internally given with the fact and experience of our common humanity, the other externally given in the life and teaching of Jesus of Nazareth. Each pole must interact with the other. The mystical element of religion, characterised by a dim, unfocused awareness of the divine, seeks out a concrete, explicit and clear expression of the divine and finds it in Jesus the Christ. If this mystical element is lacking, no encounter with the Jesus of history can give rise to a salvific faith. This human sense of the need for God and his truth is present in the lives of all men and women and is salvific even when, for one reason or another, they fail to arrive at an explicit knowledge of the historical Jesus.

The truth that Christ died for *all* of the human race, and not merely for an élite, is at the heart of Christian faith in spite of the many efforts down the ages to shrink its scope, application and effectiveness. Von Hügel's point is that when Christ is preached, something far more profound than the transmission of sacred information occurs. The gospel does not arrive on our doorstep unannounced and unprepared for. The very fact that we are human is already a preparation for it. We already have some idea of what salvation is because we already experience the need for it. The encounter with Jesus of Nazareth is a coming home. 'This is eternal life, that they know thee the only true God, and Jesus Christ whom thou hast sent' (Jn 17:3). Jesus is God's self-gift to creation, which in men and women has become capable of responding to God's offer. In order to respond to this offer men and women have to enter into a distressing awareness of their own inability to become what they ought to be. To be whole, or holy, is to be healed of the wounds inflicted by every kind of estrangement we experience in life: estrangement from ourselves, from our fellow human beings, and from the environment in which we live. Estrangement from God occurs on one or other, or all, of these fronts; and it is God who takes the initiative in offering and bringing about the healing and reconstructing process which with scriptural warrant we call the new creation. He does it most specifically in Jesus of Nazareth.

Relating Jesus to the cosmos is a necessary task for any Christian theology which wishes to keep the doctrine of creation in fruitful relationship with the doctrine of salvation. It means accepting the challenge of relating a particular series of historical events to the whole evolutionary course of created nature. That has always been and will continue to be the intellectual scandal of Christian faith. It is the existence of this scandal which makes gnostic stratagems a lasting temptation for those who are intellectually embarrassed by the particularity of Christian faith.

It is possible to regard the notion of a cosmic Christ as little more than a poetic conceit, a playing with metaphor, or a fanciful attempt to bring religion and science closer together. I believe, on the contrary, that it is consonant not merely with Alexandrian christology but also with powerful if mysterious New Testament texts which have their origins in a felt need to do justice to the universal scope of salvation. That Christ should be seen to belong to the cosmos is implicit in the doctrine of his humanity: if human beings have emerged from the cosmos, then so too has Jesus who is called the Christ. Far from being a poetic conceit, the doctrine of the cosmic Christ is a ringing answer to docetism, i.e. the notion that Jesus only appeared to be a man. That Christ is to be seen as Lord of the cosmos stems not only from his divine status but also from the fact that God responded to his humanly sacrificial obedience by raising him from the dead, highly exalting him and bestowing on him the name which is above every name (Phil. 2:9). It is God *the creator* who constitutes Jesus as Lord of the cosmos. This insight is in its turn a reflection of what the Antiochene Fathers were anxious to enshrine in their doctrine of the two natures in Christ.

The doctrine of the cosmic Christ is a corollary of the doctrine of incarnation. If God's Word and Son has become a human being, and if human beings are not merely the summit of creation but are physically, chemically, and biologically related to the rest of creation, then it must follow that the cosmos itself is taken up into the sweep of God's salvific purposes. Finally, if Christian soteriology is to proclaim the universality of salvation, it must undertake to show that the message, work, and meaning of Christ extend far beyond the particularity and cultural restrictions of the life of Jesus of Nazareth without ever being severed from their roots in that particularity.

There are three major Pauline texts which, when taken together, are rich in meaning and have a scope of potential reference far wider than Paul could have intended. I cite them here in considered awareness that for their original historical reference one must look to their context in three different letters.

> For the creation waits with eager longing for the revealing of the sons of God; for the creation was subjected to futility, not of its own will but by the will of him who subjected it in hope; because the creation itself will be set free from its bondage to decay and obtain the glorious liberty of the children of God. We know that the whole creation has been groaning in travail together until now; and not only the creation, but we ourselves, who have the first fruits of the Spirit, groan inwardly as we wait for adoption as sons, the redemption of our bodies (Rom. 8:9-23).

> He is the image of the invisible God, the first-born of all creation; for in him all things were created, in heaven and on earth, visible and invisible, whether thrones or

90

dominions or principalities or authorities—all things were created through him and for him. He is before all things, and in him all things hold together. He is the head of the body, the church; he is the beginning, the first-born from the dead, that in everything he might be pre-eminent. For in him all the fulness of God was pleased to dwell, and through him to reconcile to himself all things, whether on earth or in heaven, making peace by the blood of his cross (Col. 1:15-20).

For he has made known to us in all wisdom and insight the mystery of his will, according to his purpose which he set forth in Christ as a plan for the fulness of time, to unite all things in him, things in heaven and things on earth (Eph. 1:9-10)

The life and death of Jesus of Nazareth place, for Christian faith, a coping stone on the Jewish conviction that God acts in human history on behalf of those whom he calls to be his own people. Christianity, however, by its missionary ideal broke with the particularism of Jewish faith. God's action in human history was henceforth to be seen as co-extensive with the history not of one tribe alone but of all humanity. Circumcision and the Law were now to be replaced by faith. That faith was not to be merely a generalised faith in God, but one which is focused upon Jesus who is called the Christ. Christians today have a different problem from that which faced the early Jewish Christians, who were called upon to accept the disturbing implications of a break with Jewish exclusivism. Christians today have to face the no less disturbing implications of two millennia of missionary activity which has been responsible for the preaching of Christianity throughout much of the world. Large areas of that world, however, have not been won over to the lordship of Christ but have retained their own traditional faiths. They have their own ways to God which do not envisage Jesus the Christ.

In addition, much of the Western world, formerly described as Christendom, has either defected from its ancestral religion or else observes it in a purely formal manner. The need for evangelisation, within quite as much as outside 'Christendom', is as urgent today as it was two thousand years ago. There is, however, a significant difference, which Kierkegaard has noted in his characteristic way.

> It is easier to become a Christian when one is not a Christian than to become a Christian when one is a Christian; and this latter task is reserved for him who is baptised as a child.[10]

Christendom resulted from the attempt to baptise a culture. The lesson of that attempt may be not so much that it should never have been made—though there are good reasons for thinking this—but that living in an *apparently* Christianised culture can blind one to the need for conversion and evangelisation. Christianity consists not in numbers or in formal practices but in quality of faith. Christendom, on the other hand, was an attempt at spiritual totalitarianism. Close relations between Church and State often corrupted the Church and seduced it from its prophetic mission. In Chapter 10 I shall argue for a 'high' doctrine of Church, but the Church I am envisaging has nothing to do with authority structures, clerical control, concordats with states, or any of the other trappings of power. It is that body of men and women 'who experience what is supremely important as bound up with Jesus'.[11] Such a Church is inescapably ecumenical not merely in its inter-Christian relations, but also in its relations with men and women of other faiths and of no faith.

The Christian Church is charged with preaching the crucified Christ in freedom. It is *not* charged with making all men and women formally Christian at all costs and by any means. In true Christian evangelisation, means are as important as ends; and means which are not purified of all trace of coercion, physical or moral, conscious or unconscious, are a betrayal of the ends. A culture cannot be baptised; only a person can be baptised. A culture can of course benefit from the Christian ideals of those who shape it; but a culture always reflects to some degree the personal and social fragmentation of those who contribute to its shaping. A culture does not become more Christian by reason of the numbers who contribute to it. Preoccupation with numbers may serve as a diversion from the real task which needs to be undertaken. Jesus Christ is Lord of history not by reason of the number of men and women who profess to follow him but by reason of his obedience to the Father's will. What Jesus of Nazareth did was *historically* limited by the circumstances of his time. Historical limitations however, are not limitations upon ontologically and transcendently valid consequences, when the one who acts is uniquely the Son of God. The existence and acts of Jesus are the existence and acts of the Christ who transcends the circumstances of his age.

Teilhard de Chardin saw the paradox of this and stated it bluntly: 'To be the alpha and omega, Christ must, without losing his precise humanity, become co-extensive with the physical expanse of time and space'. Teilhard unfolds the paradox in terms of cross and resurrection. The cross 'has been placed on the crest of the road that leads to the highest peaks of creation'.[12] It is 'the symbol of the pain and toil of evolution rather than the symbol of expiation'. Christopher Mooney cites this remark with the comment that Teilhard has a 'strange tendency to depersonalise sin when speaking of Christ's work of redemption'.[13] This was because he feared that concentration on the expiatory character of Christ's death would obscure the cosmic implications of salvation. Mooney explains this fear by reference to the theology of original sin which prevailed in the Roman Catholic Church of his age. In Chapter 7 I shall outline a theology of original sin which I believe would go some distance towards allaying this fear by viewing the Fall (in Teilhard's own words) 'not as an isolated event, but as a general condition affecting the whole of history'.[14]

To see in the crucified Christ the centre of the universe is not an act of religious imperialism. This is the empire of a man who is crowned with thorns and nailed to a cross and who dies in utter abandonment, the victim of every kind of alienation which marks the cosmos from its physical beginnings to its human defiance of what God wants it to be. This empire rejects all the values which make other empires fearsome, exploitative, and power-obsessed. This empire is one of freedom; and it has to be brought about with the same freedom as that with which Jesus sought the will of his Father. Golgotha was the result of one man's response to the gift and call of the creator. It was a perfect response, a triumphant justification of all that God the creator has in mind for his creation. It demonstrated once and for all that the cosmos in its human manifestation *can* be all that God expects. Jesus of Nazareth showed how it was possible for *homo sapiens* to be perfect as God himself is perfect. For this reason God raised Jesus from the dead and made him Lord and Saviour.

In advancing the doctrine of the cosmic Christ we must take care to give no grounds for suspicion that we are encouraging a flight from the particularities of history. It is precisely *historical* events which faith sees as having cosmic meaning; for, as Teilhard rightly observed, Christ must become alpha and omega without losing any of his historical particularity. This is a hermeneutical task of formidable difficulty and delicacy. It is difficult, because, as Lessing pointed out long ago, history deals in contingencies while universally valid reason deals in necessities. It is a delicate task, because its implementation inevitably looks like imperialism to those who are not Christians.

Teilhard sees in the risen Jesus a cosmic triumph.

> Christ must be kept as large as creation and remain its Head. No matter how large we discover the world to be, the figure of Jesus, risen from the dead, must embrace it in its entirety.[15]

5

Resurrection and Salvation

> If a man has committed a crime punishable by death and he is put to death, and you hang him on a tree, his body shall not remain all night upon the tree, but you shall bury him the same day, for a hanged man is accursed by God; you shall not defile your land which the Lord your God gives you for an inheritance. (Deut. 21:22-3)

> The Messiah of Israel could never at the same time be the one who according to the words of the Torah was accursed by God. It was perhaps for this very reason that the leaders of the people and their clientele had pressed for the execution of Jesus by crucifixion. This was the most obvious way to refute his messianic claim. (Martin Hengel)[1]

THERE is a note of tragic finality about a crucified Messiah. Calvary witnessed the death not only of a good man but also of an intense and brief hope. Jesus had preached a kingdom in which the poor, the neglected, the despised, and the outcasts would be at home under the benign rule of God. Those who entered this kingdom would experience it as a condition in which they were healed, forgiven, accepted, and liberated. Such a kingdom would empower the powerless and fulfil the dreams of many in Israel. Those dreams were nailed to the cross together with the man from Nazareth who had given them currency and plausibility. To nail a dream is to proclaim an illusion. Hence Luke depicts the two disciples of Jesus remarking in disillusioned tones, 'We had hoped that he was the one to redeem Israel' (Lk 24:21).

During the hours which followed the trauma of Calvary the followers of Jesus were in total disarray, lacking, as they did, a mandate for action and a goal towards which to direct their

95

lives. Bereft of their friend and master, whom they had betrayed or abandoned, they were like travellers without map or compass. Some of Israel's liturgical prayers, which they had heard since childhood, may well have become a poignant reality for them in their desolation.

> Vindicate me, O God, and defend my cause
>   against an ungodly people;
> from deceitful and unjust men deliver me!
> (Ps. 43:1)

> Thou hast made us the taunt of our neighbours,
> the derision and scorn of those about us.
> . . .
> Rise up, come to our help!
> Deliver us for the sake of thy steadfast love!
> (Ps. 44:13,26)

> My heart is in anguish within me,
> the terrors of death have fallen upon me.
> (Ps. 55:4)

> I am weary with my crying;
> my throat is parched.
> My eyes grow dim
> with waiting for my God.
> (Ps. 69:3)

> I consider the days of old,
> I remember the years long ago.
> . . .
> Has [God's] steadfast love for ever ceased?
> Are his promises at an end for all time?
> (Ps. 77:5, 8)

Then all was utterly changed by a happening which lies at the heart of Christian faith and life. It inspires both intense joy and intense speculation—often in the same person. It ended the fear and desolation of the disciples. It sent them out joyful and confident into the very world from which they had been hiding. It convinced them that God had not abandoned his servant whom they now proclaimed with triumphant publicity as the Messiah, the Christ, the Annointed of God. 'He is risen', 'God has raised him up', 'We have seen him'. From this moment 'alleluia' (praise the Lord), becomes the anthem and principal *leitmotiv* of Christianity. Liturgies will ring with it as they celebrate what happened in the small hours of the third day after that terrible Friday. The Church will make it a night of lights, and warmth, and music, and gaiety. In the northern hemisphere it will coincide with the ending of winter, so that nature itself will be drawn into the feast by revealing the new life of growing things beneath the receding ice and snow. The days will lengthen and darkness will be banished.

Elemental things will be used in the Easter liturgy: charcoal, wood, wax, water, and—above all—fire. Fire, perhaps the most strikingly elemental of all these gifts of God, is a powerful reminder of creation. 'And God said "Let there be light"; and there was light.' In Haydn's oratorio, *The Creation*, after a dark and subdued representation of chaos these words are sung *pianissimo* until the word *Licht,* light, explodes in a dramatic *fortissimo* with an effect unsurpassed by any romantic composer.

Light is the most powerful of all symbols. It banishes the terrors of the night. These terrors are perhaps less real to us who command light at the touch of a switch. But it was not always so. Fire enabled our ancestors to survive two ice ages. It gave them warmth and it lit the frightening hours of darkness. It continues to symbolise the faith-inspired conviction that creation is good in spite of its layers of darkness. It is the primary symbol of what happened on that first Easter night when God once again said 'Let there be light' and there was light—the light of Christ. *Lumen Christi* is proclaimed by the deacon in a darkened church which will shortly flame into an exultant confession of faith in the risen Lord.

No one has caught the blend of exultation and warm domesticity of this night better than the ninth-century Irish scholar and poet, Sedulius Scottus, whose *Carmen Paschale* has been brilliantly translated by another Irish scholar and poet, Helen Waddell.

> Last night did Christ the Sun rise from the dark,
> The mystic harvest of the fields of God,

And now the little wandering tribes of bees
Are brawling in the scarlet flowers abroad.
The winds are soft with birdsong; all night long
Darkling the nightingale her descant told,
And now inside church doors the happy folk
The Alleluia chant a hundredfold.
O father of thy folk, be thine by right
The Easter joy, the threshold of the light.[2]

From this point on, the wayfarer's path is lit by a light which faith makes inextinguishable. It does not so much banish darkness as conquer it and rob it of its intimidating powers. We are now able to celebrate human existence as a gift from God which is not rudely snatched from us by death. Death, 'the last enemy', is defeated by the victorious Christ. Faith in the resurrection does not remove death or our natural aversion from it. Faith in the resurrection is not a kind of metaphysical whistling in the dark. It is rather a quiet and heartfelt recognition that what happened to Jesus of Nazareth will happen to all of us, and that although it is an uncovenanted gift, it none the less responds to our deepest yearnings. The resurrection puts death in eternal perspective.

One short sleep past, we wake eternally,
And death shall be no more. Death, thou shalt die.[3]

The liturgy of Easter is a celebration of life itself. It brings together the panorama of creation and the revivifying powers of God's Spirit moving once again over the face of the waters (Gen. 1:2) and breathing into the dead body of the Son of Man the breath of life, making him once again a living being (Gen. 2:7), this time translated to a new realm of existence beyond time and space yet capable of communicating in a mysterious way with time- and space-bound men and women. St Paul is very clear that when we celebrate the resurrection of Jesus we are celebrating the resurrection of all humanity.

Critical study of the resurrection of Jesus is a minefield. Exegetical and philosophical analysis of the resurrection narratives can easily leave the reflective believer paralysed and incapable of venturing upon any interpretation of what happened. This is a ridiculous and indefensible posture for any believer. One simply has to take a stand somewhere among the discrepant interpretations.

The debate has been largely controlled by one's view of the relationship between the Jesus of history and the Christ of faith. In general those theologians who emphasise the discontinuity between the historical Jesus and the Christ proclaimed in the kerygma can afford to disregard the historical significance of the life and death of Jesus. For them faith in the proclaimed Christ is what matters and it colours every account of what Jesus said and did. There is no way back to the Jesus of history. The New Testament narratives, especially of the resurrection, have the character of myth and cannot be treated as sources for knowledge of what actually happened. In this view it is in effect the faith of the disciples which rises. Death on Calvary put Jesus beyond the reach of history. After Calvary he lives on in the faith of his followers. If the articulation of their resurrection faith seems to suggest a historical dimension, this is only because myth has to borrow the garments of history. As soon, however, as logos gets to work on mythos, the garments disappear and we are left with pure faith having no point of historical reference apart from the interior dispositions manifested by the disciples.

Today for a variety of reasons there is widespread reaction against this view of the resurrection of Jesus. Its conception of history is seen as too positivistic and its dependence on existentialist philosophy leaves it vulnerable to the charge of tying itself to an ephemeral philosophical fashion. A faith which begins in historical particularity can hardly reach its culmination in a kind of latter-day gnosis severed from all historical anchorage. Bultmann and Marxsen have the merit of challenging all Christians, even those who profoundly disagree with them, to accept that there is a significant discontinuity between all that happened before Calvary and all that happened afterwards. There is, after all, an important truth contained in Bultmann's remark that the proclaimer became the proclaimed and that this change in the focus of faith had far-reaching implications for the content of faith. This truth is particularly important for soteriology. The risen Christ is God's answer to the worst that his creatures can do to his creative designs. It inaugurates a new age with new perspectives. It calls for and empowers a new vision of what is possible and what is to be done. The risen Jesus is at the heart of the new age.

The word 'new' could mislead here. It does not imply an abolition of the old but rather its transformation. It is a 'new creation' but, unlike the first creation, it is not *ex nihilo*. The new creation is what the Spirit of God does to the first creation. The first creation does not cease with the arrival of the new. On the contrary, it continues, lit now by a new light which reveals new possibilities and powered by new energies which make those new possibilities a reality. Something of profound importance for creation has happened in the life, death, and resurrection of Jesus of Nazareth. The first Christians know this intuitively and seek to express it, as we shall see, through a variety of images and analogies borrowed from ordinary human experience. Something has happened—*and it has happened in the first instance to Jesus of Nazareth.*

It is precisely at this point that the issue of continuity between the Jesus of history and the risen Jesus becomes inescapable. In terms of creation, leaving aside the issue of redemption, there has to be this continuity. Something *cosmic* has to happen if there is to be redemption in any real sense. A Christ who arises only in the human heart cannot meet the demands of a universe in travail. He may indeed inspire the apostles to go out without fear to preach salvation to a fallen world; but if his resurrection is no more than their re-focused faith, then he himself is reduced to a glorious memory recalled and utilised in a surge of apostolic determination. What happened to Jesus of Nazareth *does* matter, even though we lack the language to describe it. The faith of the Church has been from the start that what was raised from the dead was a *body* and not simply a soul, a spirit, a memory, or an inspiration. The trouble is that we have no language to describe a 'body' which is no longer in our time and space, just as physicists have no language to describe what may have preceded the Big Bang. The comparison is deliberate. I am not suggesting that the cosmic explosion with which our universe would appear to have begun is necessarily the moment of creation. I am, however, suggesting that Christians have no business taking refuge in gnostic dualism as a stratagem for dealing with problems of creation *ex nihilo* and bodily resurrection from the dead. We may not know how to describe a risen body, but that does not license us to disregard its existence. We may be puzzled and embarrassed by the gospel descriptions of a body that can pass through solid matter like doors and walls, to say nothing of its appearing and disappearing at will, and yet can be touched. Revelation tells us nothing about the physical properties of risen bodies, and physics tells us nothing about the state of affairs before the singularity in which the universe began; but such proper agnosticism is not a denial that there *is* a state of affairs to be accepted if not accounted for. To profess faith in the resurrection of the body, as Christians do in the creed, does not entail the ability to describe the characteristics of a risen body. Equally, to express ignorance about the characteristics of a risen body does not prohibit one from professing faith in bodily resurrection.

Real, if indescribable, continuity exists between the historical and the risen Jesus. Soteriology itself depends on such continuity. The circumstances of Jesus' death and resurrection, however difficult they are to recover from the historical evidence, are of signal importance to a convincing and effective theology of salvation, precisely because these circumstances occur regularly in human history. If salvation is to have cosmic meaning, it has first and foremost to mean that the creator is not defeated by the worst that men and women can do to each other and to those who come in the name of the creator, including especially, his own Son; nor is he limited by the physical conditions which obtain in our universe. A risen body is a body translated from the conditions characterised by entropy. This is, after all, the substance of hope. The world will pass away but not before the new creation has been completed by the transforming action of God's Creator Spirit. If Christ is at the heart of this transforming action, then the life, death, and resurrection of Jesus are integral to it. This in turn means that we cannot be content with a faith which is exclusively located in what happened within the minds and hearts of the disciples of Jesus. I say 'exclusively' with deliberation. There is no *historical* way back to *either* the Jesus of history *or* the risen Jesus except through the faith of the disciples after Easter; but this limitation, however frustrating it may be, does not license the believer to profess lack of interest in either. Least of all does it license the believer, in the name of faith, to profess a virtuous disregard for the historical character of what happened in so far as this can be recovered. To be sure, there are daunting interpretative problems to be met. How could it be otherwise where the historical anticipates the eschatological in the resurrection of Jesus of Nazareth?

To attend primarily to the apostolic and early Christian experience of the risen Christ in no way implies attenuation of belief in the reality and objectivity of what actually transpired. It merely recognises that apostolic and faith-inspired interpretation of the event is an indispensable part of the event itself. This recognition is particularly important for any soteriological apprehension of the meaning of the risen Jesus who is proclaimed in the kerygma to be the Messiah, the Christ, the Annointed of God. Salvation which is not experienced as salvation would be without meaning. Yet salvation is more than experience. It has objective reference. Something transformed the scattered and demoralised disciples of the earthly Jesus into a joyful, directed, and determined band of men and women dedicated to proclaiming the glorious news that Jesus lives and acts now through God's Spirit at work in the world, and that he is present in the proclamation and serving spirit of the Church—that is, the body of believers commissioned to go out into the world announcing that God in Jesus has reconciled the world to himself (2 Cor.5.19). The theological task entailed by this proclamation consists in a variety of attempts to give this truth negotiability and meaning in all the circumstances in which men and women find themselves in any age. Soteriology is the complex of such attempts. As we shall see, it is largely expressed through symbolic narratives or models borrowed from human experience. Such narratives and models have all the imperfections of any attempt to express the inexpressible through analogy with experiences on which we have direct empirical purchase.

The disciples experienced the risen Jesus primarily as the

friend and master who understood how they felt after their denial of him and their flight from the scene of danger after he had been arrested. Clearly he had not returned to life in the sense of simply taking up again his former life. Whatever the resurrection narratives are trying to convey, it is not simple univocal continuity of life after a brief and terrible interval. This is the same Jesus, to be sure, but in a very different mode.[4] According to the evangelists he possesses some of the qualities of historical existence such as location and tangibility, but even these properties are modally different, for his body is apparently not subject to ordinary physical laws. The resurrection narratives leave a score of questions unanswered about this new mode of existence and they can scarcely be harmonised with one another; indeed their incoherence has been invoked as an argument against the reality of the whole phenomenon they are trying to describe. This incoherence of the narratives can, of course, also be invoked in favour of the truth of what they seek to describe: we should be rightly suspicious of too coherent or clear an account of an event which of its very nature defeats the power of language to capture it. Jesus in his risen state belongs to a different realm of existence, though he can make contact with his historically situated followers. He belongs to 'the age which is to come', the 'end-time'.

His followers, however, belong to time and space. This fact alone makes it impossible to describe the resurrection without nuance or qualification as 'historical'. We have already noted that the word 'historical' does not simply mean 'what really happened', as if there was no interpretative process involved in the concept of history. The resurrection of Jesus is an eschatological event with historical implications. Jesus does not return to his former life, though according to the gospels he can and does make limited empirical contact with those who knew him 'in the flesh', as Paul puts it. Paul believes it important to observe that Jesus is no longer 'in the flesh' that is, time- and space-bound, as he had been before his death. Yet those who met him risen were insistent that they had not met a wraith, a ghost, a spirit. Those who report him as risen make no attempt to give a coherent account of 'risenness'. They were not reporting back to laboratories, to conventions of philosophers, or to students of paranormal phenomena. Yet we are conscious today that Christian faith is legitimately open to scientific, philosophical, and psychological questions. It is this divergence of interest (in the fullest sense of the word) between their approach to the resurrection and ours which creates theological problems for us today. Once we have abandoned the naïve realist view of resurrection as the resuscitation of a corpse, we have no choice but to admit our inability to provide simple unqualified answers which will meet all the demands of science and critical thought.

One may be willingly agnostic about the mode of existence enjoyed by Jesus of Nazareth after his resurrection, but one cannot simply dismiss it as irrelevant merely because it poses unanswerable questions. For this reason the debate over the empty tomb remains important. Accepting the basic historical reliability of the report that the tomb was empty does not of itself commit one to the view (a) that resurrection is the resuscitation of a corpse, or (b) that belief in the resurrection would be fatally compromised by any clear demonstration (if such were possible) that the tomb was not empty. Exegetes distinguish between the tradition of the empty tomb and the tradition on which the appearance narratives are based. The distinction is important even for those who accept both traditions—apparitions and empty tomb—as authentic.

Edward Schillebeeckx, however, goes much further by postulating an experience which *precedes* both tomb and appearance phenomena. For Schillebeeckx the primary Easter experience is one of conversion, first of Simon Peter, then of the other apostles.[5] This conversion arises directly out of the experience of forgiveness.

> May it not be that Simon Peter—and indeed the Twelve—arrived via their concrete experience of forgiveness after Jesus' death, encountered as grace and discussed among themselves (as they remembered Jesus' sayings about, among other things, the gracious God) at the 'evidence for belief': the Lord is alive? He renews for them the offer of salvation; this they experience in their own conversion; he must therefore be alive.[6]

This intimation of forgiveness was what Ian Ramsey would

have described as a 'disclosure experience'. The apostles, probably inspired by Peter, come to a realisation that they are forgiven for deserting Jesus in his hour of greatest need; but 'a dead man does not proffer forgiveness': *therefore* Jesus is risen.

It is that 'therefore' which leaves one uneasy and vaguely suspicious of being in the presence of an unintended sleight of hand. It is an important insight which Schillebeeckx offers us—too important to rest upon what has the feel of a logical flaw. That they could have reached the conclusion that the Jesus they had known *would have* forgiven their infidelity is not in question. That they could through prayer and discussion become convinced that the God he addressed as 'Abba' now forgives them is also not in question. That they could conclude from the interior conviction of forgiveness to the reality of the risen Jesus is, however, a different matter. For Schillebeeckx the conviction of forgiveness, together with the conversion it inspired, is the controlling Easter event. The appearances and the empty tomb are appendices to the main event. Schillebeeckx is asking us to believe that a dawning conviction, strengthened by discussion, of Jesus' will to forgive constitutes the major element in the change which came over the frightened and demoralised apostles. It is an attractive proposition, but it hardly convinces. Could such an experience have been free of doubt and of an anxiety lest it be self-deception? Could it have relieved them of their fear and sense of having been abandoned? What Jesus *would* have done is not the same as what he actually *does*. If he *does* it; he is risen. But can this 'does' be no more than a matter of dawning conviction? Surely something more tangible, more immediately present and—dare one say it?—more convincingly 'objective' (in the sense of 'outside themselves') is called for to account for the change in them? The conversion of which Schillebeeckx speaks is a strikingly pertinent and appropriate *preparatio evangelica* for the encounter with the risen Jesus. One can hardly take it for the main event.

It may indeed have predisposed them for an encounter with the risen Jesus (though this remains speculative, since the New Testament says nothing about it). What is attested to by the gospels is their conviction that the resurrection is an event of forgiveness. The risen Jesus is the forgiving Christ who

105

establishes the Church as a body of forgiven sinners with a mission to communicate this forgiveness to others.

Schillebeeckx is here engaged in a dialectical task, namely, that of correcting the excesses of 'empiricist objectivism' without capitulating to the subjectivist interpretations of Bultmann and Marxsen.[7] He explicitly repudiates the notion that the resurrection of Jesus consists merely in the conversion and renewed faith of the disciples. The resurrection is indeed something which happens to Jesus personally, but it cannot be dissociated from its effects on the disciples. For Schillebeeckx the resurrection is radically soteriological: it brings salvation, healing, new hope, and, above all, forgiveness. The resurrection, the sending of the Spirit, and the foundation of the Church are one and the same event.

> Therefore one cannot speak of Jesus' personal resurrection without speaking at the same time of his saving presence in our midst as experienced here and now and articulated in belief in the, resurrection: Easter experience, renewal of life and reassembling or 'being the Church'.[8]

This view of the resurrection is in keeping with Schillebeeckx's philosophy of experience.[9] 'Experience', he writes, 'is always interpreted experience'. In the neo-Scholastic theological schema the resurrection was interpreted in a markedly empiricist and objectivist manner. It was seen as the greatest of Jesus' miracles and therefore as the most important authentication of his claim to be sent by God. The closest model for this view is photography of the kind which allows for no interpretative processes. It simply registers what is 'out there' by pointing the camera in the right general direction and hoping for the best. Viewed this way, the resurrection lacks soteriological content and becomes a kind of divine magic specially performed by God to show that he is still in charge. It does not speak to the human condition, it merely says, 'Look, only God can do this sort of thing (i.e. raising people from the dead), therefore give the assent of your mind to all that Jesus has taught in God's name.' Many years ago Maurice Blondel characterised this approach as 'extrinsicism'—a concept of revelation and grace which lacked both mystical and moral reference. Catholic theology since Vatican II has had to recover this mystical and moral dimension by learning to appreciate the implications of subjectivity in the whole salvific process. Schillebeeckx in his two great books on Jesus Christ makes a major contribution to this enterprise.

The disciples, then, do not simply register the fact of the risen Jesus as one might register the fact that today is a sunny day. For the apostles the resurrection was an overwhelming experience of love, trust, reconciliation, healing, and forgiveness. The friend and master whom they had in their different ways betrayed and abandoned was alive again, bringing direction where there was indirection, joy where there was sorrow, confidence where there was diffidence, resolution where there was irresolution, and, above all, forgiveness where there was self-recrimination and a paralysing sense of guilt. The road had been closed for them; now it was open and shining before them. A new Paraclete had come among them, sent by both Jesus and the one whom he had taught them to call 'Abba'. They were overpowered by the experience of forgiveness, of being accepted by God and recognised by the risen Christ. They were forgiven and sent out to forgive. Sin would still be present in their own lives and in the lives of those they met, but God in Jesus had conquered sin. They would have to face death, but God in Jesus had conquered death. They had a glorious message, based upon their own experience of their reconciling encounter with the Lord, and they were commissioned to spread that message abroad in the world. The Spirit of Jesus and the Father would be with them and their disciples to the end of time. They had not been left orphans but were now learning to interpret all that Jesus had taught them, and moreover to interpret it in the light of his death and resurrection.

His earthly teaching now took on a new and urgent meaning. They could now understand much about Jesus which had previously escaped them. In this sense the proclaimer indeed became the proclaimed. He had proclaimed the Kingdom of God; they were now learning, through their own experience of reconciling love, the profound lesson that to proclaim God's Kingdom is to proclaim Jesus as the Christ, the Lord of all creation. This is what it means to be Church: to recognise that an undistinguished band of men and women had been formed into a brotherhood and sisterhood of people upon whom the Spirit was resting and among whom Jesus was present. And it was all pure gift, utterly unmerited, unexpected, and wholly wonderful.

James Mackey has suggested that many of the resurrection encounters took place in a Eucharistic context (Emmaus is the paradigmatic instance).[10] It would follow from this that the Eucharist remains the primary setting for an encounter with the risen Jesus, which in turn means that salvation is experienced and celebrated primarily in the Eucharist. If, of course, it is not being experienced in daily life, there will be nothing to celebrate in the Eucharist.

What is beyond dispute is the fact that the first Christians proclaimed Jesus not merely as risen but as *saving*. What could this mean? We have here the first and controlling question of soteriology. Like so much else in the gospel message, it was susceptible of 'spiritualisation', i.e., of exclusive location in the world to come. The word 'exclusive' is important here. Christian faith affirms that salvation is *finally* and completely expressed in a realm beyond history; but death merely places a seal on what has already been taking place in this world.

All sorts of circumstances prompted the early Christians to see this world as a vale of tears and consequently to look to the world beyond death as the real world. The Platonism of the Church Fathers gave philosophical underpinning to this attitude even after Constantine and Theodosius had brought this world into the Church as a political reality. It is, however, one thing to regard the world to come as one's real home and quite another to contract out of the abrasive realities of life here below. The world is not saved by an individual or even communal yearning for the delights and consolations of heaven. The world is saved by exposure to the Word of God expressed in human terms in the words and deeds of Jesus of Nazareth, now risen and acting through the mission of the Holy Spirit. It is the Holy Spirit who gives new life and new effectiveness to the words and deeds of Jesus preserved in the memories of those who knew him in the days of his flesh and proclaimed by them in the light of his resurrection. That memory and that proclamation are historical to the core. They originated in the restrictive circumstances of time and place and they are directed to those who live in the restrictive circumstances of time and place. That is why we speak of salvation *history* and not merely of salvation, which would be much easier, as gnostics of every age realise. Salvation does not come simply through a privileged gnosis or cosmic awareness that good has conquered evil in and through the death and resurrection of Jesus. Of course such an awareness is crucial to the mission of the Church. Gnosticism has at least the virtue of pointing to a contemplative dimension in the doctrine of salvation; but no one is saved by knowledge alone. It is faith which saves, and faith has to be lived out in historical circumstances; which means that it has to interact with events in space and time and not merely contemplate an other-worldly drama taking place beyond the reach of space and time. There is a history to be redeemed, because history did not come to a halt with the death of Jesus.

In theological terms history is sinful by virtue of being human. It does not cease to be sinful after Calvary. Even those who are redeemed contribute to the world's sin. Human beings bring their fractured condition to every enterprise they undertake. Every human enterprise needs redemption, because the men and women who engage in it need redemption. There seems to be a contradiction here: the believing Christian is redeemed yet is in continuous need of redemption. Jesus wins the world for the Father on Calvary, yet the harvest remains to be gathered in. Sin is denied its final victory but not its intermediate power. The death of Jesus is a once-for-all event, but its efficacy is spread across the span of history. The resurrection of Jesus speaks of victory, but the fruits of that victory have to be appropriated by faith and then worked into the fabric of a continuing history. It is this conviction which gives rise to the thorny question of how salvation history is to be related to universal, secular, history.

By all expectation the resurrection of Jesus ought to have signalled the end of history. The Messiah was expected to be a figure of the end-time, a leader who would conduct Israel to its theocratic apotheosis. And so the first Christians eagerly awaited the imminent coming of the Lord. The faith of Israel was that a Messiah would come. The faith of the first

Christians was that he had indeed come, had been rejected by his own, but would come again. Everything suggested that his second coming would be soon, since the coming of the Kingdom meant the end of history. But he did not come again, as months lengthened into years, years into decades, and decades into centuries. The Christian Church has as its charter a hope deferred. The Church exists as a group of men and women inspired with the thought that there is a world to be saved, and charged with the conviction that the history of salvation, so far from ending with the death of Jesus, has begun a new and challenging chapter which has its centre in the risen Christ.

The Church is living in the end-time and has been doing so for the last two thousand years. In short, the existence and mission of the Church are eschatological. It is not easy to make sense of an end-time which has already lasted so long and in principle could last for millions of years more. It was easy for the first Christians to expect the end of time. For their successors there is the problem of plausibility. Universal history has shown no sign of an impending end. From time to time it has had its prophets of imminent doom. On the whole, however, those who proclaim that the end is nigh are likely to be seen as cranks. Even in an age like ours when we have the power to blow our planet apart or exterminate all life with deadly man-made bacteria one cannot plausibly speak about the end of history without adding 'as we have known it'; and that is not what the Bible understands as the end. The need for salvation transcends bombs and bacteria. The death and resurrection of Jesus will continue to have a bearing upon whatever human life might survive the criminal lunacy of unrestrained warfare in the late twentieth century. The continuation of history after Calvary constitutes the same theological problem for Christians today as it did for their earliest predecessors. The questions remain the same: Why did Jesus die on Calvary? How does his death affect the lives of men and women? Why did God allow it to happen? Above all, what implications did his death have for the relations between God and humankind? The answers to these questions, however halting and tentative, constitute that branch of theology known as soteriology. Before turning to enquire into the meaning and scope of salvation it may help to reflect briefly on its deepest symbol—the cross.

If it is true that our universe began in an explosion of unimaginable power, then the cross of Christ was, for the Christian, already implicit in that primordial manifestation of creative energy. It is no accident that the cross became the most powerful symbol of both creative and redemptive power. From being a sign of contradiction and degradation the cross has become the very geometry of self-sacrificing love, or rather of the price which God is prepared to pay so that love may become the most powerful energy in the universe. The cross is probably the most all-embracing and pervasive symbol ever produced by a religion. Its symbolism, however, is shot through with paradox. In origin a symbol of shame, it became a symbol of glory. In origin a symbol of utter powerlessness, it became a symbol of transcendent power. In origin a symbol of degradation, it became the symbol of triumphant and healing gladness.

The symbolic transmutation which took place in historical imagination in respect of the cross is a fascinating illustration of what a symbol is, or rather, of what a symbol does, and of how it receives its meaning and its ability to address the imagination by suggestion, intimation, and general impression. There is nothing intrinsically noble or holy about the pattern produced by an upright post with a bar across it. Its geometrical simplicity lends itself to investment with different meanings, good and bad. (One has only to recall that the swastika is a cross). Until in the early fourth century Constantine banned crucifixion as a method of execution, the symbolic impression made by a cross would, even for Christians, have been one of shame. To use the language of a later theology, the cross would have been firmly associated with the historical Jesus who was nailed to it, since that was how the Romans executed the worst of their criminals. Only subsequently would it be emblematic of the triumphant Christ. The fact that the Christian eye has grown accustomed to the cross as one of its holiest symbols makes it difficult for the later believer to recapture its original historical association with degradation and powerlessness.

When we come to consider, not the cross as a geometrical

symbol, but the crucifix with its figure of a tortured man with outstretched hands, we shall see that the possibilities for symbolism grow richer still. We easily underestimate the feat of imaginative interpretation which is called for whenever the Christian looks at a crucifix and sees it as a numinous phenomenon. We scarcely realise the extent of what happens when the baptised imagination is able to dwell on the tortured body of a crucified man not merely without repulsion but with a profound sense of the holy. An unbeliever was once heard to say to a friend that she wondered how Catholic parents could leave such a frightening object where children could see it. Such remarks are salutary for all of us who are liable to allow our sacred iconography to become a cheap grace through convention.

Let us here in conclusion return to the empty cross and derive from it one last, but powerfully suggestive, piece of symbolism which has striking relevance for soteriology. Paul, preaching in the synagogue at Antioch, reminded his hearers of what had taken place in Jerusalem a few years earlier. The rulers and people in Jerusalem, 'though they could charge [Jesus] with nothing deserving death, yet they asked Pilate to have him killed. And when they had fulfilled all that was written of him, they took him down from the tree, and laid him in a tomb' (Acts, 13:28-9). Here the word *zulon* can mean 'tree' or 'gibbet'; and it spontaneously suggests an extension of the theme of the two Adams on which Paul liked to dilate. It generates a myth of graceful and apt symbolism.

John Donne, in the grip of what he believed to be a terminal illness, gives this myth a classical expression:

> We thinke that Paradise and Calvarie,
> Christs Crosse, and Adams tree, stood in one place;
> Looke Lord, and finde both Adams met in me;
> As the first Adams sweat surrounds my face,
> May the last Adams blood my soule embrace.[11]

This in turn reflects the Preface for the liturgy of the Holy Cross:

> The tree of man's defeat became his tree of victory;
> Where life was lost, there life has been restored
> Through Christ our Lord.

112

The Christian imagination has often delighted in the antithetical correspondences between the two trees, one bringing slavery and death, the other bringing deliverance and life. The first Adam's sin launched him and his descendants on a pilgrimage of sweat, blood, and tears. The second Adam's sacrificial obedience, through sweat, blood, and tears, opened up a new road to salvation and hope for all who are prepared to find the wellsprings of faith and joy in the spectacle of a crucified man opening his tortured arms to a world grown cold and apathetic. There is cosmic meaning to be found in this terrible scene; but it has to be found by acts of interpretation made possible only by the startling belief that the Creator of all things 'has highly exalted [Jesus] and bestowed on him the name which is above every name, that at the name of Jesus every knee should bow, in heaven and on earth and under the earth, and every tongue confess that Jesus Christ is Lord, to the glory of God the Father' (Phil. 2:9-11).

How Original is Sin?

ONE of the major difficulties about the word 'sin' is its semantic instability. It is more than usually dependent on its context for its meaning. Like creation, it should have an exclusively theological reference, but it has also been secularised, usually with prejudice to its original meaning. Tabloid newspapers use it in salacious reference to unconventional sexual activities. The phrase 'to live in sin' has a ludicrously restrictive reference, hardly ever being applied to those who, for example, habitually abuse power or engage in shady business deals. Religious moralisers sometimes claim that we have 'lost the sense of sin'. This may indeed be true but perhaps not as they understand the phrase. The most serious ambiguity of all is that the word 'sin' may be used to describe an offence in its objective reference (George killed James) or to describe the effect that an offence is deemed to have on the offender's relationship with God (George 'committed a serious sin'). This ambiguity is particularly evident, for example, in the case of offences committed by the mentally sick or the emotionally disturbed. The absurd legal phrase 'guilty but insane' enshrines the ambiguity in an expression which lacks logical coherence in its subjective reference. To perform an act which is objectively wrong does not necessarily mean that the performer is subjectively culpable. If an act is not free in the sense that the agent was capable of knowing that what he did was wrong and was free not to do it, then he cannot be properly described as guilty, unless the word 'guilty' is being incorrectly used to mean simply that what he did was wrong.

In its theological usage, then, the word 'sin' is not synonymous with wrong-doing, and still less with illegality. One classical definition of sin is 'any offence against the law of

God'. This definition suffers from some of the defects noted above. Wrong-doing is properly called sin only when it is related to God the creator. Sin is not a synonym for wrong-doing or crime. In a court of law sinners are to be found on the bench, among the jury, and in the witness-box quite as much as in the dock. Indeed there are cases in which the sinfulness of the accused may be far more in doubt than anywhere else in the court-room. If George who is mentally ill to the extent of having little if any control over his acts and emotions, kills James, his act, viewed from the standpoint of a healthy imagination, comes under the category of tragedy rather than sin. It can indeed be properly described as evil, because theologically the concept of evil has a built-in ambiguity which embraces suffering as well as wrong-doing. The relationship between offence and culpability is mysterious and sometimes profoundly and disturbingly ambiguous. Much of the older type of moral theology, while allowing that there might be 'lack of advertence' or less than 'full consent' in individual circumstances, proceeded on the general assumption that offenders know what they are doing, know that it is wrong, and are perfectly free not to do it.

One thing, however, is quite clear: human beings treat each other for both good and ill in a way not possible for electrons, algae, or antelopes. *Homo sapiens* possesses possibilities for good and ill which do not belong to other species. Men and women can care, know that they ought to care, and experience remorse when they do not care, for their fellows. The sense of right and wrong is one of the most remarkable developments in evolutionary process. J. H. Newman regarded the presence of conscience quite simply as a 'first principle'. In his *Grammar of Assent* he refuses to try to prove its existence. He merely tells us that if we look at our own experience, we shall find it there, for it is plain for all to see. Conscience, he remarks, 'does not repose on itself, but vaguely reaches forward to something beyond self, and dimly discerns a sanction higher than self for its decisions'.[1]

Conscience 'is a connecting principle between the creature and his Creator; and the firmest hold of theological truths is gained by habits of personal religion'.[2] The existence of conscience is a signal of transcendence. It inspires us to ascend through our own experience to the existence of One who gives conscience its final meaning. More than anything else it defines our species as orientated to God whether we like it or not. This orientation is of course not restricted to conscience. It manifests itself as a pervasive sense of incompleteness, of yearning and of unsatisfied aspiration. Nevertheless conscience, in the sense of knowing that some deeds are good and others wrong, has a remarkable ability to suggest the transcendent. It does, as Newman claims, link creature and Creator in a very particular way. In evolutionary terms it belongs to culture rather than to nature. The existence of moral consciousness is particularly resistent to reductionism. One can speak anthropomorphically of 'selfish' genes, but the power to love transcends genetic programming. The power to love, however, presupposes freedom; and freedom entails the power to refuse to love.

'Man', said Goethe, 'is the first conversation which nature holds with God'.[3] In men and women creation arrives at a point where God can offer it an invitation to intimacy. Hominisation, however, means freedom to refuse as well as to accept. Sin is refusal of, or apathy towards, the offer. Redemption is not a new offer, but the original offer coloured by the refusal. Creation, sin, and redemption form part of the one sweep of divine love and they should not be considered as temporally successive happenings. The drama should therefore be laid out in the present continuous tense: God is creating; men and women are partly cooperating and partly rebelling; and God is offering forgiveness, reconciliation, and healing.

Did something go wrong at a critical stage in human history? This question will tend to divide believers into those who think that orthodoxy demands that we affirm an actual, and by implication a specially serious, sin committed at the dawn of history, and those who recognise the anthropological implausibility of such a special sin. It is one thing to affirm that man has sinned since the dawn of history and quite another to hold that our remote ancestors committed one specific sin the cosmic effects of which were handed on biologically to each succeeding generation.

The doctrine of original sin was once, and in certain Church circles still is, advanced in a way which invites rejection by critically-minded believers and gratuitously exposes Christian faith to ridicule by non-believers. The Genesis account, if taken as a literal description of an actual historical event, runs counter to what is known about the origins of human life. Furthermore, if the genetic model (i.e., the inheritance of sin 'by generation') is pressed, it can offend against the most elementary sense of justice. Finally we must note that the very phrase 'original sin' is highly problematic because of its associations with a frequently misunderstood mythology and also because the word 'sin' in the phrase 'original sin' is semantically most peculiar. The task which faces the Christian theologian today is to show how one can and must accept the reality of the situation which the phrase 'original sin' was designed to cover, but to do so without an appeal to what Newman called 'some terrible aboriginal calamity'.[4] If the classical doctrine of original sin is not re-interpreted, there is a danger that the reality it seeks to describe will fail to be recognised by those who reject its traditional mythology when it is presented as literally true.

The doctrine received its classical formulation from St Augustine, who also coined the phrase 'original sin'. Perhaps the best way of understanding how the doctrine in its traditional formulation came into existence is to look briefly at the matter as Augustine saw it at the beginning of the fifth century.

Augustine is one of those theologians whose theology is born out of personal experience carefully observed. This is passionate theology, not always systematically consistent, but expressed in a style which pays noble content the compliment of graceful expression. Augustine would have instinctively felt that if you are going to write about a sublime subject like the Trinity, you should be able and willing to match your language to your topic. His *De Trinitate* shows that he did so. Any reader who ever studied a neo-Scholastic treatise, *De Deo Trino*, will recall what can happen to style when a topic is drained of passion and poetry and has as its main concern the avoidance of verbal heresy. Augustine was a stylist through and through, and stylists are often particularly susceptible to images. They aim their writings at the imagination—that is, they write with instinctive awareness of that mode of mental activity which is often impressionistic, alert to the existential power of metaphor, and capable, as the poet Ted Hughes puts it, of relating the 'outer world' around us to the 'inner world' of human experience.[5] There is danger as well as power in this kind of writing. The author can be carried away by his emotional involvement in his subject. Augustine writing about Adam and Eve and their fall from grace, was writing with a fervour born of his own emotional experience. When he was a young student in Carthage, he came under the influence of the Manichees, who played on his youthful inexperience, his disenchantment with the Bible, especially with the 'barbarous' tales in the Old Testament, and above all on his growing obsession with the provenance of evil. If creation is good, where does evil come from? The Manichees (followers of the Babylonian religious leader, Mani) professed a radical dualism of good and evil in the full Gnostic tradition. This appeared to settle the question of the origin of evil as a problem in theodicy. Evil, according to the Manichees, comes from the primal figure of Darkness and inheres in the physical world. What Manicheism left in serious doubt, however, was the omnipotence of the God of Light, who could hardly be said to be doing well in the cosmic battle. It was a convenient doctrine for someone of Augustine's passionate make-up. One was a passive spectator in the cosmic battle taking place all around, and even within, oneself. 'I . . . held the view that it is not we who sin but some other nature within us.'[6] Manicheism continued to hold his allegiance while he remained in Carthage until, having been finally disillusioned by the inability of Faustus, one of its leaders, to answer his many questions, he became first a sceptic and then a Platonist. Finally under the influence of Ambrose of Milan he became convinced of the truth of Christianity.

What happens next is crucial to an understanding of Augustine's doctrine of sin and grace. Neoplatonism had inculcated in him a deep respect for virtue as knowledge. If one really *knows* the good, one will inevitably follow it. That confident belief did not match Augustine's experience. He practised Platonic contemplation, his attraction to Christianity was growing daily, but he found himself powerless to take the last effective step by asking for baptism. Then came the breakthrough.

Augustine was one of those whom William James would classify as having a 'twice-born' temperament. He had a passionate conversion experience which is grippingly recounted in the eighth book of his *Confessions*. Suddenly, it seemed to him on later reflection, he was empowered to carry through into living commitment what had up to that moment been a cherished and deeply-willed but impossible ideal. Neither mind *nor will* had achieved the breakthrough. From now on his prayer to God would be *Da quod jubes et jube quod vis*, 'Give the power to carry out your command, then command whatever you wish.' Grace makes impossibility possible. But it did not explain the origin of evil. Furthermore, what Augustine was saying about grace seemed to some Christians to be dangerously passive and quietistic. These were people, many of them aristocratic, who had come under the influence of a Celtic monk named Pelagius. Pelagius has had a bad press largely because he gave his name to a heresy of great theoretical importance in the Western Church and because he was one of Augustine's most notorious adversaries. His quarrel with Augustine was a very Western affair, which Eastern Christians found difficult to understand.

The Western Church condemned Pelagius as a heretic who denied the necessity of grace; but in the centuries which followed there has been many a fierce guardian of verbal orthodoxy who has all unawares practised the purest Pelagianism. Exhortations like 'Pull yourself together' and dicta like 'Where there's a will there's a way' have a Pelagian ring to them. Muscular Christianity of the type practised in many a school and seminary might appropriately have had Pelagius as its patron. Pelagians take a no-nonsense view of the human condition. As they see it, mysticism and a tragic sense can sap the will and destroy its sense of purpose. Pelagius felt that Augustine's emphasis on the flawed nature we have inherited from Adam could serve to promote moral lassitude and quietistic resignation. Henry Chadwick puts it nicely: 'To tell people that their will was corroded to the point of almost total incapacity seemed to Pelagius fatally enervating. . . . The doctrine that everything is the gift of grace, including the very will itself, seemed . . . debilitating to the point of catastrophe.'[7]

It might be argued that temperaments can be divided into

those who instinctively side with Pelagius and those who instinctively side with Augustine. Born managers, successful entrepreneurs, effective military leaders, and dynamic football coaches cannot afford much sympathy with the tragic element in life. The Spanish philosopher, Miguel de Unamuno, was reflecting Augustine's tragic sense when he wrote that

> the most tragic problem of philosophy is to reconcile intellectual necessities with the necessities of the heart and will. For it is on this rock that every philosophy that pretends to resolve the eternal and tragic contradiction, the basis of our existence, breaks to pieces.... It is not enough to think about our destiny: it must be felt.[8]

Augustine would have concurred whole-heartedly. In his view we are defined at least as much by our desires as by our powers of intellect and will.

Augustine's doctrine of original sin is specifically an attempt 'to reconcile intellectual necessities with the necessities of the heart and will'. The trouble is that he pursued the logic of tragedy to its extremes and gave to others less passionately endowed than himself a doctrine of pessimism about the human condition which not even his equally heartfelt doctrine of grace could relieve. Augustine's God is so supremely and minutely in control of events in this world and salvation in the next that he leaves enfeebled men and women wondering in anguish whether he has decided to save them or not. John Calvin would take Augustine's premises to their logical conclusion.

It was Augustine who designed the chart that Western Christian theology would use in the centuries which were to follow. Its aim was to pilot the believer between the Scylla of gnostic dualism on the one side, and the Charybdis of Pelagian optimism on the other. It postulated an original fall from grace and from untroubled bliss into the state in which we find ourselves today. We know what is good, but we do not pursue it. To depict this disturbing gap between ideal and performance Augustine borrowed Tertullian's model of the *tradux*, a vine-shoot prepared for further growth. Tertullian had claimed that by Adam's sin 'man was given over to death, and has made the whole race, drawing contamination from his seed, a stock or breed (*traducem*) stained with his own condemnation'.[9]

Augustine tightened the argument into humankind's 'seminal' identity with Adam:

> For we were all in that one man [Adam], when we *were* that one man who fell into sin.... Not yet had the particular form been created and apportioned to us in which we were individually to live; but there was a seminal nature from which we were to be propagated.[10]

Augustine's imagination had now seized on a prolific image. A few years later he developed the notion of seminal identity further, qualifying it with legal, pathological, and botanical models:

> Hence being made an exile after his sin [Adam] also bound by the penalty of death and condemnation his own race which by sinning he had corrupted in himself as in a root.[11]

The imagery now loses all restraint:

> This therefore was the case: the damned mass of the whole race was lying, indeed wallowing, in evils, being tossed from evils to evils, and, being joined to the faction of those angels who had sinned, was paying the most frightful penalty of its wicked disloyalty.[12]

This sort of language comes easily to the trained rhetor who is intent on matching style to content. It needs to be read as poetic hyperbole. When the Scholastics got at it, they reduced it to flat, emotionally neutral analysis. Augustine's passionately deployed models became, in Scholastic hands, matter-of-fact dogmatic descriptions. Botanical and legal metaphors were employed to qualify the essentialist concept of nature, thus forming a metaphysical system which literalised them and turned them into abstractions. Augustine had employed the concept of 'nature' with little regard for logical coherence. The Scholastics employed it with abstract precision. Pelagius had said that Adam's sin had the effect of bad example. It did not *change* human nature. Pelagians such as the Italian bishop, Julian of Eclanum, protested that natures cannot be changed:

Adam did not cease to be a man just because he had sinned. Julian protested that Augustine's position was in effect a capitulation to Manicheism—a charge which stung Augustine and provoked him to make some rather snide personal remarks about Julian. It was not an edifying debate, but it witnesses to Augustine's deep emotional involvement in its outcome.

The classical doctrine was given conciliar expression at the Council of Trent which affirmed that Adam's sin 'is one in origin and is passed on by propagation not by imitation'. The council continues, 'even children who in themselves could have as yet committed no sin, are therefore truly baptised for the remission of sins, so that by regeneration there may be cleansed in them what they contracted by generation'. Trent is here simply rehearsing the teaching of the provincial Council of Carthage (AD 418), which in turn is employing Augustine's arguments against Pelagianism. It is important to remember this historical circumstance. 'Propagation' is specifically intended to be antithetical to 'imitation', while 'generation' acts as a foil to 'regeneration'. The context in which these words are used limits and defines their function. Taken out of context, they can seriously mislead. 'Imitation', as Pelagius had employed it, conveyed an environmental, purely extrinsic, conception of the origin of sin. The orthodox response was to make 'propagation' the orthodox antithesis of 'imitation' and to intend it to mean the inherent, antecedent, sinfulness of men and women even before they have been exposed to bad example and have begun to sin personally.

Regeneration is a model apt to speak with immense force to someone of Augustine's temperament; but it also led him to dramatise his entire pre-conversion existence and to concentrate the essence of that existence into the concept of generation. The result was that in his writings 'generation' takes on a semantic function of supreme ambiguity. On the one hand it is a literal description of the handing on of life; on the other it is a model designed to suggest the notion of sin. For the generation/regeneration model to become thoroughly unstable all that was needed was a further literalisation by means of the concept of concupiscence. Augustine's detestation of sexual desire made him attend more closely to the physical circumstances of generation and consequently to see in the specifically sexual element of those circumstances the very paradigm of sinful, unregenerate, activity. Although Augustine does not identify concupiscence exclusively with sexual desire, he quite plainly finds in that desire the most powerful sign and manifestation of sinful unreason. The effect on his theology of sin is notable. 'So it is that from this concupiscence of the flesh birth takes place, but it is a birth into the world not into God.'[13] Here again we notice a confusion of models. Concupiscence and birth into the world are literal; birth into God is figurative. Both are deployed in a way that may be taken to imply their one-to-one correspondence.

In order to avoid a total identification of concupiscence with sin, Augustine distinguishes between flaw (*vitium*) and guilt (*reatus*). Concupiscence is the flaw which survives baptism to remain in the baptised as both weakness and penalty. Weakness remains as a punishment while guilt is removed. Concupiscence is therefore the cause of personal sin, the weakness resulting from sin, and, in some measure, the temporal punishment due to sin. It destroys freedom but leaves free will. Martin Luther would later cut through this intricate knot of distinctions by simply identifying sin with concupiscence, thus reaching a conclusion from which Augustine finally shrank.

The doctrine of original sin remains sensitive, especially in the Catholic Church, and any attempt to re-state it in a manner which will carry meaning and relevance for modern men and women is liable to draw fire from traditionalists who see no need for such re-statement and who remain content to repeat the pre-critical formulas which were employed to express a very important doctrine which is easily betrayed by purely verbal orthodoxy. In the following chapter I shall suggest how the doctrine might be interpreted in a way which responds to the legitimate demands of a critically aware faith.

The human existence which results from a faith-inspired acceptance of the demands of Christian discipleship is an adventure in which each individual shares. The primary drama is a social one, involving the entire human race from the dawn of history down to the eschatological completion of God's plans for his creatures. The doctrine of creation is therefore at the heart of our project. The perspective is Christian but the scope is human. This is not a study of how Christians see *themselves* as participants in the drama, but of how Christians see the whole *human* drama. Christian life and human life are not two separate lives. Christian life is human life seen from the perspective of the good news of Jesus Christ.

There is a Christian doctrine of creation because of the felt need to affirm the universal sovereignty of God, the dependence of the world upon him, and the non-identification of nature with him. There is a doctrine traditionally named 'original sin', because of the need to account for the palpable admixture of evil with good wherever human beings are to be found. How are these two doctrines to be mutually related? How can we affirm that creation, coming from the hands of God, is necessarily good, and at the same time recognise the presence and pervasive influence of evil?

We have seen Augustine's dilemma: If we recognise evil as a necessary feature of existence, we thereby postulate a fissure between good and evil at the heart of being itself. This Gnostic view, adopted by the Manichees, makes human beings tragic spectators caught up by virtue of their finitude in the cosmic struggle between good and evil. To be finite is, in this view, necessarily to be evil, though with the possibility of being redeemed through a salvific awareness of what is going on (*gnosis*). Augustine rejected this view as finally subversive of the very idea of God. God is infinitely good by definition and therefore all that he does is good. Evil cannot have its source in creation itself nor can it have ontologically ultimate roots. Evil is something which happens to good, a distortion which supervenes because of the misuse of intelligence and freedom. It is historical and therefore shares in the contingency of history. It belongs not to ontology but to anthropology.

The other limb of Augustine's dilemma was the Pelagian option: human beings enter life in ontologically good and morally neutral circumstances. Their lives will be morally characterised by the free choices they make. There is no antecedent compulsion or predisposition to sin, apart from the bad example of those who misuse their freedom. Augustine rejected this sunny view of the human condition as quite simply failing to account for the facts of human moral experience. His own experience had convinced him that there is a human predisposition towards evil which he calls 'concupiscence' and which constantly threatens to subvert even the best of intentions. We therefore find him charting his course, with considerable difficulty, between Manicheism and Pelagianism. The result is a doctrine of *original* sin based on human solidarity with the first man, Adam. This doctrine was not seriously in contention during the Reformation, except to the extent that the Reformers set about emphasising the degree of corruption which has afflicted human nature since the Fall, while the Council of Trent defended the essential goodness of human nature, even though fallen.

The case against the doctrine began to be made in earnest during and after the Enlightenment, when an unbounded confidence in human ability and a disdain for dogmatic religion became a feature of educated secular thought.

The objections which can be brought against the traditional statement of the doctrine of original sin are formidable. In its classical formulation the doctrine is heavily dependent for its credibility upon a literal and pre-critical interpretation of Genesis, coupled with a particular reading of Romans 5. In depicting a state of original innocence, understood historically, it flies in the face of what we know about human origins. In literally attributing the guilt of the first man's sin to all his descendants it offends against even our most rudimentary sense of justice—an offence which is intensified when the doctrine is applied to unbaptised infants.

I have been implying that a careful examination of the language employed in the traditional statement might enable us to distinguish between the substance of the doctrine (which is unnegotiable) and the manner of its formulation (which is subject to cultural change). In the light of this distinction three doctrinal truths can be recognised as belonging to the substance of Christian faith. (1) Christ is central to the whole divine economy, which includes creation, revelation, and redemption. (2) Every human being is in need of the redemption won for the race by Christ. (3) The need for redemption is antecedent not merely to the commission of personal sin but also to exposure to sinful influences: this antecedence is the most fitting meaning we can attribute to the word 'original' in the term 'original sin'. As long as these truths are safeguarded, the accompanying images and arguments can, I submit, be modified, re-interpreted, and in some cases even abandoned without infidelity to divine revelation or Catholic doctrine.

Critical biblical study has established the character and purpose of Chapter 3 of the Book of Genesis. It should be read as an 'aetiological myth', that is, as a symbolic story told to account for the situation in which human beings find themselves. The myth of the Fall is an imaginative attempt to explain, through symbolic events, how it is that we find ourselves in our present moral situation both as individuals and as a race. Human existence is a bewildering amalgam of good and evil. Each one of us knows himself or herself to be capable of good and bad deeds. As a result, the societies of which we are members bear all the marks of our divided selves. Sometimes the social expression of division appears to take on a life of its own which is additional to the divided selves of those who share in it. Human experience and action is often morally ambiguous and sometimes psychologically ambivalent. We rarely come up to Kierkegaard's idealistic injunction to 'will one thing'; indeed it is doubtful that we ever could do so. Our seemingly disinterested acts frequently conceal interested motives of which we are perhaps unaware. This ambiguity and ambivalence can be seen in children long before they are capable of moral response in the adult sense. Thus a child embraces a baby brother leaving the observer in some doubt as to whether the embrace is an affectionate hug or a hammerlock designed to deal with the inconvenient challenge of a rival sibling. The correct interpretation may well be that it is *both*. Social constraint will later teach the child overtly to eschew (and probably repress) the aggressive element. In the adult who is in touch with his or her feelings such ambivalence can be disturbing and distressing, so much so that many of us repress the aggressive element and concentrate on the caring and rational element in our attitudes and actions. In an age like ours, which is characterised by awareness of the human subconscious, we have fewer excuses than our forebears for ignoring the presence within us, both individually and socially, of forces which can be given an expression that is positive and life-enhancing or negative and destructive. Conscious moral response to these forces will determine whether our attitudes and acts will in fact constitute good or evil.

The sense of division experienced by normal human beings as they contemplate their essays in moral behaviour is classically expressed in the seventh chapter of the Letter to the Romans in which Paul in somewhat breathless prose seeks to explain a characteristic piece of Jewish psychology to the Greek mind.

> I do not understand my own actions. For I do not do what I want, but I do the very thing I hate. Now if I do what I do not want, I agree that the law is good. So then it is no longer I that do it, but sin which dwells within me (Rom. 7:15-17).

Paul is doing two things here. He is drawing attention to the phenomenon of the divided self, which any person can discern by introspection and social observation. (Some commentators on Romans advert here to Ovid's *video meliora proboque, deteriora sequor*, 'I see and approve of what is better, but I pursue the worse course'.) Paul goes further than merely observing the phenomenon of the divided self; he seeks to explain it by appealing to a force called 'sin' dwelling within us. He comes startlingly close to personalising this force and making it responsible for the evil we do in spite of our better selves.

Following this Pauline lead, the Pastoral Constitution, *Gaudium et Spes* of Vatican II observes:

> Man therefore is divided in himself. As a result, the whole life of men, both individual and social, shows itself to be a struggle, and a dramatic one, between good and evil, between light and darkness. Man finds that he is unable of himself to overcome the assaults of evil successfully, so that everyone feels as though bound by chains.[14]

These words are intended as a factual description of the human condition, recognisable not merely to believers but to any realistic observer of the human scene. The council is here utilising what Maurice Blondel called 'the method of immanence', that is, a modified and non-imperialistic form of apologetics which relies not on external signs and wonders but on the implicit logic of inner human experience. In a daring remark which owes much to French transcendental thought, the passage concludes:

> Both the high calling and the deep misery which men experience find their final explanation in the light of [Christian] Revelation.

Blaise Pascal had remarked that man is the glory and the scandal of the universe and is a mystery to himself. *Gaudium et Spes* reflects this thought and makes it the link between sin as the experience of individual and social division, on the one hand, and redemption by Christ, on the other. We shall consider the redemptive aspect later. Here it is sufficient to note how it can be theologically prepared for by individual and social observation. Although the word 'sin' belongs to the religious vocabulary, the phenomenon it describes is universal. In short, although one does not have to be a believer in order to be a sinner, one may have to be a believer to accept one's condition as remediable. 'Sin' is a specifically theological word and should be preserved as such. It is not a synonym for crime or wrong-doing. It identifies wrong-doing in the light of God's redemptive purposes. It is ultimately a hopeful word, because, unlike such words as 'crime', 'felony' and 'misdemeanour', it always suggests the possibility of forgiveness and newness of life as its correlative.

Forgiveness lies at the heart of God's relationship with humankind. To be human is to need saving and healing. Now it has to be admitted that this is a strange and possibly, to some ears, even a repellent claim. Augustine himself was tormented by the thought of attributing sin to infants, yet he was forced by his own logic to do so. They could not be personally guilty, so the source of their guilt had to come from elsewhere, namely, from Adam. Does one have to hold on to Augustine's macabre imagery and mythology in order to vindicate him against Pelagius and Julian of Eclanum? Or can Augustine's basic insight be retained in a demythologised form? I believe that it can, and that the way to do so is to take evolution with theological seriousness.

Some theologians hold that man rather than nature should be the object of a theology of creation. We have also seen how a theologian like Moltmann has reacted agains this existentialist anthropocentrism by emphasising humanity's dependence upon its natural matrix. Moltmann actually calls his theology of creation 'environmental' in order to draw attention to this feature. He notes that modern philosophical anthropology has chosen to start from the question, What *distinguishes* human beings from animals? He, on the contrary, proposes to begin from the question, What *links* human beings with animals and with the rest of creation? This change of emphasis is significant not merely for ecological reasons. If it is accepted that *homo sapiens* is biologically descended from animal ancestors, then it matters anthropologically *and theologically* that we take this genealogy into careful consideration when we are seeking to determine the question of what it means to be human in terms of nature's relationship with God. St Paul speaks of nature groaning for its salvation. One can interpret this either as no more than anthropomorphic projection or else as a recognition that man belongs to nature and that through man nature is given a voice to articulate its relationship with God. Paul's meaning is by no means clear, but it is almost inevitable today that we should read more into it than Paul intended to put there. Pierre Teilhard de Chardin found a great deal of inspiration in the eighth chapter of Paul's Letter to the Romans.

The link between nature, animate and inanimate, and mankind can be considered physically, biologically, and (in default of a more precise word), mystically. Our early human ancestors experienced the power of this link both physically and mystically. Their response to it was Dionysian rather than Apollonian. They did not speculate about it; they felt it, celebrated it, and feared it. It formed part of the unseen world in which they lived, reproduced themselves, and died. Later, as a result of the rise of the higher religions and of philosophy, man learned to differentiate himself from nature and nature from God. This differentiation was a necessary stage in human cultural evolution, but there was a price to be paid both theologically and anthropologically. God was recognised as Lord of creation but at the expense of a recognition of his active presence *in* creation. Man's sense of the power of dominion over the rest of creation, ostensibly legitimated by divine injunction, eventually led to a distorting and predatory relationship with his environment which, as a result of modern technology, we are now coming to see as not only unhealthy but positively dangerous to the future of mankind itself.

Any satisfactory theory of sin, especially of 'original' sin must reckon with man's physical, chemical and biological roots in his natural environment. It was, and is, precisely the 'creationist' view of human origins which disregarded, and disregards, the pervasive significance of these roots. By reducing biblical mythology to a pseudo-scientific explanation of man's appearance on earth, the 'creationists' have been forced to oppose the findings of modern scientific investigation into the origins of man. In the creationist view Adam comes from the slime of the earth, but he does so without any biological intermediaries. He names the animals to signify his dominion over them but he fails to recognise his biological inheritance from them. His animal nature appears to be autonomous and physically underived. When his descendants see an ape in the zoo they see not a biological cousin but an alien species. They simply ignore the physiological and zoological similarities and insist instead that they are on the side of the angels. Such a view is scientifically inexcusable and theologically gauche. Evolutionary theory, supported by a vast amount of empirical evidence, cannot with impunity be dismissed as theologically irrelevant. There is no choice to be made between beast and angel: the harder and truer choice is how to discern the mystery of their combination in one species.

Does modern scientific consciousness, then, mark the end of that phenomenon traditionally labelled 'original sin'? Far from it. The Enlightenment strove to emancipate itself from what it took to be the most obscurantist of Christian doctrines and it succeeded only in replacing it with a ludicrously favourable assessment of human nature and its moral possibilities. No realistic world-view can afford to ignore the dark side of human beings and their social existence. The pre-critical doctrine of original sin, for all its bizarre imagery, at least accepted the shadow before pointing to the light.

The question which faces us today is not whether we can jettison the doctrine as an anachronism, but whether we can interpret it in a way which is faithful to its basic insight that is to be human is to need redemption.

Creation and Alienation

IT is impossible to point to an exact moment when a being one can confidently label 'human' appeared on the cosmic scene. Anthropologists, by the painstaking study of fossils, can indicate the existence of a branch of apes whose members adapted better than others to life in the plains of Africa, whose bodies grew erect, who (which?) used simple tools, and most significant of all, who began to develop a language for communication.

> Nothing is more striking and more sustained in the whole of human evolution than the twofold trend towards increase in brain size on the one hand, and, on the other, towards cultural activities, cultural mastery, and indeed utter dependence on culture for survival. These two sets of changes are indissolubly linked. The chain between them may be set forth simply as follows: increase in brain size → gain in intricacy of neuronal organization → rise in complexity of the nervous function → ever more diversified and complicated behaviour responses → progressively amplified and enhanced cultural manifestations.[1]

In short, hominisation results from the mutual feedback between biological development, especially of the brain, and cultural development, especially that of increasing proficiency and sophistication of language. Man is, above all, the animal who communicates.

It was to be the nature of that communication which would determine the religious and moral character of our species. Simple instinctual communication would no longer suffice if *homo sapiens* was to fulfil the evolutionary promise of all that had gone before. With the emergence of our species a whole new range of possibilities opened up. In theological terms, if the actualisation of these possibilities were to conform to the will of the Creator, a new creation would be needed. Yet the first creation would not thereby cease. The new creation is not a new entity, autonomous and unrelated to primordial creation; it is the guiding, healing, and ennobling, in short, the transformation, of primordial creation. Medieval theologians referred to the realm of the new creation as the 'supernatural'. Later the neo-Scholastics treated the supernatural as an entity in its own right and emphasised its distinctness from nature.

Supernaturalism, the mirror image of reductionism, is not interested in, and may indeed be embarrassed by, the biological process through which our species came to be. It emphasises the discontinuity at the expense of the continuity. It is prepared to make the handsome concession that 'grace builds on nature'—a metaphor which puts nature in its place as a mere foundation to hold up the supernatural building within which the real God-inspired living is done. Such juxtaposing makes a poor image for conveying the dynamic relationship between nature (in *either* of its senses) and grace. Grace is not a detached entity; it is something magnificent which happens to nature. It is nature lit by a new light and fired with a new vision. Whatever metaphor we choose, it should convey the image of suffusion not juxtaposition. We must take careful note of the ambiguity of the word 'nature' when it is used as one limb of the nature/supernature dialectic. If we take nature to mean essence or substance, neither grace nor sin can alter the nature of *homo sapiens*. Julian of Eclanum was right to make this point against Augustine.

If, however, we take 'nature' in a non-essentialist sense, then nature *does* change, and morality as well as physical evolution depends on this possibility. It is precisely *evolving* nature which makes the *humanum* possible. Essentialism has its proper place, but it is powerless to represent *gradual* change. It waits to pounce on a new essence. It wants to decide whether *Homo habilis* and *Homo erectus* were 'human', had human souls, belonged to the race redeemed by Christ. Such questions lack scientific reference; and theology is incompetent to answer them. Hominisation was a long process (by our, if not by Nature's, standards). Whether there was a mutational leap into hominisation or whether hominisation took place gradually is partly a scientific and partly a philosophical question. It largely depends on how we define 'human'. Theologians need to move with extreme caution in this matter. No special revelation has been given about the physical detail of hominisation—which is why the monogenism/polygenism debate has been a theological cul-de-sac.

Most theological speculation on original sin has been uninterested in what preceded *homo sapiens*. Pre-critical theology accepted the Genesis myth as a factual account, so the question did not arise. Later neo-Scholastic essentialism, even when it accepted the main lines of evolutionary theory, still postulated a historical point at which a specific man and woman appeared on the scene and became the progenitors of the human race. In the light of all that has happened in scientific anthropology and biblical criticism the question of how to relate creation to the Fall arises in a pressing manner especially for Catholics, who have to reckon with the authority of doctrinal formulas they have inherited. John XXIII and the Second Vatican Council lessened the pressure here by their distinction between the substance of doctrine and the manner of its formulation. This leaves some room for re-interpretation and re-formulation. By and large, recent Catholic interpretations of original sin belong to one or other of two schools of thought, the situationist and the personalist.

Situationists like P. Schoonenberg and K. Rahner treat men and women as historical beings who experience their freedom against a social environment. Situationists draw heavily on the language and philosophical preoccupations of existentialism. To be human is to be 'situated in the world'; but this situatedness is sinful in that it is the product of sinful history. Original sin here is interpreted environmentally: man is thrown into a sinful world.[2] This school of thought has difficulty in showing how it avoids the stigma of Pelagian environmentalism, but it is well suited to a theory of sinful history.

Personalists like A. Vanneste are not interested in origins. It is enough for Vanneste that every human being *de facto* sins: He therefore finds no need to distinguish between personal and original sin: to be human is to be an actual sinner.[3] Neither

133

school of thought pays significant attention to the pre-personal disposition towards sin.

Protestant theologians are less constricted by ecclesiastical formulas than Catholics are and they therefore have greater room for theological manoeuvre. Apart, however, from this ecclesiastical circumstance, there are substantive theological reasons why Protestantism approaches the matter from a different angle. Luther's identification of concupiscence with sin, together with his doctrine of the Christian as *simul justus et peccator*, 'at once pleasing to God yet a sinner', makes it less necessary to wrestle with the problem of reconciling destiny with freedom or graced existence with moral achievement. The Christian, for Luther, is totally sinful yet at peace with God through graced faith in the redeeming Christ. Catholicism never felt the same freedom as Lutheranism to detach moral performance from graced existence—hence the Catholic doctrine of merit. Furthermore where Luther had claimed that human nature is totally corrupted by sin, the Catholic response was that it was not totally corrupted but rather 'wounded', 'despoiled', or 'damaged'.

Ecumenical study can hope to show that there is not as much difference between the Catholic and Protestant positions on justification (the process whereby God makes the believer acceptable in his sight) as might at first sight appear. Luther and the Council of Trent were speaking two different languages and were thus at cross-purposes in much that they were claiming. It might be said without too much distortion that the traditional Catholic position before Vatican II was abstract and essentialist while the Protestant position was more concrete and open to later existentialist interpretation. Each viewpoint is needed as a corrective to the other. Paul Tillich, who wrote from a Lutheran and existentialist perspective, was nevertheless able to say that essences, or universals, 'liberate [man] from bondage to the concrete situation to which even the highest animals are subjected'.[4] Tillich, however, qualifies this remark by his entire theory of what it means to be human. Men and women actualise themselves in concrete, existential, situations.

Tillich's theory of man and sin is based on the relationship between essence and existence. Essence for Tillich is not unlike a Platonic Form or Idea, except that the Tillichian essence is pure potentiality. When it is 'realised', it becomes distorted, since the reality cannot come up to the perfection of the essence. The myth of Adam and Eve in the garden is a brilliant representation of essential humanity. He calls it 'dreaming innocence'. It never actually existed but remains a synchronic myth, applicable to every stage of existence and history. The passage from essence to existence is a 'fall' into freedom. It involves the loss of dreaming innocence which, however, remains in human experience as a kind of nostalgia. The freedom brought about by the fall into human existence is partly moral and partly tragic. Man projects his yearning for dreaming existence back to his origins and finds there a state of being for which he instinctively craves but knows he cannot have. He has to actualise himself through concrete decisions, but the price he pays is loss of innocence and the painful acquisition of a state of anxiety in the face of non-being. He experiences estrangement, from God, from self, and from his environs. It is part ethical and part tragic. Man is partly responsible for it by his decision to actualise his potentialities and partly the victim of a tragedy for which he has no responsibility. The tragedy stems from the fact that he has acquired a destiny, and the acquisition is inevitably sinful. 'Creation and the Fall coincide in so far as there is no point in time and space in which created goodness was actualised and had existence.'[5]

Tillich's ideas on creation and fall have been criticised from different standpoints. He ties them so firmly to existentialist philosophy and German idealism that he leaves little or nothing for Christians who are opposed to, or at least unconvinced by, either. The most serious theological charge that can be brought against his position is that he makes sin (= estrangement) a necessary feature of becoming existentially human. For all Tillich's concern with existential actuality, he is as little interested in the biological development of man as any neo-Scholastic. In spite of these deficiencies Tillich's ideas remain stimulating. He appreciates that there is in human existence a tragic element which is easily missed by compulsive moralisers or dismissed as 'romanticism' by social realists. He also dwells on the truth that unless one has the freedom to say no to God, one is not in a position to love him either. Tillich's myth of 'dreaming innocence' has been convicted of incoherence in that it deals purely in potentiality and lacks concrete reference not merely in protology (the theology of human beginnings) but also in eschatology (the theology of human end). I would, however, wish to argue that something like dreaming innocence can be found in man's biological beginnings and that it can be invoked without necessary reference to Platonism or German idealism.

The Jungian anthropologist, Erich Neumann has written as follows:

> The essential fate of man, at least of the mature modern man, is enacted on three fronts which, though interconnected, are nonetheless clearly marked off from one another. The world as the outside world of extrahuman events, the community as the sphere of interhuman relationships, the psyche as the world of interior human experience—these are the three basic factors which govern human life, and man's creative encounter with each of them is decisive for the development of the individual.[6]

These are extraordinarily suggestive words when taken in the context of their author's philosophical position. He is, as a disciple of Carl Jung, interested in the phenomenon of individuation—that is, a process of healing which comes about through an equilibration of the conscious and unconscious. The conscious mind is rational, ordered, and structuring. The unconscious is unbridled, disordered, and unstructured. The two are constantly at war in the individual psyche. The wisdom brought by individuation enables a person to understand what is going on and to become reconciled to it.

The sociologist, Claude Lévi-Bruhl, speaks of the pre-logical character of primitive human thought. He sees primitive man as engaging in 'a network of mystic participations and exclusions'. Primitive man experienced life 'as an unbroken continuous whole',[7] agrees Ernst Cassirer, who goes on, however, to question Lévi-Bruhl's concentration on the pre-logical character of primitive human approaches to life. Cassirer is more impressed by primitive man's sense of the *oneness* of his world and his attempts to share in that oneness sympathetically. Primitive myths are an attempt to express this sympathy. They are products not of thought but of feeling.

> Primitive man by no means lacks the ability to grasp the empirical differences of things. But in his conception of nature and life all these differences are obliterated by a stronger feeling: the deep conviction of a fundamental and indelible *solidarity of life* that bridges over the multiplicity and variety of its single forms. He does not ascribe to himself a unique and privileged place in the scale of nature.[8]

Neumann, reflecting these ideas, speaks of 'man's original fusion with the world'.

> History teaches that in the beginning the individual did not exist as an independent entity, but that the group dominated and did not allow the emancipation of a separate ego. We find this state in all departments of social and cultural life; everywhere at the outset there is an anonymous collectivity.[9]

The ambiguity of this state is worth pondering. In an age of raw individualism we tend to admire its apparently harmonious and uncoerced socialism. There can, of course, be no question of our returning to it in its original form. It is no more open to us than is the tranquillity of an animal chewing the cud, unaware of its tenuous hold on life and its destiny in the abattoir. In the process of evolving creation, and especially in the human pilgrimage, there is never any going back. What Jung describes as the collective unconscious endows us with a nostalgic sense of lost peace, and our imagination does the rest.

The summers of our childhood were always sunny. Our present situation often seems to be bathed in the light of a setting sun. At such moments eschatological realism should suggest to us not a midday which has passed but a sunrise which is to come, provided we can face the intervening and transitional dark. That is the pattern of human pilgrimage. Man could not remain in the undifferentiated unity of his primitive days if God's purposes were to come to fruition. To be sure, he would continue to yearn and search for unity, harmony, and integrity in his relationship with the world, his fellows, and his own inner life, and, through all these, with the God who creates him. He had to go forward into individuality; and increasingly he came to realise that his journey was as much a fall as a progress. He had to become alienated from an earlier existence in order to arrive at his later destinations. He had to embark on a phase of evolution which is cultural rather than physical or biological. Yet he must bring the physical and biological with him. They continue to clamour within him for their own kind of peace, but the world he is making will not allow him to satisfy his atavistic yearning. He must go forward weighed down by a genetically produced nostalgia for his lost animal past, a nostalgia which is locked into his bones and flowing in his veins. This condition is therefore a much more flesh-and-blood reality than Tillich's dreaming innocence. It is not an ideal; it is a fact of life. No wonder we human beings experience life partly as exhilarating promise and partly as condemnation to a threatening freedom. No wonder we construct our myths to express and account for the ambiguity of life and the ambivalence of our feelings. We have eaten of the tree of knowledge of good and evil, and there is no turning back to a primitive innocence whose loss we feel so painfully.

It was St Augustine who, more than any other theologian, gave us the grim doctrine which amounts to what Ricoeur has called the 'massive indictment of the whole of humanity'.[10] We can, however, also discover in Augustine's writings a line of thought which accords better with our modern evolutionary awareness and with our unwillingness to think of God as the moral policeman of human existence and history.

In two remarkable chapters of his book, *On the City of God*, Augustine examines the human condition in terms of peace. Peace for Augustine is 'the tranquility of order', the harmony existing between all the elements which go to make up creation and within it the human creature. Augustine does not, of course, approach his topic from the standpoint of evolutionary biology, but he is clear and unhesitating about what man has in common with the animals, namely, a body and a soul. The passage is striking.

The peace of the body, then, consists in the duly proportioned arrangement of its parts. The peace of the irrational soul is the harmonious repose of the appetites, and that of the rational soul the harmony of knowledge and action. The peace of body and soul is the well-ordered and harmonious life and health of the living creature. Peace between man and God is the well-ordered obedience of faith to eternal law. Peace between man and man is well-ordered concord. Domestic peace is the well-ordered concord between those of the family who rule and those who obey. Civil peace is a similar concord among the citizens. The peace of the celestial city is the perfectly ordered and harmonious enjoyment of God, and of one another in God. The peace of all things is the tranquillity of order. Order is the distribution which allots things equal and unequal, each to its own place.[11]

Peace is understood here not merely in a psychological but also in a metaphysical way. It has hierarchically graded levels. In Chapter 14 of book XIX Augustine develops this theme. If we were irrational animals, he writes, we would want nothing more than the peace of the body and the peace of the appetites which belong to the irrational soul, and by satisfying these we would fulfil our purpose in accordance with God's will.

But, since man has a rational soul, he subordinates all this which he has in common with the beasts to the peace of his rational soul, that his intellect may have free play and may regulate his actions, and that he may thus enjoy the well-ordered harmony of knowledge and action which constitutes, as we have said, the peace of the rational soul.[12]

If we give an evolutionary interpretation to Augustine's insight into the levels of peace within individual men and women and within the societies to which they belong, it becomes possible to interpret the Fall in terms of the passage from one level or phase of evolution to the next. (Augustine's Neoplatonism leads him to speak in terms of body and soul, but this model is not indispensable to his argument.) One has to 'fall', or be alienated, from a lower level of peace in order to attain to the higher. Thus the appetites, instincts, drives, and energies the simple satisfaction of which brings peace to the irrational animal cannot of themselves bring peace to the rational animal, because the rational animal attains to peace only through the 'harmony of knowledge and action'. The knowledge made possible both by a larger brain and by increasingly sophisticated means and content of communication holds out the promise of a completely new destiny which can no longer be achieved by the 'harmonious repose of the appetites'. The irrational animal knows; the human animal knows that he or she knows. Self-awareness has intervened to make all sorts of new adventures possible, but it also brings in its train new fears and anxieties. Self-awareness is also death-awareness. As Theodosius Dobzhansky has put it, 'A being who knows that he will die arose from ancestors who did not know'.[13] Dobzhansky goes on interestingly to reflect on human death-awareness: 'is this the evolutionary acquisition corresponding to the Biblical symbol of Fall?'[14]

In addition to all this, the human animal has acquired a knowledge of good and evil, in short, a conscience, a sense of right and wrong, which will no longer allow him/her to rest in the lesser peace of the irrational animal. But hominisation does not separate men and women from their irrational and semi-rational origins. The human race appears to have had a long primitive existence during which cultural as distinct from physiological development took place. Moral sense would appear to have grown slowly. One imagines that rudimentary examples of altruism, of a kind not observable in animals, could be found in early human behaviour. Presumably the urge to go to the aid of someone in need, even though it put one's own safety at risk, was felt and acted upon well before it became the object of reflection and thus of conscious virtue. It typifies and illustrates Augustine's insight into the hierarchical levels of peace. The animal instinctively looks after its own interests or instinctively acts for the good of its species. This new animal, *homo sapiens*, has achieved a level of existence within which the instincts of self- and herd-preservation are no longer the only governors of behaviour. Something far-reaching and awesome in its implications has happened. Evolving nature has transcended itself to the extent that the older mechanisms for preservation and well-being are no longer sufficient either for social survival or for a peaceful relationship with the Creator who is now perceived to be addressing his creation in a way which makes new demands and offers new possibilities. Those earlier mechanisms, however, still remain to be challenged by the newly developing consciousness of right and wrong and they can reassert themselves at any time or place, as for example in the case of a hit-and-run driver whose instinct is simply to get away from a threatening situation as his pre-human or semi-human ancestors would have done in an analogous situation.

Do the instincts, drives, and energies proper to a non-human primate, then, become sin when they are found in human beings? Clearly they do not, since they too come from the hands of the Creator. They can, though, become the means, the vehicles or instruments of sin, if they are not shaped, bridled, harnessed, healed, and directed by that expression of divine providence which has been traditionally called grace. All that God does, including creation itself, is grace in the sense of gift, but theologically the word is especially associated with that unique expression of divine providence which seeks a free response in beings who have the power of rational thought and autonomous action. There is, however, a psychological price to be paid for this growth into expanding rationality and autonomy. As Jung has pointed out, the journey into greater consciousness entails for human beings a distancing from their instincts.[15] These instincts are not supplanted by reason and conscious willing. They remain, often to be ignored or repressed. Human beings can try to live their lives as if pre-human animality and race-memory played no part in their journey towards God. Notoriously, such failure to face the demands of the unconscious can result in mental and emotional disturbance, and this disturbance in turn can be an obstruction to that wholeness which in religious language is called holiness.

We must be careful about the conclusions we draw from this observation. Man has 'fallen' from the level of peace appropriate to his animal ancestors which lived instinctually. With the development of mind and consciousness, including the consciousness of good and evil, the human animal has consciously to consider the implications of satisfying his or her instincts. In some situations instinctual satisfaction may be perfectly in accord with the new and elevated level of peace (in Augustine's terms, 'the harmony of knowledge and action'), e.g. to rest when one is tired, to drink when one is thirsty, or to defend oneself from attack. In other situations the instinctive reaction will not be in accord with that harmony between knowledge and action which is both possible for, and obligatory upon, men and women, e.g. to react violently to a trivial provocation or to take what belongs to someone else merely because one experiences the urge to do so. Man is consigned to a level of peace which is both gift and demand. His instincts yearn for a lesser peace; his mind and rationally instructed will do not allow him to seek his peace at a lower level. If God may be said to 'speak' to the animals through their instincts, he speaks to men and women through their reason which, Augustine remarks, is precisely what elevates humankind above the animals.

Augustine, however, attaches the greatest importance to desire as a compass for guiding human beings towards God.[16] He frequently observes that we are defined by our desires. In his early Platonist period he was disposed to consider the advisability of seeking that stilling of desire which the Stoics called *apatheia* and which can be found in the writings of such early Christian philosophers as Clement of Alexandria. Later, Augustine moved away from this search for emotional stillness. It did not accord with his pastoral experience as bishop of a highly emotional people. He reached the intuitive conviction that to kill desire is to kill one's humanity. The Christian task is not to kill desire but to direct it into the paths willed by God for man. Man must indeed live by reason; but he cannot live by reason alone. In many respects Augustine remained a Platonist all his life, but he consciously repudiated the Platonist ideal of contemplation as an escape from the angularities and sometimes abrasive realities of life in space and time. More and more he came to see human, and therefore Christian, life as a journey to be undertaken in faith, hope, and love.

Earlier he had sought a 'stillness... of thought, free from space and time'.[17] As a bishop he sees the necessity of seeking and doing truth amid the turbulence of everyday existence. In this existence the mind must go into partnership with will and desire. The word *delectatio*, delight, plays an increasingly significant part in his thinking and teaching. The journey towards God is guided by the grace of God which delights the mind and draws the will. The initiative lies with God; and if recognition of this truth gives rise to problems about the providence and partiality of God, such problems must be pondered in fear and trembling, not evaded by a mystical leap into eternity.

> If those things delight us which serve our progress towards God, that is due not to our own whim or industry or meritorious works, but to the inspiration of God and to the grace which he bestows.[18]

That progress towards God is powered not by abstract thought or by contemplative *gnosis* but by a nostalgia for eternity. The Christian is here explicitly defined as a pilgrim whose journey is motivated by the desire for God. Prayer is the expression of that desire and 'yearning is the heart's core'.[19] The virtue appropriate to pilgrimage is faith, which in the period immediately following his conversion Augustine tended to see as the common man's substitute for the contemplative gnosis practised by an élite. He used the image of the proud man who sees from afar the land which is his destination but is ashamed to take ship with the masses. He contrasts this proud and ineffectual élitism with the condition of the humble man of faith who, though he cannot see his destination, is content to board the ship which he knows will bring him there.[20]

The human journey to God really began when the raw materials of physical existence emerged from the initial cosmic explosion widely accepted today as the event, or 'singularity', in which our universe originated. Along the way, some striking developmental leaps occurred of which the most striking was the emergence of an animal who achieved self-consciousness, the power of abstract thought, together with the ability and need to communicate rationally with other members of the species. All of nature is caught up in this tremendous adventure, because *homo sapiens* is part of nature. If, however, the rest of nature is inferior in achievement to man, it also possesses an innocence which he has lost. The advance from inorganic to organic being gave rise eventually to pain. But the advance from pre-rational and unconscious animality to a being in whom evolution became cultural was to give rise to something more traumatic: the gratuitous infliction of hurt by one member of the species upon another, by groups of members upon other groups of members, and by the whole species upon its natural environment. No wonder that man, in seeking to comprehend all that has happened since hominisation, should speak of a 'fall'.

This interpretation of the doctrine of original sin is open to the charge that it sees sin as an inevitable product of hominisation. Teilhard de Chardin attempted to answer this charge by speaking of the 'statistical' necessity of sin. As an answer it carries some force, since it points out that the emergence of human autonomy and freedom necessarily implies the possibility of sin—that is, of refusal to cooperate with God and his purposes for man. I think, however, that we can go further than this. Pre-critical Scholasticism always conceded the analogical character of original sin. In other words it appreciated that the word 'sin' was here being used in a partly equivocal sense. Yet it also claimed that there was sufficient univocacy in the word 'sin' to allow of its being employed to describe the condition of human nature itself; we enter the world in a 'fallen' condition. I have suggested that this fallenness can be found in the loss of that 'peace' which is appropriate in lower forms of life. The introduction of autonomy and freedom means that instincts, drives, and passions inherited from our animal forebears remain with us and now become disordered by reason of the fact that if they are not healed and governed under grace, they will lead us away from our divinely given destiny. More than that, they are intensified by our intelligence and freedom. In *homo sapiens* they are no longer restricted to our physical and biological makeup. They are expressed in our culture, which is the arena in which evolution continues in our species. The world we *make* for ourselves, as distinct from the natural world which is given to us, is the product of powers acquired in the cultural phase of evolution.

We now rightly speak of a fallen *history* which is also a history of salvation. Where we or our ancestors have failed to allow God's grace to heal us, we construct historical monuments to our sin, neatly and grimly symbolised in the fact that we build concentration camps. Where we or our ancestors have responded to grace, we have erected monuments to our graced nature such as hospitals. The concentration camp and the hospital are not, *tout court*, kingdoms of darkness and light respectively. There are examples of heroic virtue in camps and examples of selfishness in hospitals. The camp, however, symbolises moral evil in its design and purpose, while the hospital symbolises good in its design and purpose.

The evolution of culture has brought with it the possibility and actuality of good and evil and also the possibility and actuality of ambivalence and ambiguity. Our good acts are never entirely free of self-interest, while our bad acts frequently have a strand of goodness woven into them. The language of warfare comes spontaneously to mind when we seek to describe the human condition. The battle is cosmic, not in the gnostic sense of transcendent warfare, but in the sense that nature *in its human expression* experiences a rift within itself and therefore, as Paul puts it, it groans for salvation. Good and evil are at war within us both individually in our own psyche and socially in the communities we construct for ourselves. It is extremely difficult to descry and separate each from the other, precisely because they coexist with, and interpenetrate, each other. Even those least influenced by Luther's *simul justus et peccator* have to concede that the saint, or healed one, is only a heartbeat away from sin, while the sinner is only a heartbeat away from conversion. It is grace, not nature or culture, which makes the difference; and this fact places us before that deepest of mysteries—divine foreknowledge and design. In one moment the guard in a concentration camp can begin to care for a victim, just as in one moment a nurse or hospital orderly can mistreat a patient. No wonder, as Pascal remarked, we are a mystery to ourselves.

When the poet, Rainer Maria Rilke, was considering undergoing psychoanalysis, it was explained to him what the treatment would mean. Rilke, remembering his muse, decided against the treatment with the memorable words, 'If my devils are to leave me, I am afraid my angels will take flight as well.'[21]

Those wise words reveal a profound insight into the

ambiguity of being human. It is no accident that they were spoken by a poet. The essentialist definition of man as a rational animal is both a statement and a misstatement of what it means to be human. We are correctly defined by our rationality in that the power of abstract reason makes us different from the other animals and from our pre-human forebears. We are incorrectly defined by our rationality, if the possession of reason is deemed to set us totally apart from the other animals and from our pre-human forebears, and if its link with desire, will, and affectivity is ignored. To recognise the daimonic within us is to recognise something of what the doctrine of original sin is trying to safeguard. Augustine found it most potently expressed in sexuality because sex was the force which kept him in thrall for so long. But it is also present in aggression, jealousy, possessive love, hatred, vengeance, fear, and a host of other primal emotions which can destroy us and our interhuman relationships if we do not name these emotions and seek to come to terms with them. I say 'name' and 'come to terms' with them—not deny or suppress them. They are indeed, what the classical doctrine of original sin has called them, 'the tinder of sin' (*fomes peccati*).

They are also the raw materials of holiness. This is what Rilke saw and Augustine—at least the Augustine of the anti-Pelagian writings—did not. We would not be human without the very forces which can destroy us. To define *homo sapiens* exclusively as a rational animal may be to overlook the wide scope of the noun while dilating upon the characteristics of the adjective.

In an age which is giving us ever more sophisticated machines for calculation, classification, memory, analysis, and many of the other functions which we associate with rationality (or at least with intelligence) it behoves us to cherish our animality, together with the daimons it makes possible. In human beings reason and feeling are often at odds and always in potential tension. The tension is life-enhancing if often painful. Reason can show us the comedy of life, its unpredictabilities, its illogicalities and its ironies. Feeling, however, faces us with its tragedy, its ecstasies, and its cruelties. To be human is also to feel desire, especially the desire for that peace and fulfilment which is possible only in God. More than that,

146

to be human is to be rationally aware of our desire, to know that we experience it as an ache and a promise. To be human is to yearn for a salvation comprehensive enough to heal the abrasive relationship between reason and feeling. It is this yearning that will always set us apart from the machines we construct to do our thinking for us. We shall never be able to construct a machine which does our feeling for us, which appreciates from inner experience the need to relate reason to feeling, or which can assure us with authority that we are loved, forgiven, and accepted, though it may make a good job of simulating all these. We may be able to build a machine which retails the story of the Prodigal Son and can analyse its meaning in a clinical manner. Such a machine, however, will never know or feel the joy of a repentant homecoming. If it did, it would have ceased to be a machine and would have become—human? Computers can malfunction, but they cannot fall from grace; they can be repaired, but they cannot be saved.

8

The Dark Enigma

BELIEVERS in a provident God can all too easily underrate the sheer scandal which the existence of suffering, especially innocent suffering, poses for many men and women whose intellectual honesty prevents them from affirming the existence of such a God. Some agnostics and atheists have been filled with anger and contempt for what they construe as the blindness, insensitivity, and credulity of Jews, Christians, and Muslims who speak of a good God who provides for all his creatures. Some years ago the distinguished critic, Philip Toynbee, wrote a little book of *pensées* entitled *Towards the Holy Spirit: A Tract for the Times.*[1] In it he gives the example of an earthquake which kills a family of three. The father dies instantly. The mother dies 'in noisy anguish' during the next twenty-four hours. The child, uninjured, is pinned down between the dead and putrifying bodies of his parents and dies slowly of thirst during the next five days. If we let this dreadful scene seep into the imagination we shall hardly be taken aback by Toynbee's comment that 'Modern Christians have devoted a great deal of hard and painful thought, a great many contorted and embarrassed pages, to finding excuses for such behaviour on the part of their all-loving and all-powerful god.'

'Why', he asks, 'do they still call it the problem of evil rather than the problem of pain?'[2] He finally advances a thesis which stands four-square in the path of any believer who attempts a theodicy for our times.

> Every justification of God's ways to man proposes some covert and glorious end which more than atones for the overt and outrageous means. But it is among our sharpest moral perceptions that not even the most superb end can

justify such means as the killing of this child in those circumstances.[3]

Toynbee here states with painful bluntness the greatest single reason why so many men and women today do not believe in the existence of a provident God. On the evidence of this little book Toynbee was not an atheist; nor was he a theist in the traditional sense of the word. Materialistic unbelief left him as unsatisfied as the Judaeo-Christianity he rejects so decisively. So he settles for a Holy Spirit whose aim is 'to spiritualise the whole of the phenomenal universe'.[4]

Reviewing the book, Arthur Koestler expressed great sympathy with the position Toynbee outlines in its earlier part but could not go along with the role Toynbee gives to the Holy Spirit. 'It seems to me', wrote Koestler,

> that if the world is 'an abomination of cruelty' which the Holy Spirit is trying to improve, then the Holy Spirit is either singularly ineffectual or else it has an infernal antagonist who frustrates all its efforts. Which leads us back to the theologians' square one.[5]

Toynbee found himself caught between belief and unbelief, as critical of the brave new world of scientific positivism as he was of ancient and, to him, worn-out dogmas. He saw the need for some spiritual principle which would give ultimate meaning to the universe, but such a principle could not be an omnipotent being who had the power, but refused, to remove pain from the work of his hands. In short, Toynbee's reaction to the classical dilemma—*either* a cruel *or* an ineffectual being—was to choose the ineffectuality, since the notion of an infinite being who is cruel is intolerable to reason and instinct alike.

Any consideration of the human journey to God must at some point reckon with the problem of evil. One knows in advance that there are no answers, only an opportunity for anguished speculation. The dark mystery of evil encompasses the wayfarer at every step. The word evil itself is fraught with ambiguity, an ambiguity which can be exploited by an apologist intent on winning the case for God at all costs. Evil can describe an earthquake or a death-camp. It is in many ways a thoroughly unsatisfactory word; yet we have no other.

149

Changing the terminology leaves the phenomenon untouched. The experience of evil precedes every attempt to name it. The intellectual problem is part of the phenomenon itself. Animals experience pain but they do not have to face its mystery. They do not have to name it, to strive to find meaning in it, or to wonder how it can be related to a provident Creator. They are protected from the intellectual ravages produced by reflexive consciousness and the drive towards rationality.

Human beings who have reached the formidable conclusion that there is no God, though they have to undergo the experience of evil, are at least spared the trauma of relating it to a beneficent Being from whose hands all subordinate beings come. Only those men and women who place their wager on the existence of a creator have to endure the ache of mind and heart which is inseparable from their decision.

In Dostoyevsky's novel, *The Brothers Karamazov,* Ivan Karamazov puts the case with a passion which sears the reader by its intensity.[6] He relates several incidents of cruelty to children, bringing his recital to a climax with the story of a little boy of eight who threw a stone which injured a hound's paw. The hound belonged to a retired army General who was a rich and powerful landowner. The boy was locked up for the night. Next morning the General appeared in full hunting gear with his hounds. He had the boy stripped and forced to run. He then set the hounds on the boy. They tore the child to pieces in front of his mother.

Ivan tells this story to his brother Alyosha who is an aspiring monk. Under Ivan's insistent questioning Alyosha admits that the General ought to have been shot. Both of them knew that it was not a sentiment appropriate to a monk. What Ivan had done was simply to confront his brother with the moral dilemma inherent in the situation and to raise in painful form some of the great questions of human existence: justice, expiation, forgiveness—and the suffering of children. He admits the special pleading in his examples. 'Listen to me: I took only children to make my case clearer. I don't say anything about the other tears with which the earth is saturated from its crust to its core....' Ivan wants justice and meaning and he wants them now, not in some future golden age. The prospect of justice and meaning deferred for the sake of some great and overarching scheme of things leaves him unimpressed. Subsequent divine judgment and punishment for men like the General seem to him to be beside the point:

> I want to see with my own eyes the lion lie down with the lamb and the murdered man rise up and embrace his murderer. I want to be there when everyone suddenly finds out what it has all been for.

For truth?

> ... if the sufferings of children go to make up the sum of sufferings which is necessary for the purchase of truth, then I say beforehand that the entire truth is not worth such a price.

We need to absorb the full force of Ivan's point if we are to avoid a cheap and superficial answer to the problem he raises.

The dreadful camps in which millions of men and women have suffered and died in the twentieth century rise up before anyone who reflects authentically on creation and providence. Almost automatically the theistic apologist springs to God's defence by proclaiming that these camps were the work of evil men. Certainly they were; but that claim does not meet Ivan Karamazov's point. Divine retribution for the perpetrators will not set all to rights. The deeper question remains: why has creation taken a course which allows the sort of evil to exist which makes Auschwitz possible? The theodicist does no service to God by attempting a defence which rests totally on establishing human culpability. God does not need that kind of defending, if indeed he needs defending at all. The scandal of Auschwitz infinitely transcends the immorality of its perpetrators. Auschwitz is not explained or set to rights by the eternal torment of the men who designed and ran it. Such 'moral' or forensic calculations are futile and trivial. It is the stark *fact* of Auschwitz, and not only the immorality of its architects and agents, which constitutes the dark enigma.

This is the whole point of Ivan's protest. To speak of Auschwitz or the suffering of children in terms of justice and human rights is to miss the point. The principle of retribution or revenge heals nothing, explains nothing, rights nothing. Ivan's protest could hardly be more radical. It is made against the very notion of eschatological meaning and harmony. He does not argue that the existence of innocent suffering proves that there is no God. He does not deny God; he defies him by proclaiming *as an absolute* that no final harmony or meaning can justify the existence of innocent suffering. No wonder his brother murmurs, 'This is rebellion.'

And of course it is. If Ivan is right, then there is no answer either now or later to the problem of evil. Philip Toynbee adopts precisely this conclusion: Nothing, absolutely nothing, can justify the existence of the suffering of children (which is, of course, intended to be symbolic of all innocent suffering). Toynbee concludes to the existence of an ineffectual God as the most acceptable hypothesis. We have already examined this hypothesis in Chapter 1 and found it defective by reason of the very definition of God. There is, it seems to me, only one course open to the theist who wishes to respond to Ivan Karamazov, and that is to deny him the right to make the existence of innocent suffering *an absolute*. We cannot, in our finitude and with our restricted metaphysical vision, arrogate to ourselves the right to lay down such an *a priori* barring order on the eventual discovery of possible meaning in the universe and beyond it. Meaning deferred is part of the human condition here below. If the apophatic has any role in theology, this is where it must be brought into play, or else we should abandon it altogether and have the courage and arrogance to make human judgment the measure of all things in heaven and earth.

The choice which faces us is not between an omnipotent but merciless God and a beneficent but ineffectual God. The choice is between God and no God. Affirmation of faith in God's existence has to precede the awesome wrestle with the possible meaning of evil. Affirmation of mystery is something deeper than the admission of ignorance. God does not deny us the right to protest, to agonise and to cry out for meaning. If, however, we have made our wager and opted for the existence of a provident God, we thereby assume the duty of faithful submission together with the terrifying asceticism of searching for meaning amid the tears of things. A mystery in its proper theological sense is a problem made habitable by grace. Entry into the Christian mysteries is not dependent upon prior solution of the problems they raise.

There is something unseemly about reducing this particular mystery to the status of a bracing intellectual exercise. For this reason we can hardly do better than draw upon the insights of a philosopher whose study, *The Symbol of Evil*, is now a classic. In an address to the American Academy of Religion in 1984 Paul Ricoeur returned to the problem of evil.[7] His paper is a brief but stimulating résumé of the essential problem together with a suggested way of approaching it. My intention here is not to summarise his argument but to reflect on some of the issues raised by his address, by its structural pointers, and by its conclusion.

The problem as traditionally conceived and presented is, says Ricoeur, expressed in the need to reconcile three statements: 'How can we affirm at the same time, without any contradiction, the following three propositions: God is all powerful; God is absolutely good; yet evil exists?'[8] Theodicy is a 'battle for the sake of coherence' between these three statements. But, asks Ricoeur, is this reduction of the problem to statements a satisfactory way of approaching it? Statement is only one, and indeed a late, phase in the occurrence of the problem. It fails to deal with the actual *experience* of evil, which precedes all statement. In addition it promotes a category mistake: it amalgamates the separate problems of blame and lament. Blame belongs to the category of wrong-doing. Lament belongs to the category of victim. Human history demonstrates all too clearly that the two are frequently linked. 'In its dialogical structure evil committed by someone finds its other half in the evil suffered by someone else.'[9] There is a tragic mystery involved in the intimate relationship between evil and wrongdoing and evil as suffering. Ricoeur, however, is not content to allow the mystery to rest in this relationship between wrong and lament. It is encountered at a much deeper level in the inner experience of the offender himself or herself. There is often, in the very act of wrongdoing, a curious sense of partial passivity, a sense almost of being taken over.

St Paul notices this in the seventh chapter of his Letter to the Romans. Most of us have at one time or another remarked 'I don't know what came over me' in reference to, say, an act of aggression which we later regret. It seems to us as if our rationality and freedom had temporarily been taken away from

153

us and that it was not the 'real me' who performed the act. This is not necessarily to be seen as an attempt to excuse ourselves of our wrongdoing; it may truthfully correspond to our actual experience at the time. The experience of ambivalence, which can make people hurt those they love, is both frightening in itself, but also encouraging in its implications.

It is frightening because it reveals depths within us over which we seem to have little or no control. We sense these depth-energies as both beneficent and destructive. It is their destructive power which frightens us, since it seems to demonstrate that our hold on rationality and virtue is a good deal more tenuous than we would like to suppose. Socially and politically we can experience a similar apprehension when for example violence and crime reveal to us the fragile character of civilised life under the rule of law. There have been times in history when the veneer of civilisation cracked open to reveal a dark abyss of primal and disordered passions. The behaviour of a mob is a case in point. Law and order can exist only when citizens consent to be subject to them or else when brute force is used by a totalitarian regime to enforce them. All this is profoundly threatening, and we need to respond to the threat with realism but also with hope. Such awareness is most beneficial when it demonstrates our need of healing and grace. It gives point to the often neglected petition of the Lord's Prayer, 'Lead us not into temptation', or, more accurately, 'Do not put us to the test', because it forces us to recognise that we all have our breaking point and that our consciously willed and achieved virtue is never secure from the standpoint of human effort alone. Our virtue, such as it is, is always under threat from the depths of our own psyche and from the submerged violence which exists in every association of men and women. This insecure hold on virtue is an important predisposition to the recognition of what Christian theology knows as grace.

If reflected upon with realism and hope, the experience can also be encouraging. The purely secular mind deals with it, as Freud did, by devising techniques which enable us to come to terms with the demands of the unconscious. Christianity, while in no way disregarding the benefits of psychotherapy, approaches the condition differently. Where Freud seems to disregard or discourage the notion that guilt-feelings may point to real culpability, Christianity accepts the fact that we actually do wrong and that something more than self-acceptance is needed if we are to be made whole. Christian theology calls this condition 'sin', while in the same breath it also speaks of forgiveness. Sin is therefore a hopeful word, when it is used correctly. When it is used incorrectly, it can be a dark and sinister word, threatening and diagnosing punishment in the shape of disaster and suffering.

The experienced connection between guilt and suffering has a long and disturbing history. We find it in the Bible and in subsequent religious history. In some people there is a tendency to regard misfortune as a judgment upon, and a punishment for, their misdeeds. The felt link between guilt and punishment can be found in the mythology and folklore of many peoples, and even in modern times it can shape attitudes consciously or unconsciously. It ought to be the task of sound faith to reject such thinking as rank superstition; but not merely can faith fail to diagnose and banish such ideas, it can actually underwrite them in certain types of popular religion. The causal linking of wrongdoing with punishment and the relating of the link to God is simply the obverse of regarding prosperity and good fortune as benefits bestowed by God as a reward for virtue. Thinking of God as a being who constantly intervenes in the events of everyday life, to reward or punish as the case may be, makes it impossible to come to a reasoned and faith-inspired attitude towards evil, whether as blame or lament.

Because, however, evil in both its senses is so difficult to understand and live with, reflective men and women have, down the ages, tried to find some rational structure which would make sense of it. Whence does evil originate if the universe comes from the hands of a good God? What meaning can be assigned to it in the divine plan? How should we conduct our lives in the face of it?

Ricoeur traces three stages, of 'increasing order of rationality', in the passage from experience to language:
(1) The first stage is that of *myth*. Our earliest ancestors constructed stories with the specific purpose of giving structure to the undifferentiated experience of evil in both its senses. These early archetypal myths sought to give expression to the inter-relationship between good and evil, together with the frequently

155

ambiguous mixture of both, which takes place in the individual psyche and in society. They recounted how evil entered the world through some cosmic catastrophe. They provided a framework within which human experience could be sited against a cosmic background, but they did not tackle the problem of why a particular individual or group should have to suffer. For this a further phase in theological reflection was necessary.

(2) Ricoeur calls this second phase the stage of *Wisdom*. Myth merely narrates; Wisdom asks why and seeks to argue the case in respect of individuals. It is at the Wisdom stage in the Bible that the notion of retribution is most forcefully argued. The classic instance of Wisdom thinking about sin and retribution is the Book of Job, which is an epic account of one man's suffering together with his attempt to comprehend what is going on.

Let us explore this contention further. Job raises the question of *innocent* suffering. The problem occurs on two levels. On the first and more superficial level the problem is soluble in principle. If fault can be found in Job, there is, for some religious minds, no longer any problem: there has been sin, consequently there is punishment. The case of Job, however, takes the question into the mysterious depths of existence where it is not soluble, even in principle, at least this side of the grave. Job, we are told at the start, is being tested. This is really not much of an improvement on being punished; but the story has an impetus of its own which carries it deeper than the author's myth can go.

Job does not know what we, the readers, are told at the beginning of the story, namely, that God has allowed Satan to test him. Job is a good man with whom God is satisfied, rather in the way that an artist might be with one of his creations. Nevertheless Job has to undergo a series of catastrophes as a test of his fidelity and steadfastness. First his cattle and servants are destroyed; then his sons and daughters are killed; finally Satan is allowed by God to afflict him with sores from head to toe. In great physical and mental distress Job wonders why these evils have befallen him. He is utterly convinced that he has done nothing to deserve them. He is joined by three friends who try to solve the mystery. One of them, Eliphaz the

Tamanite, puts the retribution case. 'Think now, who that was innocent ever perished? Or where were the upright cut off?' (Job 4:7). Eliphaz is smug and eminently satisfied with his powers of theological exposition as he expounds the traditional wisdom that such suffering as Job's simply has to be a punishment for some misdeed. Job listens miserably to the friend who so confidently explains his plight. If Eliphaz is of little help to Job, Bildad, his second friend, is even less helpful, with his hard-and-fast division of mankind into good and bad and his outrageous remark that Job's sons and daughters must have been very bad indeed to have suffered such a fate. The third friend, Zophar, is the worst of all. He upbraids Job for his lack of repentance and for his stubborn protests of innocence. Job fiercely resists the arguments of his friends. There must be some other explanation, he insists. The three friends now turn vindictive. By refusing to admit his guilt Job is challenging their theology of retribution. If Job is right, they have some painful rethinking to do. After an intervention by another character, Elihu, who restates the Wisdom case, God speaks.

It is a highly dramatic moment, opening with the powerful words, 'Who is this that darkens counsel by words that lack knowledge?' It is as if God is silencing an insignificant squabble among children. He makes no attempt to comment on the arguments that have gone before; nor does he offer to console Job or commend him for his steadfastness. Instead God launches into a paean on creation. Where was Job when the marvels of the cosmos came into being? God proclaims his provident care for the animals and asks whether Job can match this providence. The book closes with Job's total submission to the divine lesson, and he is thereupon restored to prosperity. No answer is given to the question of innocent suffering. God in effect ignores both the reasonableness of the question and the emotional distress of the questioner.

God's proclamation of his own omnipotence and, by comparison, Job's powerlessness can be legitimately seen as the only possible, if extremely oblique, answer to the problem of innocent suffering. It does not point the way to a theodicy which attempts to reconcile such suffering with the provident care of a good God. Instead it affirms the existence of an infinite gap between God and man: God understands the

157

cosmos; man cannot. Insofar as the Book of Job proclaims that God knows what he is about in creating a world where innocent suffering occurs, the book provides a radical, and probably the only spiritually satisfying, answer to the deepest and most acute of all theological problems. Insofar as the author portrays a God who acts and speaks like an oriental despot, the message of the book is more problematic. Job's God can seem very like the God of the medieval nominalists, a God whose absolute power and freedom terrified Martin Luther and drove him to an anguished search for a God of mercy in place of the arbitrary despot who ruled his life and who refused to be pleased by even the most sincere efforts to serve him. Preoccupation with divine omnipotence has on occasion led certain religious imaginations to construct the image of a being who stands off from his creatures, looking down at them from afar and always ready to judge their faults with severity. Job's God can, but need not, be seen in this way. Omnipotence, after all, need not be interpreted as arbitrariness.

Carl Jung approaches the book of Job in a most unusual and thought-provoking way. In his *Answer to Job* he treats the book as a literary critic might treat any dramatic composition.[10] This approach gives him liberty to regard Job's God as one of several characters in the drama and to take him to task for his insensitivity, accusing him of having 'an ulterior motive' in making Job 'the outward occasion for an inward process of dialectic in God'. As Jung sees it, God uses the encounter with Job as a way of laying to rest his own inner doubts: 'His thunderings at Job so completely miss the point that one cannot help but see how much he is occupied with himself'.[11]

Before we react too sharply to Jung's presumption in taking God to task, we need to remember that, for all its profundity, the Book of Job is an exercise in didactic anthropomorphism. The God who speaks forth from these pages is a humanly constructed character, not God as he is in himself. Jung, by putting him in the psychiatrist's chair, makes some shrewd theological observations. Is the God of this Wisdom author somehow afraid of human questioning? In spite of the fact that God has everything, he appears to need Job's loyalty, and he attaches importance to the way man speaks of him.[12] God praises the monster, Behemoth, in extravagant language, but he says nothing about man, his greatest creature. Why should that be? Jung ponders the question and concludes: 'The real reason for God's becoming man is to be sought in his encounter with Job.'[13] Jung pursues this intriguing idea. God, he says, has suffered a moral defeat at Job's hands.[14] Wisdom thereupon suggests to God the desirability of becoming man. God then makes his awesome decision. Later, when Jesus is dying on the cross in utter abandonment, 'God experiences what it means to be a mortal man and drinks to the dregs what he made his faithful servant Job suffer'.[15] This, says Jung, is God's answer to Job.

It is perhaps symptomatic of Jung's interpretation of the Bible that it can but need not be taken in an orthodox Christian sense. Jung complained more than once that theologians have simply ignored the contribution of empirical psychology. Whatever Jung's intentions may have been, he has written a book from which orthodox Christian theology can borrow many fruitful insights. Consider this one:

> [God] has equipped his human creatures with a modicum of consciousness and a corresponding degree of free will, but he must also know that by so doing he leads them into the temptation of falling into a dangerous independence.[16]

What better description of sin, 'actual' or 'original', could one hope to find than this:

> [God] also overlooks the fact that the more consciousness a man possesses the more he is separated from his instincts (which at least give him an inkling of the hidden wisdom of God) and the more prone he is to error. He is certainly not up to Satan's wiles if even his creator is unable, or unwilling, to restrain this powerful spirit.[17]

As we shall see, the Fathers of the Church took this truth with a greater literal reference and intensity than most believers can do today. We have allowed ourselves to be intimidated by the process of demythologisation, and in consequence, by dismissing the myth we may have lost sight of a profound truth which can be conveyed only by means of myth. In our flight from the symbolic expression of truth we have closed off an important avenue of divine communication with us. In breaking the myths we have unwittingly jettisoned the truths they bear. We have sacrificed our imaginations to the demands of a speculative intellect which has been under siege since the Enlightenment. We have thus lost not only our intellectual innocence but also much of our ability to respond imaginatively to the God who approaches us in symbols.

(3) Ricoeur's third stage in the journey from experience to language is that of *Gnosis*. Gnosticism advanced the process from Wisdom to theodicy by creating a radical ontological dichotomy between good and evil and by pitting each against the other in cosmic battle. The gnostic challenge appears to take the emphasis off suffering by its preoccupation with the impersonal values of cosmic struggle. Man here becomes a more or less passive element in the battle of giants. It was Manichean gnosticism which occasioned Augustine's denial that evil is a substance with positive existence. Whatever is is good. Evil must therefore be a negation, a non-thing. Augustine's denial of substantiality to evil had the effect of withdrawing the debate from the sphere of the ontological and of locating it instead in the sphere of knowing, willing, and acting. Ricoeur draws an important conclusion: '*This purely moral vision of evil leads in turn to a penal vision of history.*'[18] Augustine's logic drives him to the inexorable and awesome conclusion that *all* suffering is retribution for sin. If this is so, it follows that sin must be co-extensive with human existence. This conclusion sends him to Genesis 3 and Romans 5 for biblical substantiation of his anti-Manichean thesis. With this 'massive indictment of the whole of humanity' the question 'Whence evil?' replaces the Wisdom question about the existence of innocent suffering.

Since the entire human race stands convicted of sin, all kinds of suffering must be seen as chastisement. Augustine never really concerns himself with the uneven distribution of suffering. The fact that some men and women have to bear more than their fair share of it while others seem in large measure to escape is for him simply taken up into the whole scheme of things which God has designed. God sees things which we cannot. If the reasons for much of what happens are hidden from us, can we rightly allege injustice? For Augustine every manifestation of suffering has a divine purpose.

His large book, *De Civitate Dei*, which took him thirteen years to write and publish, was initially planned as a response to the pagan charge that Rome had fallen to the Goths because of Christian infidelity to the Roman gods. The sack of Rome in AD 410 had shocked the civilised world. The sacking of cities was usually a brutal affair, but Alaric's conquest of Rome set up symbolic shock-waves which were out of all proportion to the event itself. How was the fall of Rome to be related to divine providence? Both Christians and Pagans believed in direct divine intervention in terrestrial affairs. Both agreed that the fall of Rome was an appalling disaster; therefore each party interpreted the event in a manner favourable to its own interests.

Since Augustine's purpose is to discern the hand of God in all that has happened, he is constrained to see divine retribution in the suffering inflicted on the citizens of Rome by Alaric and his hordes. Some Christians and some pagans had been killed; some Christians and some pagans had escaped. Augustine has a moral justification for each case. If they died, it was a punishment for sin of some kind. The Christians may, for example, have been cowardly in failing to rebuke the pagans for the error of their ways and so were punished by God through the instrumentality of Alaric.[19] Those who escaped were beneficiaries of God's mercy: they were chastised so that they might be brought to repentance,[20] and so on. Augustine is antecedently committed to finding a good theological reason for everything that happens, and this for him means finding a good *moral* reason. It is all willed by God who foresees every possible consequence of every possible act. Evil, both physical and moral, is permitted for a variety of reasons, some of which we may suspect, some of which remain beyond our ken. Augustine is in general more concerned to proclaim God's omniscience and omnipotence than to reconcile either with divine love and providence. He has, however, left us a principle of theodicy which has reappeared frequently in Christian thought: '[God] judged it better to bring good out of evil than not to permit evil to exist at all'.[21]

This principle retains its validity even for theologians who hold no brief for Augustine's obsessive moralism. It can be understood non-moralistically and in a way which does not envisage a God who makes a practice of intervening directly in the causal chain of historical events. Throughout the Middle Ages and beyond, Christians sought to interpret historical events, especially natural catastrophes, as divine chastisement for sin. This kind of interpretation was a direct consequence of the penal view of history. It was operating as late as 1908 in the religious press's reaction to the Messina earthquake. It remains a commonplace of fundamentalist religion today.

In the eighteenth century, the age which prided itself on its devotion to reason, there was a reaction against this interpretation of history in terms of sin and divine retribution. This was the age of Deism, a philosophy of religion which accepted the existence of a Supreme Being but removed him from any continuing involvement in his creation. The early Enlightenment therefore banished the problem of evil by declaring the universe to be rationally constructed and therefore radically good. The doctrine of original sin was declared to be a particularly benighted example of Christian obscurantism. All the world's ills could be cured by the application of reason and by the abandonment of dogmatic intransigence and pessimism.

In the first half of the eighteenth century there was a disposition to 'optimise'—i.e. to place the best possible construction on—everything. Gottfried von Leibniz set the scene with his *Théodicée*, published in 1710. Leibniz constructed a philosophical system in which harmony plays a controlling role. The world as we have it was created by God from an infinite number of possible units, not all of which are compatible with one another. God chose those 'possibles' which would combine with one another in the best possible way. The resultant world is the best possible out of an infinite number of different combinations. Leibniz's 'optimism' does not imply a belief that ours is a near perfect world. He is well aware of the existence of suffering and moral evil, but he sees these as belonging to the best of all *possible* worlds, because God as infinite wisdom has reviewed all the possible alternatives and decreed the world we actually have. God could not have done otherwise, since he is himself infinitely wise and good. Leibniz was in this respect firmly in the Augustinian tradition, but his metaphysical 'optimism' lent itself to the confident spirit of the age and also to superficial popularisation.

Alexander Pope had already enshrined in poetry the conviction, born of the scientific revolution, that the universe we actually live in is the best possible, because it combines the maximum of variety with the maximum of order. Pope had therefore expressed with the emotional satisfaction made possible by poetic language what Leibniz later expressed in the more sober language of philosophy.

> All Nature is but Art, unknown to thee;
> All chance, direction, which thou canst not see;
> All discord, harmony not understood;
> All partial evil, universal good;
> And, spite of Pride, in erring Reason's spite,
> One truth is clear; whatever is, is right.

That truth may have been clear to the age of reason, but it became rather less clear as the eighteenth century drew on. On 1 November 1775 there occurred in Lisbon a terrible earthquake with subsequent fire and flood in which two-thirds of the city was destroyed, with an estimated loss of 30,000 lives. The shock of the catastrophe was theologically heightened by the fact that, because it was a great feast-day, the churches of the city were full. (This detail prompted the irreverent to ask why God was so remiss in looking after his own.) The following year Voltaire wrote his *Poem on the Disaster of Lisbon*, in the preface to which he severely criticised, not Leibniz himself, but the superficial philosophers who misinterpreted Leibniz by their claim that everything that happens is always for the best and who told the people of Lisbon that the heirs of the dead would come into their fortunes, masons would grow rich rebuilding the city, and so on. 'So don't worry about your own particular evil; you are contributing to the general good'.[22] Three years later Voltaire published his satirical masterpiece, *Candide, or Optimism*, which mercilessly lampooned the fashionable optimism of the age, and which Frederick II described as 'Job in modern dress'.[23]

Immanuel Kant had undergone something like the same dis-illusionment as Voltaire. Initially he had supported Leibniz, but later he came totally to disavow his support for the ideas of the *Théodicée*. Kant was in full sympathy with the basic spirit of the Enlightenment. He subscribed to the dictum, *sapere aude*—have the courage to think for yourself. He also believed, however, that the duty to think for oneself brought in its train certain serious intellectual and moral obligations. Not for him the effervescent irreverence and iconoclasm of the French Enlightenment. Rationalism has challenged the main tenets of dogmatic Christianity; David Hume had put the case for radical empiricism; Kant, awakened, as he said, from his dogmatic slumbers by Hume, put himself to the task of providing a critique of reason which would set out the limitations imposed on reason by the conditions necessary for knowledge. Kant's critique had devastating implications both for traditional dogmatic theology and for the natural theology which was so assiduously cultivated in the eighteenth century as a foundation for all religious belief. Its effect was to place a barring order on all cognitive communication between God and man. God cannot communicate with man without becoming one among other phenomena, and thereby ceasing to be God; nor can man arrive at any natural knowledge of God, because causality is not to be invoked in the transcendent, i.e. non-phenomenal, cases of God, freedom, and immortality.

In the light of Kant's critical conclusions about revelation and natural theology, it came as a shock to some of his contemporaries that he was prepared to speak of 'a *radical* innate *evil* in human nature'.[24] Kant, as we might expect, dismisses as 'inept', the notion that one can account for moral evil in man by reference to it as an inheritance from the first man and woman. Everyone begins from a state of innocence and is personally responsible for his or her evil acts. Experience demonstrates, however, that the human condition is indeed marked by innate and radical evil. Kant affirms, but cannot account for, this evil. He can find 'no conceivable ground from which moral evil in us could originally have come',[25] yet he does not shrink from affirming its existence, much to the disgust of some of his contemporaries. Goethe, for example, complained bitterly that Kant had 'criminally smeared his philosopher's cloak with the shameful stain of radical evil...so that Christians too might yet be enticed to kiss its hem'.[26]

Karl Barth, who commends Kant for his honesty and sombre realism, draws a thought-provoking comparison between Kant and Mozart, who were contemporaries. 'In Kant's philosophy, as in the music of Mozart, there is something of the calm and majesty of death which seems suddenly to loom up from afar to oppose the eighteenth century spirit.'[27] To appreciate what Barth means one has only to think of the Countess in *The Marriage of Figaro*, or the autumnal moments in *Così Fan Tutte*, where a truly farcical plot is darkened into aesthetic plausibility by moments of fleeting anguish which are perfectly caught by the sombre beauty of the music.

'I had to deny knowledge in order to make room for faith', Kant claimed. Faith as Kant understood it is very different from the traditional understanding of faith as a response to God who reveals himself by means of miracles and other external manifestations. Faith for Kant is a practical matter that has to do with pursuing one's duty. It means addressing the question of what one *ought* to do. To be human is to be conscious of being under obligation. Kant is a very stern moralist but he is also a dedicated enemy of heteronomy, the concept of being morally bound by norms derived from *outside* oneself. The moral law is to be discovered within one's own experience. Duty is its own guarantor. There must be no question of reward or punishment involved in one's motives for doing good or avoiding evil. To be religious, says Kant, is to view our duties as divine commands. Note the order: they are duties before they are divine commands. We conclude to the existence of God not through proofs from causality or design, but from examining the implications of having the experience of duty. This examination Kant describes as the exercise of *practical* reason. Moral experience provides the only road to God. We must of course note that Kant's concept of moral experience is highly individualistic, but it is open to social and political accommodation. Liberation theology today can be said to have a strong 'practical' basis in that it grounds its concepts of revelation and faith in action on behalf of the poor and oppressed.

Kant himself was not concerned with the classical problems

of theodicy. Both his denial of the possibility of knowing God and his preoccupation with moral experience and the concept of duty made the problem of theodicy superfluous. Nevertheless Ricoeur finds continuing importance in the Kantian shift from theoretical to practical reason. Evil is better seen as a challenge to action than as a speculative problem. Indeed in seeking to meet the challenge we may find ourselves advancing some way along the road to meeting the problem. Today's Political theologians would be in sympathy with this approach. Response, they would say, is more important than intellectual solution. Action takes precedence over thought. If the problem of evil inspires men and women to seek to overcome it, then a new meaning can be discovered in Augustine's claim that God 'judged it better to bring good out of evil than not to permit evil to exist at all'. If evil, both as guilt and lament, becomes the occasion of another great leap in cosmic evolution, then such a prospect allows it at least provisional meaning in the human journey towards God. I say 'provisional', because we cannot yet perceive where such a leap might lead. We can, however, approach the enterprise with a hope that is both eschatological and historical, both otherworldly and this-worldly. Such an approach is eschatological in that it professes trust in the overall design of divine providence. It is historical in that it implies a recognition that the enterprise of hope has a social and political dimension. The two are inextricably intertwined in the Christian vision of pilgrimage.

What happens to the problem of evil when we concentrate on action rather than on thought, on the task to be undertaken rather than on the problem to be solved? Ricoeur, having pointed out that evil committed by one person is evil undergone by another, writes

> If we were to remove the suffering inflicted by people on other people, we would see what remained of suffering in the world, but to tell the truth, we have no idea of what this would be, to such an extent does human violence impregnate suffering.[28]

The point is important when we look at the tears with which the earth is saturated from its crust to its core. The worst sufferings are man-made, because they often incorporate malice of some kind. Malice adds a dimension which is not present in the suffering which comes from nature. Pain which comes to us from the vast indifference of the universe is easier to accept than pain which is inflicted by fellow human beings endowed with the power to love.

Utilising Freud's essay, 'Mourning and Melancholy', Ricoeur invokes Wisdom as a form of mourning. Just as mourning for a loved one eventually frees one for fresh attachments by teaching the mourner how to let go of former attachments, so the Wisdom stage in the handling of the problem of evil (i.e., the stage in which we ask why an individual or group should be thus afflicted) offers an opportunity for converting lament into complaint ('Why me?'). Complaint in turn offers an opportunity for integrating into the work of mourning the very lack of a ready answer. There are three subsidiary phases in this stage. The first is to resist the (often irrational) urge to seek for a moral cause of the distress, as Job's friends did. Some people have greater need of this phase than others. It involves as a final outcome a firm subscription to the conviction that God does not 'send' affliction as punishment. Afflictions come to us unbidden from the world which God has made. We do not know why this should be, but the fact that it is so offers us the opportunity of entering into the dark mystery and of seeking to transcend it and, if possible, to grow through it towards God and our fellow men and women.

The second phase consists in allowing one's profound unknowing to develop into a 'complaint against God'. Jewish theology has always been better at this than either Christian or Islamic theology. Islamic theology would find the very notion of complaint against God to be blasphemous, as would indeed some kinds of Christian spirituality. Jews, however, have a strong sense of the covenant between God and his people: God too has his responsibilities. Complaint of this kind rebels against any theodicy which speaks easily about divine 'permission' of evil. Permission is, after all, merely a weaker form of willing, and appeal to it does nothing to resolve the enigma. Jewish prayer practises a real freedom before God which a sound Christian theology and spirituality ought to be able to share. We are dealing with a heavenly Father who *cares* for all his creation. If we really believe in a caring God, how can we avoid the sort of complaint we find, for example, in the psalms? 'Our accusation against God is here the impatience of hope. It has its origin in the cry of the psalmist, "How long O Lord?"'[29]

The third phase envisages integration of complaint and indignation into the suffering itself. Through it we 'discover that the reasons for believing in God have nothing in common with the need to explain the origin of suffering'.[30] Although Ricoeur does not say so explicitly, we should note that this phase of integration is a function of prayer even more than it is a function of theology. It is an act of profound trust which is prepared to hope against hope. It inspires us to trust not only the God who made us but also the very structures of the world he has given us as our environment. He comes to us not only in the serenity of the world which so often delights us but also from out of the whirlwind of threat, pain, and discontent. He teaches us to discern him through mist of tears as much as in the tranquillity of order. It is a hard lesson, and we instinctively kick against it. In this phase, theology melds with prayer and is simply helpless and ineffectual without it. In this phase the notion of 'the best of all possible worlds' is simply transcended in the recognition that the finite mind can devise no credible theodicy which offers a theoretically satisfying explanation of why nature is red in tooth and claw, why one species lives off another, or why it can happen that small children die in torment.

To the unbeliever this attitude will look suspiciously like a case of wish doing duty for rational thought. Theistic believers can only respond that, having opted for the existence of a provident God for other reasons, they are prepared to commit themselves in faith, hope, and love to that God who, because he is God, can be credited with reasons which lie beyond the grasp of finite minds. It so happens that many believers have testified that in enduring suffering they have unaccountably grown in love for their fellow men and women and consequently for God also. This experience is not an answer to the intellectual problem of innocent suffering, but it does witness to the conviction that the final reason for the existence of the cosmos is love and that real love always costs. In the next two chapters we shall consider the price which God himself in Christ was prepared to pay in order that the world might believe and so be saved.

Redemption in Scripture and Tradition

'GOD was in Christ reconciling the world of himself' (2 Cor. 5:19). Paul's words constitute probably the most literal statement that can be made about the being and work of Jesus. Its two limbs are distinguishable, though indissolubly linked. (1) God was in Christ, and (2) this presence was a reconciling one. The first part is christological and gives the simplest possible description of the relationship between God and Jesus. Later ages were to speculate, with the help of Greek philosophy, about *how* God could be in Christ. Did God express himself fully as this man, Jesus of Nazareth? Did God share a divine 'nature' with Jesus? If so, did that nature take the place of the human nature or did it co-exist with it? If it co-existed with the human nature, how was it that Jesus was not two persons, one human, the other divine? The ontological constitution of Jesus thus became an occasion for extremely subtle metaphysical speculation. The schools of Alexandria and Antioch, each with its own characteristic concern about the ontological constitution of Jesus, pressed for either the unity and divinity of Jesus (Alexandria) or the need to assert the distinction between his humanity and his divinity (Antioch). Each, when taken to its extreme, produced a heresy. The Alexandrians tended so to stress the unity and divinity of Jesus that their radical members in effect denied his real humanity (Monophysitism). The Antiochenes tended so to stress the duality and distinctness of the divinity and humanity that their radicals in effect denied the personal unity of Jesus (Nestorianism). The Council of Chalcedon (AD 451) attempted a definition which would accommodate the concerns of both schools, but like most ecclesiastical definitions, especially those intended to accommodate two conflicting viewpoints, it could be interpreted with a bias in either direction. Eventually, at least in the West, the Chalcedonian formula was usually interpreted with a Monophysite bias, and the humanity of Jesus was in consequence frequently lost to sight. One might be forgiven for wondering why it was necessary to move from the beautiful simplicity of St Paul's 'God was in Christ' to abstruse philosophical speculations about the manner of this presence.

John Henry Newman ascribes the eventual complexification of such doctrines to 'that loving inquisitiveness which is the life of the *Schola*'.[1] There is indeed a certain inevitability about the scholarly enquiry into the ontological constitution of Christ. A price, however, has had to be paid, especially by a Church which treats its defining formulas as part of the deposit of faith, even though these formulas are couched in terminology which can lose its original sense and reference by reason of the natural obsolescence and transformation of language. We need constantly to remember with Aquinas that faith is directed in the last analysis not to the form of words but to the reality which the words try to articulate.

Strangely, however, the second limb of Paul's remark (' . . . reconciling the world to himself') did not lend itself to comparable speculation. There are no elaborate philosophical theories about the transcendent meaning of what Jesus was *doing* when he suffered and died on Calvary. There is unanimous agreement that whatever it was that he did, he did it 'for us'. Just as he had gone about Galilee doing good to his fellow men and women, so at his trial and on Calvary he completed this work by undergoing condemnation, torture, and death for his fellow men and women. There are no early Christian metaphysical theories about this achievement; instead we have been left a number of compressed narrative models which attempt to convey by means of analogy what Jesus achieved by his suffering and death. Thus although the christological speculations of the first six Christian centuries were indeed influenced by soteriological considerations (e.g. the conviction that human nature must be present in its entirety in Jesus if it is to be redeemed), there was remarkably little conceptual development of the doctrine of salvation. Salvation was deemed to be a concept whose meaning was transparent. There were no conflicting theories about it, merely different analogies and metaphors for illustrating it. The New Testament provides seminal examples.

The language of soteriology is replete with burnt-out metaphors; but then so is any dictionary. Development of language could never take place if metaphors retained their pristine effervescence. It is in the nature of language that its metaphors, once brilliant and stimulating, should cool and fade with time and use until at last they become prosaic nouns, verbs, and adjectives. With their fading there fades too a feeling for the world from which they originated. Metaphors are the product of culture, and cultures change. The culture of Palestine in the first century is available to us only through historical research and reconstruction. Even in its most specialised forms, such research can scarcely represent to us the resonances which words like 'redemption' or 'expiation' had for first-century Christians. Through the New Testament our Christian forebears have left us their words as frozen records of what they thought and felt about the life and death of Jesus. We have to guess imaginatively at how those thoughts and feelings were actually experienced. As J. H. Newman said, they have left us their impressions expressed as notions from which we have to try to reconstruct the experiences which gave rise to them. Even if we could perform this task adequately, there would remain the further task of determining whether those experiences are either possible for, or relevant to, the world we live in today.

Is there an identity of experience which is capable of renewed expression in successive ages? In short, is there a univocal, universally valid, element which survives the linguistic limitations of a word like 'salvation'? I wish to argue that there is, but that it survives only through the use of what David Tracy has called the 'analogical imagination'. Without the analogical imagination, tradition in its theological sense becomes impossible. The experiences of the first Christians are not available to us today except through historical reconstruction, which is at best tentative and provisional, and imaginative representation, which is utterly dependent upon our ability to interpret images analogically.

The first Christians lived in a geocentric world peopled not

171

only by men and women but also by unseen powers, both benevolent and malevolent, which contended for the souls of time- and space-bound men and women. When the first Christians used a word like salvation, it was in reference to a world that was embodied in myths which structured human existence. We no longer structure our experience by reference to those myths. We no longer see our world as bounded by a bright canopy of equidistant stars above and a dark and menacing underworld beneath. The word 'salvation' does not have the same mythical resonances for us as it had for the first Christians. We have, to be sure, our own myths (which can lack the emotional vividness of earlier ones). We treat our myths with self-conscious scepticism and suspicion, when indeed we are aware of them at all. The very ambiguity of the word 'myth' predisposes us to use it with suspicious care. Our post-Enlightenment sophistication makes us wary and uncomfortable with any experience which is dependent on myth for its articulation. Our forebears in the faith were not so constrained or self-conscious. The intellectual innocence which made their myths credible and apt is scarcely possible or desirable for us today. So we are left with their myth-derived metaphors and an uncertainty about how to understand and use them.

The task which faces contemporary soteriology is one of partial deconstruction, which is relatively easy, and partial reconstruction, which is formidably difficult. We have to search for the element of univocation which will allow us to employ the language of tradition while discounting the element of equivocation which necessarily arises out of a world that has changed so dramatically during the last four centuries or so. Such attempts at deconstruction and reconstruction constitute some of the principal tasks of theology. We have no business re-inventing the wheel; but neither can we continue to use the wheel in its primitive form. That there is a univocal element in such words as 'salvation' and 'redemption' can hardly be doubted, even when we have weighed all the implications of cultural innovation and the natural tendency of metaphors to die. We cannot, however, simply re-possess and re-articulate the old myths. What we can do is study how they functioned in an age which found them credible and then ask whether we in our age can create vehicles of expression which function in a comparable way and with a comparable effect on the Christian imagination.

The intellectual dimension of Christian pilgrimage is for the reflective believer one manifestation of the cross of Christ. Adaptation, including re-interpretation, of models and metaphors to be found in Scripture and Tradition, is an uncomfortable activity. Today's Christian has to concede the discontinuities as well as affirming the continuities between the early formative centuries of Christian belief and the world in which he or she must practise a living faith. These continuities and discontinuities challenge the imagination even more than they do the speculative intellect.

The New Testament itself contains most of the soteriological models which were to be subsequently exploited by the Christian imagination. Naturally one does not expect to find there the more finished theological syntheses of a later age; but it is to Scripture that the Christian must in the first instance look to find the sign-posts for any authentic soteriology. The disciples of Jesus had experienced his presence and acts as saving. The death of Jesus initially appeared to put an end to his salvific work.

Luke represents the two disciples on the road to Emmaus as somewhat lacking in soteriological confidence and hope: ' ... we had hoped that he would be the one to liberate Israel' (Lk. 24:21). Indeed the apostles themselves had not made much more soteriological progress after the forty days of apparitions and prayerful waiting for the Holy Spirit. They were, according to Luke, still locked into a narrow and provincial understanding of the scope of salvation. 'Lord', they asked Jesus just before his ascension, 'will you at this time restore the kingdom to Israel?' (Acts 1:6). For Luke, as for John, it is the coming of the Holy Spirit that makes all the difference. Christian soteriology arises only after the Holy Spirit has made it possible to see history from a new perspective. Again it is Luke who shows us the Spirit-filled Peter on the day of Pentecost laying the foundations for all subsequent soteriological thinking: ' ... this Jesus, delivered up according to the definite plan and foreknowledge of God, you crucified and killed by the hands of lawless men' (Acts 2:23). Peter is here assuring his audience that what happened on Calvary was not a merely contingent historical event brought about by human malice. It took place 'according to the definite plan and fore-knowledge of God'. Now this appeal to a divine plan, while it solved one problem, namely, the apparently meaningless contingency of Jesus' death, set a new and challenging agenda for the first Christian theologians. By invoking a divine plan they achieved transcendent meaning; but there was a formidable theological price to be paid for this achievement. What could God have been doing when he handed over his servant Jesus to be condemned for blasphemy by the leaders of Israel and executed for treason by the Roman administration? The question prompted them to look into their own history and into the texts which had grown out of and shaped that history. Paul therefore recounts the events surrounding Calvary as having happened 'according to the Scriptures'. Here, then, was the context within which those events were to be understood, believed in, and preached. The life *and death* of Jesus were to be seen as being of a piece with the covenant made by God with Abraham and Moses. God had rescued his people from Pharaoh. He had done the same in Jesus. It was a bold stroke of theological thinking. It provided both continuity and novelty. It envisaged a new covenant sealed with the blood of the crucified Jesus. The old had foreshadowed the new. The Day of the Lord, foretold in the Scriptures, had arrived in Jesus, whose death represented the last assault of the powers of darkness upon God's salvific will. The former covenant was buried with Jesus in the tomb. The analogical imagination made it possible to utilise, in this new context, all the old soteriological terms; but now they would be invoked against a firmly eschatological background. New Testament soteriology is forged in the conviction that the Last Age has come. The resurrection of Jesus is at its heart. This needs to be noted in view of the fact that later Western soteriology often virtually ignored the soteriological implications of the resurrection.

Paul exhorts the Thessalonians 'to wait for [God's] Son from heaven, whom he raised from the dead, Jesus who delivers us from the wrath to come' (1 Thess. 1:10). Salvation is in the first instance from the satanic forces which brought about the death of Jesus (1 Cor. 2:8) and are intent on the destruction of humanity. This background is apocalyptic and consequently not easily assimilated by modern believers; but it was to prove a fertile source of inspiration to the patristic and medieval imagination.

There are, however, other New Testament models and metaphors some of which transcend their first-century cultural provenance better than the apocalyptic myths. Some reflection on these models is indispensable to any serious study of Christian soteriology.

Redemption, Ransom, Liberation

The metaphor of redemption, so vital in the Hebrew and Greek worlds, though more accessible than apocalyptic models, is not easily grasped by the modern mind. It derives its impact from social circumstances which were different from those of the modern Western world. Today, for example, the word ransom is primarily associated with kidnapping—a fact which tends to rob the metaphor of its original power, since payment of a ransom can be construed as an act of weakness. In the Old Testament it fell to a man's next of kin to buy back the freedom he might have lost, say, through debt, or to redeem him from slavery (Lev. 25:47-54). Thus when God is described as 'redeemer' (Heb., go'el) the image invoked is less that of a powerful rescuer than of a kinsman who has an obligation to come to the assistance of his afflicted relative. Redemption is therefore a reminder of the Covenant between God and Israel. God's principal redemptive act on behalf of his people was of course his rescuing of them from Egyptian bondage. Jewish Christians spontaneously looked to the Exodus, and to the paschal liturgy which commemorated it, when they sought for images and models to depict the work of Christ.

In the New Testament the context of redemption is Messianic and eschatological, that is, it is firmly set within the expectation of what God would finally do for his people (in the first instance for Israel and then, by Christian extension, for the whole of humanity). In Mark's gospel we find Jesus saying 'For the Son of Man also came not to be served but to serve, and to give his life as a ransom for many' (Mk. 10:45). The Greek word *lutron*, meaning ransom, comes from the same root as the

175

word *apolutrōsis*, meaning redemption or liberation. The implication is, of course, that every rescue-operation costs something, whether in terms of money, risk, suffering or even death. Some commentators believe that when Jesus speaks of giving his life as a ransom for many he has in mind the Suffering Servant texts of Second Isaiah. Chapter 53 of Isaiah contains a powerful description of the man of sorrows who was despised and rejected by men. 'Surely he has borne our griefs and carried our sorrows.... But he was wounded for our transgressions... upon him was the chastisement that made us whole, and with his stripes we are healed' (Is. 53:4-5). Jesus has paid the price for our liberation by his suffering and death. Significantly Paul describes Christ not as redeemer but as 'our redemption' (1 Cor. 1:30).

Neither Paul nor the other New Testament writers speculate about the recipient of the ransom. They are content to employ the metaphor without driving it beyond its limitations. Many of the Fathers, as we shall see, were unable to exercise this restraint and went on to ask the theologically fatal question 'To whom was the ransom paid?', concluding that it must be the Devil, and thereby opening up a line of enquiry which produced an exotic and unbiblical mythology centred on 'the Devil's rights'.

Propitiation, Expiation, Purification

We have here as dangerous a clutch of theological nouns as can be found anywhere. The possibilities for misunderstanding and misuse are abundant. In an age when taboos presented a formidable challenge to religious purity and integrity, the notions of expiation and purification contained a highly emotive charge. They offered the possibility of putting things right again after wrongdoing or after the contracting of some ritual impurity. The association of expiation with the shedding of blood was of course a commonplace of Jewish worship and it had parallels throughout the contemporary world. Blood is an enormously powerful symbol, suggesting as it does the very life-force of human beings. The danger of misuse lies in the ambiguity which results from our not always being able to determine whether the word is being used literally or metaphorically. As a symbol for self-sacrificing love the phrase 'to

176

shed one's blood' possesses nobility and exaltation of purpose. To understand it literally, however, is to reduce it to a crude superstition which credits the *physical* reality of blood with mystical powers. Such a reduction is a powerful temptation in time of war or, more usually, of rebellion against tyranny. It lends itself to demogogical rhetoric and an unhealthy pre-occupation with violence inflicted and received.

Two years before the French Revolution Thomas Jefferson wrote in a letter, 'The tree of liberty must be refreshed from time to time with the blood of patriots and tyrants. It is its natural manure'. The words are informal, dry, even perhaps cynical. Jefferson was, after all, a child of the Enlightenment. In the hands of a romantic like Padraig Pearse, however, the same metaphor is given an exalted tone intended to inspire and nourish patriotic determination.

> Bloodshed is a cleansing and sanctifying thing and the nation which regards it as the final horror has lost its manhood. There are many things more horrible than blood-shed; and slavery is one of them.[2]

This sort of language is dangerous precisely because it speaks so powerfully to the Dionysian element within us. There has been a general feeling of benevolence among Irish Catholics towards Pearse's fervid interweaving of patriotic and Christian sentiments. It seemed to be no accident that the Rising took place at Easter when the Church was commemorating the death and resurrection of Christ. Pearse's 'bloody protest for a glorious thing' still has the power to stir Irish hearts even in an age when violent republicanism has sickened the vast majority of Irish men and women. Pearse's blood-mysticism, however, extended significantly beyond the cause of Irish freedom and cannot be simply classified as patriotic hyperbole. Reflecting on the carnage in Flanders during the 1914-18 War, he uses Jefferson's image with chilling intensity and without Jefferson's deflationary humour: 'The old heart of the earth needed to be warmed with the red wine of the battlefield. Such august homage was never before offered to God as this, the homage of millions of lives given gladly for the love of country.'[3] This sort of ultra-romantic glorification of blood-sacrifice was utterly rejected by Pearse's fellow-patriot, James

Connolly: 'No! we do not think that the old heart of the earth needs to be warmed with the red wine of millions of lives. We think anyone who does is a blithering idiot.'[4] Connolly's robust realism provides a much needed corrective to Pearse's blood-mysticism, collapsing a potent metaphor into literal reference.

The reservations expressed here about the language of blood-sacrifice are to a large extent the product of modern consciousness schooled by post-Freudian psychology with its warnings about sado-masochistic attitudes. It would be anachronistic to read them back into ancient literature, including the New Testament. Blood sacrifices were an important feature of ancient, including Jewish, worship. The Letter to the Hebrews works out an elaborate soteriology on the analogy of Temple sacrifice. Indeed the Letter to the Hebrews appears to abandon symbolic for literal language when it says 'For if the sprinkling of defiled persons with the blood of goats and bulls and with the ashes of a heifer sanctifies for the purification of the flesh, how much more shall the blood of Christ, who through the eternal Spirit offered himself without blemish to God, purify your conscience from dead works to serve the living God' (Heb. 9:13-14). Commenting on the Old Testament idea of blood-sacrifice, Roland de Vaux remarks, 'Blood expiates because it has or because it is life.'[5] The passage from Leviticus on which he is commenting is striking.

> For the life of the flesh is in the blood; and I have given it
> for you upon the altar to make atonement for your souls;
> for it is the blood that makes atonement, by reason of the
> life (Lev. 17:11)

De Vaux believes that it is this text which inspired the author of Hebrews to observe that 'under the law almost everything is purified with blood, and without the shedding of blood there is no forgiveness of sins' (Heb. 9:22). The blood of Jesus had indeed been shed unto death. Many reflective Christians of Jewish background or influence found it natural to make the connection between the Lord's passion and death and the contemporary consciousness of blood-sacrifice. Adolf von Harnack has observed that the New Testament notion of blood-sacrifice gave Christian soteriology an entrée into the contemporary world.

The point about these terms which denote purification is that in a certain sense they by-pass the rational processes and address something deep within the pre-rational human being. When I described them as dangerous terms I was far from dismissing them but merely noting that they need to be deployed today with the greatest care and historical sophistication. They make their appeal to the instinctive and unconscious element in our psyche and as such they can stir deeply-entrenched emotions not all of which are amenable either to rationality or to healthy spirituality. The fact is that the urge to expiate certain of our offences is a deep-seated one. In everyday life we speak of the need to make up, or atone, for our offences against others. This felt need has an instinctive authenticity about it, but it can easily lose that authenticity and become disordered and neurotic. Guilt-feeling may or may not correspond to reality. Masochistic self-hatred can masquerade as repentance. The felt need to make reparation, in itself a healthy reaction to the sort of wrong-doing which has seriously harmed others, can degenerate into a neurotic desire for punishment. This degeneration of what may be in itself a healthy impulse into an irrational desire may issue in certain theological interpretations which have in point of fact played a regrettable part in later Christian soteriology. The worst of these interpretations turns on the notion of an offended God whose anger needs to be propitiated by human suffering. The suffering and death of Jesus have sometimes been interpreted as salvific precisely because they were deemed to have satisfied the anger of a vengeful God.

Those who held this view of God were simply blind to its implicit blasphemy. Carried away by reflection on human wickedness, these interpreters indulged a twisted view of how things are between God and man. They projected on to God some of the meanest and most ignoble of human passions and thus they achieved a vicarious, if unconscious, satisfaction of their own darker and unrecognised passions.

Sacrifice

The word 'sacrifice', together with the images it may conjure up, has much in common with those we have just considered. It is a word with powerful emotional resonance but also with many possibilities for ambiguity. It has had a long and influential history in Christian soteriology. Its role in Eucharistic theology is notoriously controversial. We have already noticed how the author of the Letter to the Hebrews deploys it in relation to the death of Jesus, which he interprets by reference to the Temple sacrifices. If taken as a virtual synonym for propitiation, it risks the same distortions as can beset the latter word. In common with the phrase 'the shedding of blood', it is vulnerable to the confusion of literal and symbolic interpretation. Eucharistic theology has proved to be a prolific source for this linguistic confusion. Catholic neo-Scholastic theology addressed itself to the question of how the Mass could be a sacrifice, as defined by the Council of Trent. Of the many theories put forward in the manuals, that of Maurice de la Taille may be singled out as a particularly apt example of how symbolic thinking can degenerate into a manifestation of what Paul Claudel described as 'the tragedy of a starved imagination'. De la Taille described his theory as 'mystical slaying'. He saw the consecration of the Eucharistic elements as a symbolic representation of the 'separation' of Christ's blood from his body. It would be hard to find a better example of a failed imagination than this bizarre theory. It reduces the symbolic image of the shedding of blood to a literal one-to-one correspondence with the two-fold consecration of the bread and the wine. De la Taille's theory was much admired in the period after it was published in 1921, but one needs to remember that response to symbol was not a developed practice in Catholicism at that time, and the adjective 'symbolic' was generally employed in a weak, indeed pejorative, sense since the condemnation of Modernism.[6]

I mention this theory mainly as an illustration of what can happen in theology when one facet of a mystery is cut away from its proper setting and then subjected to an intense and detailed scrutiny which lacks final credibility and persuasiveness because it robs the mystery of a context which would give it meaning and reference. This sort of analysis is rather like looking at a newspaper photograph through a powerful magnifying glass: you don't see greater detail, you see bigger dots. To concentrate on the Eucharistic elements at the expense of the overall setting within which the elements play their part and derive their meaning is to fail in that imaginative and intuitive use of the mind which Pascal called *l'esprit de finesse.* The mathematical mind is incompetent to register the scene as a whole. It asks the wrong questions. It speculates on the liturgical relationship between the Last Supper and Calvary in a way which invites the destructive dissection of a mystery. It strips the petals from a rose in an attempt to discover the source of its charm. Pre-Vatican II Catholic theology of the Eucharist was preoccupied with the ritual character of sacrifice. As J. Ratzinger pointed out twenty years ago, however, Luke and Paul interpret the Last Supper as a victory for the prophetic spirit 'over cultic ritual and sacrificial practices'. 'Criticism of ritual worship has assumed its definitive shape, and the Temple has become superfluous.'[7] Neo-Scholasticism, in reaction to the Reformers, returned in effect to the Temple—not the Temple in Jerusalem but a temple constructed by minds preocupied with the ritual minutiae of sacrifice often at the expense of the integral meaning of the life, death, and resurrection of Jesus.

Much present-day soteriology places less emphasis on the cultic associations of the word 'sacrifice' and instead ponders the message of the Philippian hymn: 'And being found in human form [Jesus] humbled himself and became obedient unto death, even death on a cross' (Phil. 2:8). Placed in the concrete historical circumstances of his time and place, Jesus, through prayer, sought to discern the will of his Father. This led him to the conviction that he must go to Jerusalem and confront his enemies with the Gospel. This decision was sacrificial to the core and it culminated psychologically in his prayer to the Father in Gethsemane, 'Not my will but thine be done'. The crucifixion was the final outcome of his obedience in historical terms.

From the standpoint of worship, the crucifixion is a supremely liturgical act. How we relate the Eucharist to Calvary is a separate question, though one of immense importance for the Christian Church. It is the sacrificial obedience of Jesus to the Father, carried out in the historical circumstances of his time, which grounds all subsequent interpretations, including those of the New Testament; and it is in these circumstances that we must seek the primary meaning of sacrifice as it applies to the life and death of Jesus. Talk about the destruction of victims as a way of pleasing God and of showing our dependence upon him has lost much of the cultural relevance it had for our forebears. What has not been lost, however, because it has perennial relevance, is the notion of a sacrificial victim who gives up his life in order that others may live. The author of the Letter to the Hebrews, though living in an age which could still think authentically in terms of ritual sacrifice, nevertheless transcends the cultural limitations of the age and arrives at a nobler and more universally relevant concept of sacrifice when he applies the words of Psalm 40 to Jesus.

> Consequently, when Christ came into the world, he said,
> 'Sacrifices and offerings thou hast not desired,
> but a body has thou prepared for me;
> in burnt offerings and sin offerings thou hast taken no pleasure.
> Then I said, "Lo, I have come to do thy will, O God",
> as it is written of me in the roll of the book.'
> (Heb. 10:5-7)

Reconciliation, Atonement, Satisfaction

Nearer to literal than metaphorical derivation, the word 'reconciliation' is perhaps the soteriological concept with the widest possibilities for relevance in a variety of cultures. It envisages a situation where people have become estranged, either bilaterally or unilaterally. When applied to the relationship between God and man, the alienation is unilateral, for it takes place only on man's side. God remains faithful to his covenant in spite of all that man can do. It is God who takes the initiative and ends the estrangement which man has inflicted on himself. The word 'estrangement' is an immediate reminder of its antonym, 'atonement'. By reason of its acquired associations, however, the word 'atonement' is not an exact synonym for reconciliation. Atonement (literally, at-one-ment) has acquired the meaning of expiation: to atone is to make up for an injury inflicted on another. When applied to God's salvific intention towards men and women, reconciliation is pure grace, and like all grace, it costs. The crucified

Christ is the price that God pays for bringing men and women back from the alienating effects of sin. God grants us peace as an absolute gift through the sacrifice of Christ on the cross. The figure hanging on the cross is the historical outcome of human sin, but God transforms it into an offer of forgiveness and loving acceptance. As we shall see, this interpretation of reconciliation as pure unilateral free gift was often subsequently lost to sight, with attention falling increasingly on the concept of satisfaction.

To approach the Church Fathers for guidance on the Christian understanding of Christ's eternal achievement is to enter a world which can be strange, at times even bizarre, to us today. In saying this I am not implying any superiority on our part, merely cultural difference. We are faced therefore with an interpretative task. One often finds in the Fathers a curious mixture of myth and metaphysics, neither of which translates easily into language which has cultural relevance for us today. Myth is addressed to the imagination, that is, to that function of the mind which responds to story and symbol and especially to that combination of both which characterises myth. Many of the Fathers were educated in the thought of Plato, and this education led them to speculate philosophically on the nature and person of Christ. However, the metaphors and models employed in the New Testament to depict the saving achievement of Christ did not lend themselves to philosophical analysis.

The hellenistic mind was more at home with the notion of a God who *is* rather than with that of a God who *acts* in history. From their hellenistic background the Eastern Fathers derived something like an obsession with divine immutability and impassibility. The doctrine of redemption, however, clearly postulates divine interventive action in and through Christ. The dilemma is to some extent met by the Antiochene Fathers in their emphasis on the Son of God 'suffering in his human nature'. The danger here, as with all Antiochene theology, was a dualistic Christ whose godhead is in some sense a spectator of his manhood's suffering. The Alexandrian Fathers, on the other hand, were anxious to avoid this danger of dividing the unity of Christ. They therefore concentrated so firmly on the divine unity of Christ that they tended to find redemptive efficacy in the very uniting of divine and human natures in his person. This could have the effect of playing down the redemptive importance of the passion and death of Jesus.

Greek thinking from Irenaeus onwards is preoccupied with corporate considerations. Redemption comes to human *nature*. What Christ achieves *in* his human nature becomes an achievement *of* that nature. As Irenaeus puts it, 'In the second Adam we were reconciled, becoming obedient to God.'[8]

St Irenaeus of Lyons was something of an intellectual maverick who still resists the customary labels. A Greek translated to the West, and arguably the first Father to merit the description 'theologian' as distinct from philosopher-turned-Christian, Irenaeus continues to divide commentators in their estimation of him. He made two notable contributions to theology in general and to soteriology in particular. The first was his preoccupation with a divine plan. More historically sensitive than later Greek Fathers, he developed the New Testament kerygmatic insight into the need to recognise that the life, death, and resurrection of Jesus must be seen against the background of a divine dispensation which governs all history from the creation to the end of time. Irenaeus' God is splendidly free of the arbitrary severity which we find in many of the later Fathers and medieval theologians. God does not need man, says Irenaeus. This divine independence, however, issues not in holy despotism, but in loving generosity. Everything God does for man is done 'not because he had need of man, but that he might have a being on whom to lavish his benefits'.[9]

The non-moralising serenity of Irenaeus' soteriology is the counterpart of his understanding of what came to be known as original sin and serves as a reminder of the mutual relationship between one's theology of sin and one's theology of atonement. A purely ethical view of sin will often have as its counterpart a penal or forensic view of redemption. A God who is angered by sin will not surprisingly turn out to be a God who needs to be appeased by blood sacrifice. Irenaeus is quite free of this urge to project on to God some of our meanest and most spiteful human tendencies. Adam and Eve were seduced by the Serpent. This, says Irenaeus, was no difficult task for the Serpent, for they were children.[10] The First Sin was one not of pride or malice but of immaturity. Adam and Eve were induced to jump the gun and forestall God's plan for them and their descendants. God's reaction to the First Sin was not anger at man's rebellion but compassion for his weakness. And so God 'designed a plan of salvation like an architect'.[11] Gently removing man from Paradise and the Tree of Life, so that man would not be eternally imprisoned in the consequences of his transgression, God arranged for death as a merciful release.[12] Man would now have to undergo a programme of recuperative education under which he would learn 'the knowledge of moral discipline, then attaining to the resurrection from the dead, and learning from experience what is the source of his deliverance', would 'always live in a state of gratitude to the Lord'.[13]

By becoming a man the Word of God, says Irenaeus, 'recapitulated in himself all the dispersed peoples dating back to Adam . . . '[14] and procured for us a comprehensive salvation. As mediator between God and man Christ was able 'by his connection with both parties to bring them again into peace and friendship, presenting man to God and revealing God to man'.[15] By passing through every age of human growth from childhood, through youth, to full manhood, Christ redeemed humanity in all its stages.[16] Humanity—to us almost inevitably an abstraction—was to Irenaeus a term denoting the solidarity of all men and women of every age. A great deal of liberal Protestant discomfort with Irenaeus' soteriology centred upon its alleged suggestion of automatic redemption with no strong ethical ingredient. Human nature here seems to be redeemed by its sheer conjunction with divine nature in Christ. The fact, however, is that we have here a soteriological principle which was to dominate Greek, especially Alexandrian, theology: only that which is assumed can be redeemed. The point was later to be made against the Alexandrians themselves when they seemed to be suggesting that in Christ the divine nature took the place of the human soul. If the human soul was not assumed, the Antiochenes claimed, it was not redeemed.

Irenaeus' doctrine of recapitulation set a pattern which Alexandrian soteriology consistently followed: the Incarnation is itself redemptive. The West has never seemed at ease with the doctrine of deification. Abstract, mystical and ontological, with an apparent smack of pantheism about it, the doctrine of deification has not seemed to speak convincingly to literal and legalistic minds such as are not uncommonly to be found in the West. Western Christianity has traditionally given it lip-service before switching the drama to the court-room, where the real business is done. Protestantism has tradi-tionally disliked its mysticism and its alleged lack of ethical seriousness. Many commentators have felt that in some way it weakens the role of the Cross and consequently the glory of the resurrection. Perhaps the best answer to this charge is to note that in thinkers like Irenaeus the incarnation, passion, and resurrection of Christ are all of a piece, all taken up into the one sweep of divine love for man.

Irenaeus' theological scheme is replete with parallelisms and symbolic correspondences. He delights in the Adam/Christ parallelism, a device which some of the nineteenth-century liberals disliked but which is nevertheless biblical and important for keeping the theology of salvation in close relationship with the theology of sin. Sin, as Irenaeus sees it, is a malady from which man needs to be healed rather than a crime for which he merits punishment and purification.

Before turning to the characteristically Western concern with divine penology let us consider briefly an area of patristic soteriology which has embarrassed, exasperated, or amused commentators for a long time. I refer to the 'Devil's rights', or 'transactional', theory of atonement.

The metaphor of ransom can be found in the New Testament. The biblical writers were content to deploy it without specifying the recipient of the ransom. Not so the Fathers, who fell upon the image with relish. Origen claimed that since the ransom could not be paid to God, the only other possible recipient was the Devil.[17] Gregory of Nyssa prefers the notion of the Devil's deception. Most of us are amused today by Gregory's view of the humanity of Christ as bait and the divinity as fish-hook.[18] Nineteenth-century liberal commentators were profoundly shocked by this attribution to God of immoral, or at least frivolous, behaviour. The Fathers seem to have had a sense of humour totally lacking in the liberals. They genuinely enjoyed the spectacle of the deceiver deceived. There is a certain low humour running through the patristic theme of the Devil's deception which continued to

186

engage the medieval mind and fascinate its imagination. The role of the Devil was one feature of Greek soteriology which passed over to the West and enjoyed a thousand-year run, until Anselm put paid to it at the turn of the eleventh century and gave us in its stead the stern theory of satisfaction.

The Eastern theology of sin borrows its characteristic models from pathology; while the Western theology of sin has borrowed its characteristic models from the world of crime and punishment. Accordingly, Eastern soteriology conducts the patient to the hospital; while Western soteriology lands the criminal in the dock of a court-room. Gregory of Nyssa's fish-hook may be crude imagery, but Gregory's fisherman saves the whole catch. Augustine's mousetrap is no less crude, and, in addition, Augustine allows us to understand that much of the food saved from the mouse is destined to putrify anyway.

It has often been pointed out that many of the West's leading theologians were trained as lawyers. Legal models and metaphors have, of course, their rightful claim in Christian theology. After all, much of Paul's language was forensic. It had to be, since he was combating pharasaical legalism. The point at issue is not the presence of legal and forensic figures of speech in the language of Christian theology, but their degree of prominence in relation to other figures. Much depends on how you run your courtroom. Tertullian's judge is unlikely to remand the prisoner for a medical report. Tertullian was a rigorist with regard to post-baptismal sin and, like his fellow-African, Cyprian, an exclusivist in his attitude to the Church. 'Every sin', says Tertullian, 'is discharged either by pardon or penalty, pardon as the result of chastisement, penalty as the result of condemnation.'[19] The sinner must satisfy the Lord.[20] Although Tertullian is sometimes credited with the introduction of the legal terms 'merit' and 'satisfaction' into the language of theology, he limits their use to personal morality and does not base a Christian soteriology on them. The North Africans, however, did bequeath to Western Christianity an image of God as a stern lawgiver and severe judge, and this image was later to call forth a matching soteriology from the pen of Anselm of Canterbury.

One other matter deserves mention before we turn to Anselm. This matter arises out of what Gustaf Aulén has called the 'Classic' theory of atonement. Aulén's book, *Christus Victor*, published in 1931, was quickly recognised as a work of scholarship and originality.[21] Aulén tackles his subject historically, but he has two axes to grind. First, he sets out to show that Luther's doctrine of the atonement, if properly understood, is a faithful reflection of the 'Classic' patristic teaching. Second, he proposes to repair the damage done to soteriology by liberal Protestants like Ritschl and Harnack. Aulén's thesis is that the customary classification of atonement theories into 'objective' and 'subjective' is seriously defective. In effect he subdivides the so-called 'objective' typing into 'Classic' and 'Latin', while he refers to the subjective' type as 'humanistic'.

Critical comment on Aulén's book has generally agreed that he exaggerates his thesis and does not do full justice either to Anselm or to the liberal Protestant tradition. Nevertheless his distinction between 'Classic' and 'Latin' has become part of the vocabulary of soteriology. He outlines the 'Classic' theory as follows:

> ...Incarnation and Redemption belong indissolubly together; God in Christ overcomes the hostile powers which hold man in bondage. At the same time these hostile powers are also the executants of God's will. The patristic theology is dualistic, but it is not an absolute Dualism. The deliverance of man from the power of death and the devil is at the same time his deliverance from God's judgment. God is reconciled by His own act in reconciling the world to himself.
>
> Thus the power of evil is broken; that is to say, not that sin and death no longer exist, but that, the devil having been once for all conquered by Christ, His triumph is in principle universal, and His redemptive work can go forward everywhere, through the Spirit who unites men with God and 'deifies' them.... It can also be said that death is changed from an enemy to a friend.[22]

In effect Aulén demythologises the demonology and claims to find under the gothic imagery a profound appreciation of the drama of redemption in which God is always the principal actor. Aulén is a vigorous opponent of the 'Latin' theory, precisely because in this theory *man* plays an active role and seeks thereby to placate a just and offended God by satisfaction, sacrifice, and merit. In this respect Aulén becomes a forceful apologist for some characteristically Protestant contentions and is consequently open to the charge that he reads back into patristic and medieval times the convictions and polemics of a later age. Nonetheless one can hardly deny that his theory of dramatic encounter between God and the forces of evil is a fair summary of general patristic soteriology.

One thing is clear: this unrefined and mythical view of redemption fitted early medieval culture like a glove. Rarely can a theological construction have been so in harmony with contemporary culture as the 'Classic' theory of redemption was with the culture of the early middle ages. Crude it may have been; but in an age like ours when theology and even liturgy find it extremely difficult to forge a convincing link with contemporary secular culture, we can ill afford to look with condescension at an age that did so with effortless success. In this respect at least we have something to learn from the so-called dark ages.

What one most notices about this period is the epic character of its dominant values. Military prowess was widely seen as the supreme achievement of secular life. The poetry of early medieval Europe is the poetry of the battlefield, of honour satisfied in deeds of arms, of comradeship in war and in the winning and losing of great causes. That at least was the ideal, however wide the gap may have been between it and concrete reality. The warrior-hero was the ideal archetype of noble ambition. His prowess was celebrated in story and song and recited unremittingly in the banquet-halls of the great. All this was reflected in theological and devotional life. Christ was portrayed as the Warrior-Hero going into battle against Satan. Artistic representations of the crucified Christ during the age between the sixth and twelfth centuries protray not a suffering man but the stylised grandeur of the *Rex-Sacerdos*, the King-Priest, in the act of inflicting defeat on the ancient enemy.[23]

The advent of feudalism enabled certain refinements to be made to the understanding of redemption. In view of the fact that the word 'feudalism' is so often employed today in a pejorative sense, we need perhaps to remember that as a

189

politico-military system feudalism rescued European society from anarchy. It specified the relationship between lord and vassal with clarity and severity. It introduced rules and ritual into a situation which had been a political and military free-for-all. The Church, having warded off the secularising dangers of lay investiture, was quite ready to sacralise the military values of feudalism by dispatching to the First Crusade some of Europe's principal brigands and by blessing a campaign designed to make the Holy Land safe for Christian pilgrims. Theologians found relevant models and metaphors in the political and military structures of the age. Both 'Classic' and 'Latin' theories of redemption drew naturally upon feudal culture. This is not to say that feudalism created a new soteriology; it merely supplied refinements to a model which the Fathers had already constructed from biblical materials. At the end of the eleventh century the theory which prevailed in the schools presented redemption more or less as follows.

By the sin of disobedience, man withdrew from the service of God and offered fealty to the Devil in an act of defiance of God (*diffidatio*, defiance, was a technical feudal term). This meant war; but the war had to be fought by the rules. God could not use his divine power against the Devil who had acquired rights in justice over man. Man was powerless to do anything for himself, and therefore his only hope lay in the Devil's breaking of the rules. Precisely in not discerning the divinity of the God-man the Devil overreached himself. He laid claim in justice to the life of Christ who had never been guilty of defiance of God. Thus was the Devil's imperium broken. God was now 'free' to reinstate man.

This soteriological thesis held the field until it was insouciantly dismissed by St Anselm in his book, *Cur Deus Homo*. Anselm's contribution to the theology of redemption has remained the subject of continuous debate. He had a genius for magnificently flawed arguments which continue to fascinate minds which not merely reject them but in some cases are actually uninterested in their subject-matter. (The ontological argument for the existence of God is perhaps the best-known example.) In the case of his soteriology there are those who argue that his position is quite simply patristic, while others argue that his ideas are taken from the world of feudalism. What is less disputable is that he demolished at a stroke the universal acceptance of the theory of redemption which rested on the notion that the Devil had acquired rights over the human race. Acts of theological demolition can create serious hazards for faith, as we today know only too well. To remove the Devil from his central role in the drama of salvation was to break with tradition and popular religion and consequently to create a theological and spiritual vacuum. 'The empire of the Devil in nature and supernature was a matter of daily experience: the Devil's empire and the daily breaches made in it by Christ provided the framework of history. The contemplation of God's triumphant strategy satisfied imagination and piety alike.'[24]

In place of the theory of cosmic warfare between God and the Devil Anselm put the theory of satisfaction which, following the best lights of the age, aimed at being strictly rational. The immediate cultural background was feudal, but by Anselm's time its epic character was beginning to wane. The courtroom replaced the battlefield. Anselm's soteriological thinking is dominated by reflection upon the damage done to God's majesty and honour by sin. He is extremely severe on any attempt to take lightly the divine justice or the offence given to it by sin. Every effort to take a more benign view is met by the stern words, 'You have not yet considered how weighty a matter sin is.'[25]

The main lines of the Anselmian argument are well known: Man was created for the blessedness that comes of total submission to the will of God. But man disobeyed, thus offending against the justice and honour of God. The situation could be remedied only by a satisfaction greater than the disobedience. Man, however, has nothing supererogatory to offer God, since anything he is able to offer he already *owes* to God. Only God can make the sort of reparation (*satisfactio*) called for; but there is no obligation (*debitum*) on God to do so. Hence we reach an impasse: man *ought* to make retribution but cannot. God alone *can* make the necessary reparation but has no obligation to do so. The stalemate is broken by the offering of the God-man; and the question posed in Anselm's title is answered.

Anselm's soteriology was thus also a striking essay in

theological relevance to his own age. It is perhaps too easy to react in disfavour today against precisely those elements in the feudal theory which were most relevant to their time. They spoke to their age about realities which transcend the ability of any age to give them permanent expression. There is, after all, permanent significance in Anselm's attempt to show that 'there is nothing arbitrary in God'.[26] The trouble is that words like 'justice', 'honour', and 'satisfaction' can sound grimly calculating when they are detached from the culture which provided them. Especially do they lose their austere grandeur when they are thought of not as martial and governmental, but as commercial, models. It is arguably no accident that the rise of banking and other sophisticated forms of commerce in the later middle ages coincided with a decline in theology. Feudal contractual customs offer some possibilities as theological models. The contractual arrangements of commerce sound a note of dissonance with the gospel from the start. If salvation is seen as the final outcome of paying off a mortgage throughout life, it becomes virtually impossible to forge a theology of faith and grace as pure gift.

There is a serene objectivity about both the 'Classic' and 'Latin' theories of redemption. They pay little heed to the subjective experience or historical character of the lives of men and women who need salvation. It was Peter Abelard who recognised that neither the 'Classic' nor the Anselmian theory did justice to the roles played by experience and history in matters of salvation. They reduced men and women to spectators at a cosmic drama. Abelard appreciated that salvation must bear upon human experience and human history and that the believer must participate in, and not merely look out upon, the drama of redemption. Thus Abelard took up a neglected patristic theme, that of Christ the Illuminator, and in a much quoted passage of his commentary on Romans gave his interpretation of Christ's redemptive work. God's Son 'took upon him our nature and in it taught us by word and example and so endured unto death, and thus bound us closer to himself by love'. 'Therefore our redemption is that supreme love which is in us through Christ's passion... so that we fulfil all things from love rather than from fear of [God]'.[27]

Bernard of Clairvaux was the first, though by no means the last, critic to accuse Abelard of Pelagianism.[28] On the other hand, the nineteenth-century liberals adopted him with all the surprised enthusiasm they reserved for the mavericks of the middle ages. 'At last', wrote Rashdall, 'we have found a theory of the atonement which thoroughly appeals to reason and to conscience.'[29] Both responses are partial, if not indeed tendentious. Today we are perhaps in a better position to appreciate that Abelard was rejecting neither the doctrine of grace nor the notion of a supra-historical drama. He was supplying a much needed corrective to an exclusive concern with that drama as bearing upon, but extrinsic to, man. As Richard Weingart has put it, Abelard's concern was to interiorise both man's predicament and Christ's correcting of that predicament. Abelard's 'teaching on the atonement has been justly praised for its insight into the nature and cure of man's alienation from God'.[30] He took seriously the psychological and moral dimension of salvation, which is why he strikes an answering chord not only in the liberals, but in twentieth-century theologians also.

Redemption in Contemporary Perspective

The just man...will be scourged, tortured, and imprisoned, his eyes will be put out, and after enduring every humiliation he will be crucified, and learn at last that we should want not to be, but to seem just.[1] (Plato)

But you denied the Holy and Righteous One, and asked for a murderer to be granted to you, and killed the Author of life, whom God raised from the dead. To this we are witnesses. (Acts 3:14-15)

Holy bright King, although Thou hadst strayed from Heaven tormented amongst us in ways that can never be measured, Thy love Thou hadst hidden, O Christ, till the lance tore a mansion secure in Thy heart for the whole world.[2] (Tadhg Gaelach Ó Súilleabháin)

In the quotation from Plato's *Republic* Glaucon is discussing the virtues and fate of the truly just man, that is, the man who is not concerned with the appearance and conventional behaviour expected of someone with pretensions to being just, but who is actually just—just to the core of his being. A really righteous man will bring destruction on himself because his fellow human beings will stand convicted by his very presence among them. Written about 380 BC, Plato's words have an uncanny relevance to the death of Jesus of Nazareth nearly four centuries later. In the quotation from Acts of the Apostles Peter is addressing the people outside the Temple in Jerusalem, accusing them of calling for the death of Jesus, the truly righteous man. What Glaucon had said would inevitably happen to such a man happened in fact to Jesus. The confrontation between radical goodness and conventional virtue allied to political convenience brought about his passion and death.

From the earliest age of the Christian Church the death of

Jesus was seen as being 'for us and for our salvation'. An act which had its immediate context in Roman and Jewish history was soon to be seen as an act of cosmic significance. Jesus was soon to be presented as Mediator between God and man. Whatever regional limitations governed the earthly life of Jesus (e.g. Mk. 7:27), in the moment of his agony he drew all humanity to himself (Jn. 12:32). Tadhg Gaelach Ó Súilleabháin gives poetic expression to this universalising circumstance of Christ's passion when he speaks of the centurion's lance opening up a mansion in the heart of Christ which would henceforth contain the whole world.

One of the principal contentions of this book has been that creation and redemption belong together in any balanced theological treatment of anthropology, and consequently of the relationship between God and man. If cosmology shows us an evolving universe and scientific anthropology shows us the stages in the process by which *homo sapiens* has emerged as a species, what each reveals must be germane to any theological reflection on the nature of man. In effect, the *physical* circumstances of our coming to being as a species, while not belonging formally to historical revelation, are nevertheless on the agenda of any serious attempt to narrow the gap which used to exist in Christian theology, both Catholic and Protestant, between creation and salvation. Creation prepares the way for redemption by dint of its evolutionary drive towards complexification. As soon as evolution becomes cultural, as it has done in the human species, a need is created which was not there before. In men and women creation unfolds *ad Deum*, in a Godward direction which is *consciously* recognised. God now speaks a new creative word which can be heard resonating in the very fibres of human being (i.e., God is transcendentally present in all human depth experiences). That word can be listened to as address in the historical explicitness of the life, death, and resurrection of Jesus of Nazareth. God's Word offers salvation to a species which knows itself to be oppressed by many of the circumstances of being human, not least by the sense of moral fragmentation and powerlessness (Romans 7).

As soon as one registers the fact that man is the product not merely of biological but also of chemical and physical developments, one can no longer proceed theologically on the assumption that only the *discontinuity* between human beings and the rest of creation matters when one comes to consider the meaning of salvation. That meaning is intimately bound up with *both* the continuities *and* the discontinuities occurring in the evolving universe. It is within the dialectical relationship between these continuities and discontinuities that we must find the experiences which provide the materials for soteriological reflection. Alienation and reconciliation constitute perhaps the two major antithetical experiences which dominate the human condition. The relationship between them, however, is not merely antithetical, it is also at many points ambiguous. Alienation is both necessary for development according to God's plan and potentially salvific when a complementary reconcilation is seen to belong to the same plan. That which has been divided, fragmented, and disjointed by natural processes has to be re-united at a higher and, in human beings, at a conscious, level. In this sense alienation precedes morality. Alienation occurs but is not consciously registered in pre-human existence. Initially, therefore, it has no moral component. In men and women, however, it becomes conscious and therefore acquires an inescapable moral component.

With the advent of *homo sapiens* God's evolutionary plan takes a new direction signalised by what Christian theology customarily refers to as revelation. Faith, a condition impossible to earlier forms of creation, now becomes not merely possible but necessary, if God's plan is to continue to unfold towards an ingathering into God himself. Faith is made possible in the cosmos by a new creative initiative taken by God and traditionally referred to in Christian theology as grace or supernatural life. The new creation, unlike its primordial matrix, is not available to be examined by the tools of empirical science. In men and women creation enters into free and creative partnership with a God who is seen to be not only one who creates but also one who saves. The prospect of salvation, implicit from the start, now becomes consciously recognised and aspired to. Salvation promises meaning and glory, but only through struggle, pain, and the constant threat of failure. More than that, it actually incorporates struggle, pain, and failure into its very fabric. For Christians the historical and symbolic manifestation of salvation through struggle, pain and failure is the cross of Christ lit by the glory of the resurrection. When this light suffuses the cosmos, all become grace.

How is all this, then, to be given concrete reference in the lives of human individuals and societies? It is in attempting to answer this question that we encounter different myths, theories, and points of emphasis. In the last chapter we saw how our biblical, patristic, and medieval forebears in the faith were able to express their perception of salvation through myths and concepts which reflected their culture and spoke with meaning and power to them. It is, however, extremely difficult to speak effectively in traditional terms about salvation to modern men and women. Traditional soteriology, which in former ages spoke with imaginative effectiveness and power, now seems to inhabit a world of its own which appears to be sealed off from daily modern experience. 'Modernity' is a term that describes a situation which is in itself neither good nor bad. It just is; and it is where we today, whether we like it or not, have to do our living, thinking, and praying. There is no point in sighing for the real or imagined simplicities of an earlier age. Christian theology is always concerned with giving a contemporary relevance to the traditional truths of revelation. This concern involves an intellectual asceticism which the Christian must school himself or herself to understand as a sharing in Christ's cross. There are no short-cuts; there is no gnostic possession of eternally pre-packaged truths. There is no credible or authentic appeal to human authority to relieve one of one's intellectual responsibilities, once these have been recognised. Each age has to achieve its own purchase on the great truths of Christian revelation by working out its own appropriate ways of subjecting itself to them. The great soteriological truth that Christ died to save us from sin has to be constantly grappled with if it is to reveal its meaning and effectiveness in successive ages; and it is in our actual lived experience that we find the concrete means for living and understanding the realities we proclaim, most of all the reality of salvation.

There can be no understanding of what salvation might mean until we are clear about the condition from which we long to be saved. The fact is that we feel oppressed in ways which are both similar to and dissimilar from the ways in which our ancestors felt oppressed. Mere brandishing of the word 'sin' is of little help here unless we are prepared to re-examine the character and scope of what we mean by sin. If we hold a trivial or purely individualistic view of the meaning of sin, we shall in consequence hold a trivial and merely individualistic view of salvation.

It will not do simply to continue repeating the classical formulas of Christian soteriology as if they possessed self-evident meaning and had merely to be invoked catechetically or intoned liturgically for their effect to take place. The reality to which they refer has to be experienced in all the contexts which go to make up any human life, however seemingly humdrum. If salvation is understood in exclusively private terms, or if it is taken to refer exclusively to life beyond the grave, the resulting soteriology will have little of theological substance to say to or about life in this world. It will stimulate the expression of other-worldly pieties and emphasise the demands of private morality. It will also encourage the poor and the downtrodden to accept their lot with patience and sub-mission and to pray to be released from this penitential vale of tears and admitted speedily to the joys of heaven. In the past this prayer came naturally to those who were life's victims, and it easily induced in them a resignation to the political and social circumstances which so often were the cause of their misery. They found in their faith and trust in God a reason for living and hoping. Salvation for them could have only an other-worldly reference, for it was precisely from the injustices and miseries of the present world that they hoped to be saved. Political powerlessness had become a controlling element in their piety.

Today we are witnessing a wide-scale and intense reaction against religiously sanctioned passivity in the face of injustice, persecution, and exploitation. Political theology, both in the Northern hemisphere and in Latin America, is already proving to be a powerful agent in the cultural rejuvenation of soteriology. Political theologians remind us that sin is not merely personal but systemic. It colours language, the means of communication, and it denatures the socio-economic and political structures by which society is governed. We have therefore witnessed a recent shift of moral and soteriological emphasis from the private to the social, from individual to structural sin. The trouble with structural sin is that efforts to diagnose culpability for it tend to be theoretical and ideological and therefore less amenable to exhortations to repentance and amendment of life. Political theologians are also vulnerable to the charge of treating a specific political ideology as being mandatory for all Christians. In the Northern hemisphere Political theologians are uncomfortably aware of the accusation of Third World theologians that they (the Northerners) are in effect armchair revolutionaries who do their writing and teaching within structures such as universities and seminaries which are the product of a socio-political system badly in need of reconstruction. Third World Liberation theologians occupy the high moral ground here, and they are not slow to exploit their sense of moral superiority by carrying out forays on those who, like Metz, Moltmann, and Schillebeeckx, are, and ought to be seen to be, their natural allies in the fight against greed, injustice, and exploitation.

The Liberationists, as Schillebeeckx has pointed out, are 'not as afraid of "totalitarianism" as Western theology'.[3] Western theology since the nineteen forties has to be done in the shadow of Auschwitz and Stalin's Gulags. Latin American theologians, in their passionate desire to bring about political and social change, are less anxious about the style of politics adopted in pursuit of, or likely to emerge after, the needed revolution.

The phrase 'option for the poor' is widely accepted today by both Northern and Third World theologians as the foremost moral imperative. Poverty and oppression are tangible manifestations of sin on a macro-scale. Liberation, redemption, and salvation are accordingly seen as having an inevitable political dimension, since nothing less than political action can bring about the changes necessary for the alleviation of poverty and oppression. Although there is widespread agreement on this, there is also a painful hesitancy about attempts to quantify and give concrete identification to the concept of poverty. Can it, for example, be treated as an absolute; or is it to be seen as irreducibly relative? If we concede its relativity, is such a concession not in danger of defusing the urgency of revolutionary fervour? The facts, after all, are there on a global scale. Millions of our fellow men and women throughout the world live in sub-human conditions, go hungry to bed, and are kept in subjugation by brutal regimes operating on behalf of an affluent and privileged few.

Third World theologians, for whom the existence of brutal dictators and callous oligarchies is a fact of everyday life, are understandably impatient with Northern confrères who find that their own situation is much less clear-cut. Poverty in Northern liberal democracies is certainly real enough, but its causes are less easily identified than those which obtain under Third World dictatorships and oligarchies. The Latin American liberation model cannot with impunity be imported *en bloc* into an average European or North American state. Attempts to apply it in Northern Ireland, for example, could give a seriously distorted reading of the actual situation where two divided communities feel themselves to be oppressed by each other. Interpretative subtleties, inappropriate perhaps in a Latin American context, are altogether necessary in any truly salvific approach to the needs of Northern Ireland where people are oppressed not only by poverty in its conventional sense but also by the sheer divisive existence of two communities separated from one another by a historical inheritance of hatred and distrust. Despair, surely one of the worst kinds of oppression, is possibly a greater temptation in Northern Ireland than in, say, Brazil or Peru, where the issues, for all their gravity, are more clear-cut, where the struggle is more readily identified as being between right and wrong, and where there is real hope that change can and will come. In Northern Ireland such hope is far harder to keep alive, because one community's dream is the other's nightmare. Where the Liberationists can speak freely of abolishing the oppressive regimes against which they are campaigning, in Northern Ireland one must speak of redeeming history by reconciling its memories.

Perhaps the problem really lies in forcing people into making choices which are exclusive of one another. There is material poverty in Northern Ireland, signalised, for example, by the scale of unemployment; but that poverty is relative in the sense that it would look like affluence if placed alongside the poverty of a Latin American shanty-town. The sad fact is that discrimination and oppression exist at every level and in various contexts of human social life, and one should not be forced to choose between these contexts. The campaign for the equality of women, for example, is not an alternative to the campaigns for racial equality or for the abolition of material poverty, though there may be tensions between them.

The notion of liberation, then, has received a new and reinforced lease of life. It is clearly an apt partner for religious faith. Consequently it provides the strongest contemporary candidate for the role of leading model in soteriology. This candidature is strengthened by the fact that the very word 'liberation' has belonged from the start to the vocabulary of soteriology.

There is, however, a serious and easily unnoticed drawback in this fortuitous circumstance, namely, the age-old one of confusing literal with metaphorical usage, of finding one-to-one correspondences between lived historical reality and the analogical models employed by traditional Christian soteriology. Just as Augustine was able to shuttle ambiguously between the notions of generation and regeneration in his theology of original sin, because 'generation' was open to literal as well as analogical reference, so too 'liberation' can be referred to either or both of two levels, the historical and the eschatological, thus enabling liberation preachers and teachers to exploit its possibilities by blurring the distinction between them. This can be done in a variety of ways, not least of which is the possibility of interpreting biblical events, notably the Egyptian and Babylonian captivities of the Jews, in such a way as to force an identification with modern repressive situations. Thus General X becomes Pharoah or Nebuchadnezzar. Such identifications have been made often before, but they were not erected into theological systems.

There is an ambiguous relationship between salvation, in its full eschatological reference, and the various spheres of activity which provide soteriology with its characteristic models and metaphors. The ambiguity lies in the fact that there is an overlap between the literal and the analogical, and between the historical and the eschatological. To be healed, ransomed from captivity, liberated from oppression are all historically actual or possible events which can be *literally* salvific in a sense which is partly historical and partly eschatological while at the same time serving as *models* for an understanding of salvation in its *full* eschatological reference. The ambiguity resulting from this overlap between the literal and the analogical is a happy and useful one, as long as we remember the restraints of the 'eschatological proviso', which forbids us to identify any historical event or situation with all that the Bible means by salvation.

Liberation is by no means the only soteriological concept which risks ignoring the eschatological proviso. Reconciliation and healing are no less vulnerable. Thus, for example, psychological alienation of one kind or another is a normal feature of personal life. Post-Freudian analysis of the individual psyche has revealed a profusion of psychological pressures by which individual men and women feel themselves to be oppressed. Psychotherapy, which aims at alleviating these pressures, usually by teaching people how to live constructively with them, is clearly salvific in an immediate, this-worldly, sense. Psychotherapy, like political liberation, offers an obviously relevant context from which pertinent modern models of salvation can be borrowed. We today tend to find our demons within ourselves rather than in an unseen world around us. The imagery formerly employed to describe spiritual oppression works just as well when it is applied to the inner world of psychic experience. Each of us has to wrestle with his or her personal demons, many of which are unknown to anyone else. In this powerful and threatening realm we experience the forces which make for alienation within our own personalities. We know, therefore, that if redemption is to carry meaning for us, it must bear upon these forces and redeem us from their destructive power. Once again, however, we must register the eschatological proviso. Psychic healing belongs to, but must not be, even by the most fervent believer, identified with, salvation in its full eschatological sense. Holiness, or wholeness in its full sense, is not synonymous with mental health. Neurosis can be a contributory factor to holiness. Healing here will often consist in learning to live constructively and hopefully with a neurosis which we have learned to identify and accept as something which perhaps cannot be changed but which when courageously recognised and faced up to, can be transformed by grace into a stepping-stone on the journey to God. Only at journey's end will it be finally removed.

From the standpoint of Christian faith, salvation is transcendental: it begins here on earth and may indeed be embodied in human acts, natural events, and aesthetic experience, but these embodiments always point beyond themselves to an absolute future. Eliot's image of the hospital is a case in point. It has literal as well as figurative references. A hospital is a place where people are healed; but, if the needs of the whole man or woman are considered, the healing is provisional and temporary. When Eliot describes the earth as our hospital, he goes on to observe that 'to be restored, our sickness must grow worse', and that the final healing comes with death. Nothing can take away the prospect of that last and gravest of events which leaves us totally defenceless in the hands of the God who made us for himself. We cannot be saved from death as an historical event, though we can be saved from a crippling fear of it. This happens when we invest it with meaning and find in it the last and greatest of the alienating experiences through which we have to pass on our journey to God. It has to be named and faced down in the faith-inspired confidence that Christ has conquered it. Hope in resurrection is central to the notion of salvation.

There are Christians who profess not merely agnosticism about life beyond the grave but even a lack of interest in it. They manage to convey the impression that such an interest is a kind of individualistic self-indulgence. There are also those who say they do not fear death. The two positions are of course not identical. One can believe in survival beyond the grave and still fear death and all the circumstances which accompany the act of dying.

Miguel de Unamuno, with perhaps greater realism and honesty, locates the fear of death in consciousness itself:

> For consciousness, even before it knows itself as reason, feels itself, is palpable to itself, is most in harmony with itself, as will, and as will not to die.[4]

Knowledge that we must die is one of the most salient points of discontinuity between the non-human animals and ourselves.

All animals die; only human animals *know* that they must die. That knowledge is an integral element in nature's progress towards God. It came with hominisation and it is intensified by all the precautions, both sensible and neurotic, which modern men and women take to ward it off. In the twentieth century there is also a widespread tendency in the secularised Western world to do everything possible to banish its manifestations and repress all conscious thought of it. A hearse passing through a busy modern thoroughfare can be instinctively experienced as an unwelcome intrusion upon normal life. Thus the last enemy, seen by faith to be conquered by Christ, can, in a secular age, regain the palm and return in triumph. A world without faith is likely to be a world that is oppressed by the prospect of death. Only faith can rob death of its sting. (I do not restrict faith here to an explicitly religious faith. There are forms of humanistic faith which function in a manner similar to religious faith.) The best that a faithless world can do with death is to regard it as an obscenity and repress it as far as possible. Yet even those without faith need a ritual to deal with it, and such a ritual will almost always take on the trappings of religion. Even in a radically secularised world death bespeaks religion and intensifies the transcendental longing for salvation.

The critical philosopher, Walter Benjamin, found himself reflecting on the fate of past victims in history, unwilling to conclude that 'the past is closed' (i.e. beyond the possibility of being eventually put right). Something in him cried out for a redemptive justice which would reach backwards and bring both solace and justice to victims. Secular eschatologies such as Marxism had nothing to say on the fate of those who had suffered in the past; and this worried Benjamin, whose yearning for cosmic justice was eschatological to the core—so much so that his colleague, Max Horkheimer, told him that his position was 'theological', a description which among Marxists would have had the force of excommunication. What Benjamin had been forced by his own compassion to conclude was that in some way solidarity with victims had to include the past; but such a conclusion ran clean contrary to orthodox Marxism. In effect Benjamin had been forced to conclude that death does not have the last word in matters of justice and suffering. Solidarity with victims of every time and place, however, demands an unclosed past; and an unclosed past is necessarily eschatological.[5]

Christian faith renders explicit the implicit religiousness of death by relating it to the death of Christ. Salvation comes to us because God himself in Christ faced the terrors of death, underwent them, and thereby drew their sting. Belief in resurrection does not obviate the need to mourn; we owe to our dead the homage of our tears; but faith allows the light of the resurrection to be reflected in the tears. A truly Christian funeral is an occasion both for mourning the dead and for celebrating the completion of a pilgrimage. It is salvific precisely because it knows how to combine both.

The traditional Irish wake, now fast disappearing, was often condemned because it occasioned intemperate drinking, with the consequent danger of irreverence to the dead and insensitivity to the feelings of the bereaved. Indecorous many a wake may have been, but by making death a familiar it prevented repression and gave social expression to a faith which affirms the transience not only of life *but also of death*. It was a genuine rite of passage which brought the community together and integrated the liturgy into the fabric of social life. There is something of it still to be found in the general Irish attitude to death, but one cannot help wondering how much of it will survive advancing urbanisation and secularisation, which affect the unconscious attitudes of believers as well as unbelievers.

Death, however, is only the last in a series of alienations through which every human being passes. At birth we are ejected from a secure habitat into an alien and threatening world. Gradually we learn that the world is not simply there for our convenience and that, although we are stars in our own drama, we have mere walk-on parts in the dramas of others. We are sent to school and there receive our first lessons in politics (not in the classroom but in the playground). We go through the alienating experience of adolescence, the leaving of home, the loss of friends,...And so it goes on, with each crisis inflicting lacerations and bruises which combine to make an average life both an exercise in survival and an adventure story. This life of the walking wounded has its delights as well as its pains, and the very alienations which are so painful to go through often turn out retrospectively to have been points of growth and signposts to a new stretch of road.

At each stage in the inevitable and creative progression something is gained and something lost. Regression to an earlier stage is impossible, except as a pathological condition caused by an inability to live with the tensions set up by alienation. This progression is the deterministic element in creation. We are destined—in our more pessimistic moods we may experience it as a kind of condemnation—to move on to new experiences, new perspectives from which to view the world, new paradigms for classifying our experiences in it, and the consequent need to measure ourselves against new sets of problems. There is no going back, for the race any more than for the individual. Our human capacity for aggression, for example, terrifies us today because advances in our ability to observe, record, and understand nature (science) and in our power to make instruments commensurate with our scientific knowledge (technology) have provided us with the means for planetary destruction. No wonder we dream. We have entered a cosmic nightmare and we sigh for a lost innocence. Theology recognises this condition as the knowledge of sin. Christian theology, however, also recognises the radical ambiguity of the word 'sin'. Each progression is also a falling. Tillich called this a falling from essence into existence, but there are other ways of interpreting what is happening. To be human is to have partial and frightening knowledge of all that is happening to us. Our ancestors created myths to help them to come to terms with the situation in which they found themselves.

We experience ourselves as both determined and free, and our instinctive reaction to this radical ambiguity is fear and bewilderment. A world has been placed in our hands. We recognise the divine call to make it a better world for all; yet the deed is not done, or only very imperfectly and sporadically done. To be human is therefore to know our need of salvation from our own destructive tendencies. We need to be saved from a historical determinism which seems to point inexorably to extinction or at least to an unprecedented cosmic catastrophe inflicted not by physical nature but by human malice or stupidity. Each new weapon which was invented was used to pierce, batter, burn, sever, puncture, and in manifold other ways assault each other down the ages. There have been wars to end all war and weapons which would ensure supremacy and thus theoretically eliminate the need to use them; but the promise was always false and the attempts to realise it futile. Now we have weapons which can demonstrably destroy our planet. To be human is to need salvation which is earthly as well as eternal; but earthly salvation does not consist in returning to the bow and arrow on the grounds that they seem almost harmless when placed alongside the nuclear bomb. It consists in the renunciation of all weapons, including weapons intended only for defence, since in a saved world there would be no force against which defence would be necessary. Awareness of our sinful nature makes it difficult to regard earthly salvation, such as permanent peace, as anything but utopian.

In a saved world there would be no remediable poverty or hunger, no injustice left unrighted, no pain left unassuaged. In a saved world there would be ... All this is of course an indulgence in utopian dreaming, but how can we do otherwise while giving concrete historical reference to the notion of salvation? These dreams are as old as human history. The Bible frequently entertains them.

> [Yahweh] shall judge between the nations,
> and shall decide for many peoples;
> and they shall beat their swords into ploughshares,
> and their spears into pruning hooks;
> nation shall not lift up sword against nation,
> neither shall they learn war any more.
> (Is., 2:4)

If salvation means anything it means all this and more. It bestrides the here and the hereafter. It has its beginnings in history but its completion in eternity. It is experienced in history as part achievement and part promise. It always promises more than it can deliver in the here and now. There have been moments when swords were beaten into ploughshares; but there have been other and more numerous moments when ploughshares were beaten into swords. There is no evidence that our species is becoming morally better, only that different types of moral response have become technically

207

possible, and therefore necessary. Our moral obligations, formerly seen as domestic and local, must now be seen as global, and we have not yet worked out a way to meet them. The evidence of our television screens severely qualifies the dictum that charity begins at home. It makes us reach into our pockets to contribute to the work of relief agencies but it operates under the law of diminishing returns. We become inured to horror on our screens, because, apart from making sporadic financial contributions, there seems little we can do about what we see before us. It is, however, within our power to continue caring and exploring ways of converting that caring into practical action.

This kind of global caring was not possible in earlier centuries, and it should in all fairness be placed alongside the murdering hatred, the torturing, and the attempts at racial obliteration which have afflicted, and continue to afflict, our world. We belong to a species which builds hospitals as well as concentration camps. We are therefore, as Pascal observed, a mystery to ourselves. We misuse our freedom with abandon, yet we can rise to heights of heroic sacrifice. Our possibilities constantly outstrip our achievements. We could feed and house every man, woman, and child on our planet, but instead our representatives and rulers speak of free market forces and of the undesirability of interfering with these forces. We stockpile obscene weapons of destruction and call it prudential strategy. Some of our leaders actually describe the demand for disarmament as a failure in civic virtue and patriotism. They speak of 'standing tall', of not 'going naked into the conference chamber', of the grandeur of their nation's values and the perils of other nations' ideologies. Many, but by no means all, Christians would describe these attitudes as sinful while conceding that those who adopt them may be perfectly sincere and therefore subjectively inculpable in holding them. We need redemption also from our unattributable sins. Perhaps, however, our political sins of omission are more attributable than we may care to think. If, for example, we use our vote to penalise politicians who advocate greater overseas aid in their policy statements, we thereby refuse to make our own small contribution to global caring.

Much the same is true of sinful history. Later ages often have to pay for the sins of earlier regimes. Thus, for example, racial tension is brought about by the actions of former colonialists. God does not 'send' these tensions as a punishment; they come as a natural consequence of historical acts, *and they are redeemable*. Citizens of multi-racial states are slowly and painfully learning how to live together in peace and without discrimination. This represents considerable moral progress, however slow, even though some men and women refuse God's gracious invitation to racial reconciliation but instead add their own contribution to the historical pool of hatred and persecution. Often they do so in the name of distorted values conceived by diseased imaginations. Such values may even parody the values of religion and use its symbols. One has only to think of the Nazi swastika or the fiery cross of the Ku Klux Klan. The manic response of people at the Nuremberg rallies and the ludicrous prancing of small-town businessmen wearing white sheets witness not only to prejudice but also to the daimonic, pre-rational, and unhealed psychic forces which seek release in ritualised hatred, fear, and scapegoating. Children living in communities which ritualise their phobias and aggressive instincts will naturally and unconsciously take the diseased moral environment for normal. Salvation here needs to be initially expressed as exorcism, by which I mean naming the beast within one's psyche and within one's community, disowning it in the name of Christ, asking for God's forgiveness and, in the knowledge that God always answers such prayer, seeking reconciliation with the scapegoats.

Alienation is, as we have seen, an inescapable feature of cosmic activity. Things break away from their matrix and become 'other'. Complexification entails alienation, as unities are broken up so that pluralities with systemic relationships may come about. Alienation therefore precedes morality. In human beings, however, alienation, in addition to being natural (birth, adolescence, leaving home, death), also becomes potentially and actually sinful (abuse of power, exploitation of labour, racial discrimination, war). Nature heals its own alienations, usually by the establishment of systemic relationships. In human beings something new and consciously willed is needed—namely, justice, forgiveness, acceptance, and reconciliation. Just as natural alienation precedes and stimulates morality, so one may say that supernatural reconciliation similarly precedes and stimulates morality. God first forgives; and forgiven men and women respond to this gracious act by acting in a way which is in keeping with the privileged status it confers.

Jesus' offer of divine forgiveness preceded moral performance on the part of those who were forgiven. People like Zachaeus, the wealthy tax-collector, were made to feel that they belonged, though society at large treated them as moral pariahs. It was as a result of being accepted into friendship by Jesus that Zachaeus undertook to review his life in moral terms. Jesus did not insist on moral conditions *before* accepting Zachaeus; he accepted him unconditionally, and this salvific experience produced a remarkable change in Zachaeus's attitude to life and to his fellow men and women. Such an acceptance, however, was a major cause of the hostility which Jesus encountered in those who saw themselves as God's vice-gerents on earth, the repositories of his law, and the guarantors of Israel's fidelity to the Covenant. It made Jesus himself an outcast and it eventually led to his trial and execution as a blasphemer. 'God was in Christ reconciling the world to himself.' In Christ God entered the world he had created, subjecting himself to its sinfulness, its arrogance, and its brutality.

At this point in the argument we have to take a stand on the meaning of incarnation. F. R. Barry has put the matter in commendably blunt terms. 'Any defensible doctrine of Atonement would seem to require both a high Christology and a high theology of the Church.'[6] We have therefore to take a stand against the sort of reductionism which sees in Jesus no more than a good man who lived his life with complete integrity and which sees in the Church no more than a voluntary association of people who subscribe to the ideals held out by Jesus. Here we may usefully reconsider Aulén's categorisation of soteriological theories into 'Classic', 'Latin' and 'Exemplary' and ask whether all three, so far from being exclusive of one another, have not something important, even indispensable, to contribute to our understanding of redemption today.

The 'Classic', transactional, theory recognised that this world is a theatre of war between good and evil. While avoiding the trap of Manichean dualism, it nevertheless made the Devil, and not human evil, God's main antagonist. Anselm corrected this, not by denying the Devil's existence, but by recognising the need to give men and women a much more active role in the drama. Anselm's preoccupation with satisfaction still left the balance tilted towards the 'objective' significance of redemption. Abelard therefore sought to give 'subjective' human response to Christ's loving example a more significant role in the work of salvation. Thus the dialectical field was staked out by the middle of the twelfth century and its poles have remained remarkably constant ever since. In Aulén's construction of subsequent developments Luther, by his doctrine of justification by faith alone, returned to the Classic theory. The Catholic Church carried on with its basic subscription to Anselm's Latin theory. The nineteenth-century liberals adopted a modernised form of Abelard's exemplary theory. Because modern versions of the patristic and medieval theories tend to follow confessional lines, the task of finding soteriological models which are faithful to Scripture and Tradition and which at the same time can speak with relevance and force to contemporary men and women is an ecumenical one. Christians have to be genuinely seeking reconciliation among themselves if they are to bring it to the world in word and sacrament.

A high christology is necessary if justice is to be done to the conviction that salvation demands divine action because God himself is affected by what happens in creation. This vulnerability on God's part has come about not because of any imperfection in his nature but because he freely accepts the liabilities which accrue from the emergence within creation of intelligent beings with a growing and dangerous desire for autonomy. In the men and women he has created God encounters rebellion, obstinacy and arrogance, all of which are an assault on his holiness. Creation has allowed evil to challenge God, and the challenge must be met by God himself. (This is the point which the authors of the transactional theory appreciated when they deployed the myth of the Devil's rights.) God must therefore, as it were, answer to himself for what he has allowed to happen. First, he has allowed evil to assault his holiness; and, second, he has allowed suffering to afflict his sentient creatures. He must answer both the demands of his own nature and the cries of his suffering creatures. He must be both demand and response. Thus the self-emptying which begins with creation itself comes to its climax in the incarnation of God's Son in Jesus of Nazareth who is both divine Word *and* human response (the point which Anselm appreciated and enshrined in his theory of satisfaction). By demonstrating that a human life can be lived in total and absolute fidelity to the just demands of God's holiness, Jesus atoned for the assault made on that holiness by sinful creation. When men and women refused to listen to Jesus and finally turned on him not only with arrogance but with savagery, they believed that they were dealing with just another man. Such savagery had happened often before and would continue to happen throughout human history. Man's customary inhumanity to man here became man's inhumanity to God. On Calvary creation reached its point of no return. God could have responded to Calvary as the final treason ('They will respect my son', Matt., 21:37) and annihilated his creation, i.e. returned it to the 'nihil' from which it came. Instead he launched creation on a new course by taking the terrible handiwork of human rebellion—the dead body of his Son—transforming it through resurrection and, by the gift of his Holy Spirit, inaugurating the new creation. The sending of the Holy Spirit is a promissory note of God's will to forgive the very worst deeds that men and women can do. That note is redeemable by faith and hope.

It was love which conceived the whole venture; and it was love which carried it through (the point which Abelard appreciated and expressed in his theory of the exemplary action of Christ). The love of God for his creation was definitively expressed in the love of Jesus for his Father and for his fellow human beings. The message of Calvary and the Third Day is that God is not mocked nor is he defeated by the worst that man can do. God's creative purposes are triumphantly justified by his decision not only to raise Jesus from the dead but also by his gift to creation of the crucified Christ now gloriously risen and active in the community of men and women through the invisible work of the Holy Spirit.

We have already considered the mystery of innocent suffering. It is rather too easy for Christians to appeal to the sufferings of Jesus as a solution of the problem. In one way the passion and death of Jesus actually compound the problem: so pervasive of creation is innocent suffering that not even God's Son can escape it. There is, however, another way of approaching the suffering of Jesus. Nowhere in the gospels does one find Jesus treating suffering as a speculative question. He did not conduct Socratic seminars about the possible purpose and meaning of suffering. Instead he took it as a fact of life, relieved it when the occasion arose, and announced bluntly that those who wished to follow him must be prepared to shoulder it. For Jesus the matter was eminently practical: to take up the Gospel is to take up the cross. The cross is not to be sought for itself; it comes to those who respond to the demands of love. The *problem* remains unsolved; the *mystery*, however, is infinitely deepened by the fact that in Christ God has taken upon himself the pain and distress of evolving creation. Jung's insight is directed more to the imagination than to the speculative intellect: Calvary is God's answer to Job. It is not an answer in any academic or speculative sense. It *is* an answer in the demonstrative and practical sense. If God himself has chosen to share our griefs, it must follow that the existence of suffering *does* have transcendent meaning, not necessarily in itself but as a concomitant of freedom and the power to love. Without a high christology this view of suffering as salvific would not be possible.

The Church is the community to which the message of Christ's conquest of sin and suffering has been committed. It is the visible manifestation of human response to the last and greatest of God's gifts. The work of redemption must go on. That is why we need not merely a high christology but also a 'high doctrine of the Church'. This doctrine has nothing to do with either authoritarian structures or elaborate ritual. The true mystery of the Church consists in the fact that God wills to bring the life, teaching, death, and resurrection of Jesus to bear on all humanity, first, through the sending of the Spirit and, second, through the sending of the Church, the *ekklesia* or gathering of those who, under the prompting of the Holy Spirit, confess Jesus as Lord of all creation. A 'high' doctrine of the Church demands a compensating recognition of the socio-political character of all Church acts. Sent into the world with a divine mission, the Church is always vulnerable to, and often

213

guilty of, capitulation to the world's standards. The potentially corrupting effect of power, especially of power exercised in God's name, is always a hazard in Church life. The Church has first to look for forgiveness for itself before it can speak of forgiveness to the world. As long as it continues to think of itself primarily in terms of its structures, both educational and governmental, and only secondarily in terms of its members, it will quite simply fail to speak to the world with conviction about salvation, for the world will simply see it as the mirror-image of all that it recognises in itself as being most in need of redemption. The man who was God's human expression of divinity went about doing good, caring for the poor and oppressed, renouncing the attractions of structured power, and being himself marginalised by his concern for the marginalised. He placed his hopes and his commission in his 'little flock' on which the Father had bestowed the Kingdom.

The Church has long since ceased to be a little flock, but the character of its mission is not changed by mere numerical expansion. Nietzsche's jibe that he would begin to believe in Christ as saviour when Christians began to look more saved is a valuable if stinging reminder to the Church that merely to profess one's faith is not enough. It is one thing to claim that 'justification is by faith alone', or that 'the Church [meaning its senior clerics] is the voice of God'; it is quite another to act in such a way that everyone can actually see that it is a community of people who love one another and seek to extend that love to all the world.

Ideally speaking, then, the Church is a community of those who forgive because they have been forgiven. Its principal ritual is the Eucharist, in which the symbolic ambience of a family meal is fused mysteriously with the self-sacrifice of Jesus on Calvary to enable the participants to celebrate all that God has done for them and for the world by his offer of unconditional forgiveness and reconciliation. Every Eucharist is a homecoming, a relaxing in our Father's house, a celebration in symbol of all that we should be and manifestly are not. Every Eucharist is an occasion when the participants express in symbolic gestures all that God wants them to be, and thus for a brief moment they enjoy the actual occurrence of what would otherwise be purely utopian. They are therefore enjoined to put into secular practice what they have just enacted in sacramental symbol. Every Eucharist is a renunciation of violence, injustice, aggression, and lovelessness. 'Eucharistic praxis', James Mackey has written in an arresting sentence, 'is the Christian alternative to war.'[7] It is *the* celebration of reconciliation because it actually produces reconciliation, if it is entered into with the right dispositions. The splendid ecumenical statement known as the Lima Document has this to say about the Eucharist:

> The eucharist is the great sacrifice of praise by which the Church speaks on behalf of the whole creation. For the world which God has reconciled is present at every eucharist: in the bread and wine, in the persons of the faithful, and in the prayers they offer for themselves and for all people.... The eucharist thus signifies what the world is to become: an offering and hymn of praise to the Creator, a universal communion in the body of Christ, a kingdom of justice, love and peace in the Holy Spirit.[8]

Those words link creation and redemption, world and Church, within the context of the Eucharist. Because the participants in the conference which issued the document came from all the main Christian traditions, their document is a reconciling act: it seeks to bring together those who have been estranged. It is also a powerful symbol of how the Holy Spirit who rested upon the face of the deep at the beginning of creation is now the empowering force of the New Creation. He inspires to healing and reconciliation by drawing his people into the mystery of a God who by the very fact of creating enters upon a costly adventure in self-emptying which reaches its climax in the life and death of Jesus of Nazareth, Son of God, Saviour.

Glossary

Analogical, univocal, equivocal. As used in theology these terms refer primarily to the nature of statements made about God. Take for example the statement 'God is wise'. To claim that the predicate 'wise' is used univocally of God and of finite beings would be to affirm that there is no difference in kind between God and his creatures, and therefore that the word 'wise' has exactly the same sense in each case. To claim that the predicate 'wise' is used equivocally of God and of finite beings would be to affirm that God and his creation are so utterly different in kind that the word 'wise' has a totally different sense in each case. To claim that the predicate 'wise' is used analogically of God and of finite beings is to affirm that there is sufficient similarity between God and his creatures to enable us to say that if we mentally eliminate the imperfections which we find in created wisdom and mentally scale up to infinity what we mean by 'wise', then we may apply the predicate to God in a manner which is neither purely univocal nor purely equivocal but which contains within it a measure of each.

Anthropic Principle. The Anthropic Principle states the claim that the universe has the properties we observe today, because if its earlier properties had been significantly different, we would not be here to observe it.

Apophatic (or Negative) Theology. Apophatic theology recognises and even emphasises what can *not* be known, conceptualised, or imagined about God. It is more ready to state what God is *not* than what he is. Apophatic or Negative theology is particularly sensitive to the equivocal element in all statements about God (see *Analogical*).

Big Bang. Cosmologists commonly use the term 'Big Bang' in reference to the initial moments of the coming to be of our universe. The model envisages an unimaginably powerful cosmic explosion from a state of extreme density and compression. The Big Bang theory has today virtually replaced the 'Steady State' theory which postulates the continuous creation of matter to fill the voids left as the universe expands.

Cosmology: the study of the nature and development of the universe.

Epistemology: the study or theory of the origin, nature, methods and limitations of knowledge.

Ecclesiology: theology of (i.e. about) the Church.

Eschatology: literally 'discourse about the last things'. Traditional eschatology dealt with such matters as death, judgment, heaven, hell, immortality. Today eschatology is more usually seen as a perspective or interpretative framework through which the dynamism and purpose of history can be viewed. Judaeo-Christian theology is eschatological in that it relates most of its images and concepts to an end (Greek, *eschaton*) towards which creation, and especially history, is moving. The Messianic Kingdom preached by Jesus is eschatological in the sense that it envisages the arrival of the 'end-time' which Jewish prophecy and apocalypticism looked to. Theologians and biblical scholars have differed over whether Jesus saw the Kingdom (or Reign) of God as already present in himself ('realised eschatology') or as lying in the future ('consistent'or 'thoroughgoing' eschatology).

Essence, Substance. Although philosophers can and do differentiate between them, these two terms are close enough in reference to be treated as synonymous. The essence or substance of something is that which makes it what it is. The terms are metaphysical in the (inaccurately) derived sense of being beyond physical conditions. The essence, or substance, of a chair is that which makes it a chair and not a table or a kangaroo. In metaphysics (q.f.) the word 'nature' has roughly the same sense and reference as 'essence' and 'substance'.

Essentialism: that school of philosophy which is preoccupied with the essence, substance or nature of things, often to the neglect of existential or personal considerations. The perduring influence of Aristotle on Roman Catholic theology made that theology predominantly essentialist until the Second Vatican Council released it from mandatory neo-Thomism. An essentialist theology is almost exclusively concerned with the abstract (i.e. impersonal, static) character of faith, salvation, grace etc.

Existentialism. Theologically, existentialism is perhaps best thought of as a reaction against essentialism (q.v.). Whereas essentialism is concerned with the abstract features of things (including human beings), existentialism is concerned with the concrete and specific character of human existence. It emphasises human freedom in a threatening world and exhorts the individual to take charge of his/her life. Existentialist considerations have had a particular influence on the theology of revelation and faith.

Kenosis, kenotic. These words come from the Greek word 'to empty' and have their origin in the Letter to the Philippians (Phil. 2:7) in which Paul speaks of Christ as 'emptying himself' and 'taking the form of a servant'. Though all kenotic theories agree that the eternal Word and Son of God laid aside certain prerogatives that were his due (e.g. glory, honour), some affirm that he laid aside actual divine attributes such as omnipotence and omniscience.

Kerygma: the proclaimed message of salvation (Greek: *kerux*, a herald). The kerygma is the earliest proclamation of the good news of salvation.

Metaphysics: the branch of philosophy which enquires into such matters as being, time, cause, substance.

Model. A theological model is an analogy, usually expressed by a metaphor, which allows us to speak coherently if imperfectly about matters which lie beyond the powers of literal description. The metaphorical element may be obvious, as when God is called a shepherd; but it may also be less obvious, as when he is called 'Father'.

Monophysitism: the doctrine that in Christ there is only one nature, which is divine. One speaks of monophysite tendencies in any approach to Christ which emphasises his divine nature at the expense of his humanity.

Nestorianism: the doctrine that in Christ there were two distinct persons, one divine and one human.

Ontological Argument. The ontological argument for the existence of God was first framed by St Anselm. It turns on the definition of God as 'that than which nothing greater can be thought'. Something which exists in reality as well as in the mind must be greater than something which exists merely in the mind. Therefore, runs the argument, God must exist in reality. The Ontological Argument has been logically refuted many times but it refuses to lie down.

Ontology: the branch of metaphysics (q.v.) which enquires into the character and properties of being as such. It is thus the widest and most abstract of all philosophical disciplines. It deals with questions of essence and existence. The ontological constitution of Christ is the abstract relationship between the divine and the human in him. In classical christology they are described as two 'natures' cohering in one 'person'.

Panentheism, Pantheism, Deism. All three words describe a relationship between God and creation. Pantheism identifies God with nature. Deism regards God as creator of the universe but denies that he is present in it or intervenes in it as revealer or saviour. Panentheism attempts to steer a middle course between pantheism and deism by affirming that God is in the world and the world is in God.

Reductionism: the belief that all phenomena can be exhaustively explained by reducing them to their simplest and lowest component parts. An example would be the belief that men and women are nothing but a complex assembly of molecules. It is the 'nothing but' which makes a position reductionist. Men and women *are* (physically speaking) a complex assembly of molecules; but being human amounts to qualitatively more than having a specific molecular structure.

Soteriology: the theology of salvation (Greek: *soteria*, salvation).

Teleology: discourse about finality, i.e. ends or purposes (Greek: *telos*, end).

Notes

Introduction, pp. 1-10
1. See P. Tillich, *Systematic Theology,* Digswell Place 1953, I, 21.
2. This argument was first suggested to me by F. Dillistone, *The Christian Understanding of Atonement,* Digswell Place 1968, 1-16.

Chapter 1. In the Beginning God, pp. 11-33
1. J. Heller, *Catch 22,* London 1975, 195.
2. Cf. E. McMullin, 'How Should Cosmology Relate to Theology?' in A. R. Peacocke, ed., *The Sciences and Theology in the Twentieth Century,* Stocksfield 1981, 40.
3. P. Davies, *God and the New Physics,* London 1984, 39.
4. Augustine, *Confessions,* XI, 14 (Sheed translation).
5. *Conf.* XI, 20.   6. *Conf.,* XI, 23.   7. *Conf.,* XI, 27.
8. K. Ward, *Rational Theology and the Creativity of God,* Oxford 1982, 80.
9. Ward, *Rational Theology,* 81-2.
10. J. Cobb and D. Griffin, *Process Theology: An Introductory Exposition,* Belfast 1977, 8-10.
11. S. Sia, 'A Changing God?', in *Word and Spirit* 8, 20-21.
12. J. Macquarrie, *In Search of Deity: An Essay in Dialectical Theism,* London 1984.
13. Macquarrie, *In Search of Deity,* 180.
14. R. Bultmann, 'The Meaning of God as Acting', in O.C. Thomas, ed., *God's Activity in the World,* California 1983, 64.
15. Cf. M. Wiles, *God's Action in the World,* London 1986, passim, but especially p.2, where he quotes and comments on W. Kasper, *The God of Jesus Christ,* London 1984, 24.
16. J. Cobb, 'Natural Causality and Divine Action', in O.C. Thomas, ed., *God's Activity in the World,* 109.
17. K. Rahner, *Foundations of Christian Faith: An Introduction to the Idea of Christianity,* London 1978, 81.
18. Rahner, *Foundations,* 87. (emphasis added).

Chapter 2. Creation and Humanity, pp. 34-55
1. J. Moltmann, *God in Creation: An Ecological Doctrine of Creation,* London 1985, 304-5.
2. Moltmann, *God in Creation,* 306.
3. It was posthumously published in G. Tyrrell, *Essays on Faith and Immortality,* London 1914, 245-77 [to be cited as *EFI*].

4. *EFI*, 245. 5. *EFI*, 250n. 6. *EFI*, 250-1.
7. *EFI*, 254. 8. *EFI*, 257. 9. *EFI*, 259.
10. *EFI*, 260-1. 11. *EFI*, 263. 12. *EFI*, 265.
13. *EFI*, 266. 14. *EFI*, 270. 15. *EFI*, 272.
16. *EFI*, 274.
17. Moltmann, *God in Creation*, 14.
18. Ibid., 30.
19. F. Capra, *The Turning Point: Science, Society and the Rising Culture*, London 1982, 289.
20. Ibid., 302.
21. Cited in P. Davies, *God and the New Physics*, 171.
22. K. Rahner, *Foundations of Christian Faith*, London 1978, 80-1.
23. Moltmann, *God in Creation*, 250.
24. Denzinger-Schoenmetzer, no. 3896.
25. This usage of the word 'creationism' is to be distinguished from, though it has some features in common with, the view of those who hold that the theory of evolution is incompatible with the biblical account of creation.
26. D. Kelsey, 'The Doctrine of Creation from Nothing' in E. McMullin, ed., *Evolution and Creation*, Indiana 1985, 180.

Chapter 3. Matter, Spirit and Creation, pp. 56-74
1. W. Jaeger, *Early Christianity and Greek Paideia*, Cambridge, Mass. 1962 54.
2. H. Chadwick, *Early Christian Thought and the Classical Tradition*, Oxford 1966, 73.
3. O. Cullmann, *Salvation in History*, London 1967, 91.
4. Cited in K. Barth, *Protestant Theology in the Nineteenth Century: Its Background and History*, London 1972, 445.
5. F. Capra, *The Tao of Physics: An Exploration of the Parallels between Modern Physics and Eastern Mysticism*, London 1976, 53.
6. Capra, *Tao*, 58.
7. J. Monod, *Chance and Necessity*, London 1972.
8. Monod, *Chance*, 137. 9. Monod, *Chance*, 50.
10. F. von Hügel, *Essays and Addresses on the Philosophy of Religion*, II, London 1926, 106-7.
11. J. Dillengberger, 'The Apologetic Defence of Christianity', in C. A. Russell, ed., *Science and Religious Belief: A Selection of Recent Historical Studies*, London 1973, 186.
12. Dillenberger, art. cit., 187.
13. A. R. Peacocke, *Creation and the World of Science*, Oxford 1979, 87.
14. Cited in Peacocke, *Creation*, 50.
15. Peacocke, *Creation*, 90.
16. Cited in B. M. G. Reardon, *From Coleridge to Gore: A Century of Religious Thought in Britain*, London 1971, 394n.
17. Peacocke, *Creation*, 90-2.
18. Peacocke, *Creation* 95.
19. Peacocke, *Creation*, 103.

20. D. J. Bartholomew, *God of Chance,* London 1984, 82.
21. Bartholomew, *God of Chance,* 157.

Chapter 4. The Way and the Cosmos, pp. 75-94
1. Irenaeus, *Epideixis*, 22.
2. Tertullian, *De Resurrectione Mortuorum*, VI.
3. P. Teilhard de Chardin, *The Phenomenon of Man*, London 1965, 297; original italics.
4. P. Teilhard de Chardin, *Human Energy*, London 1969, 91.
5. A. Schweitzer, *The Quest of the Historical Jesus: A Critical Study of Its Progress from Reimarus to Wrede,* London 1954.
6. A. Schweitzer, *My Life and Thought: An Autobiography*, London 1966, 53.
7. Schweitzer, *The Quest*, 401.
8. L. Boff, *Jesus Christ Liberator: A Critical Christology for Our Time*, New York 1978, 279-80.
9. J. L. Segundo, *Evolution and Guilt*, Dublin 1980, 115-16.
10. S. Kierkegaard, *Concluding Unscientific Postscript*, as cited and translated by D. G. M. Patrick, *Pascal and Kiekegaard: A Study in the Strategy of Evangelism*, Vol. 2, London 1947, 240.
11. J. B. Cobb Jn., *Christ in a Pluralistic Age,* Philadelphia, 1975, 17.
12. Cited in C. Mooney, *Teilhard de Chardin and the Mystery of Christ,* London 1966, 119.
13. Mooney, *Teilhard de Chardin*, 134.
14. Mooney, *Teilhard de Chardin*, 137.
15. Mooney, *Teilhard de Chardin*, 136.

Chapter 5. Resurrection and Salvation, pp. 95-113
1. M. Hengel, *The Atonement: The Origins of the Doctrine in the New Testament*, London 1981, 43.
2. H. Waddell, *Medieval Latin Lyrics*, Harmondsworth 1952, 131.
3. J. Donne, *Holy Sonnets,* iii.
4. Dermot Lane uses the nice phrase, 'an underlying identity within transformation' to describe the relationship between the Jesus of history and the risen Christ. See *The Reality of Jesus: An Essay in Christology*, Dublin 1975, 54.
5. E. Schillebeeckx, *Jesus: An Experiment in Christology*, London 1979, 380-97.
6. Schillebeeckx, *Jesus*, 391.
7. Schillebeeckx, *Jesus*, 644.
8. Schillebeeckx, *Jesus*, 646-7.
9. A neat conspectus of how Schillebeeckx understands the word 'experience' can be found in his *Christ: The Christian Experience in the Modern World*, London 1980, 30-40.
10. J. P. Mackey, *Modern Theology: A Sense of Direction* (Oxford 1987), 78-80.
11. J. Donne, *Hymne to God my God, in My Sicknesse.*

Chapter 6. How Original is Sin? pp. 114-30

1. J. H. Newman, *An Essay in Aid of a Grammar of Assent*, London 1895, 107.
2. Newman, *Grammar*, 117.
3. Cited by F. Heer, *The Intellectual History of Europe*, London 1966, 441.
4. J. H. Newman, *Apologia pro Vita Sua*, London 1913, 335.
5. J. P. Mackey, ed., *Religious Imagination*, Edinburgh 1986, 4.
6. Augustine, *Confessions*, V, 10.
7. H. Chadwick, *Augustine*, Oxford 1986, 108.
8. M. de Unamuno, *Tragic Sense of Life*, London 1921, 15-16.
9. Tertullian, *De Testimonio Animae*, 3.
10. Augustine, *De Civitate Dei*, XIII, 14.
11. Augustine, *Enchiridion*, 26.
12. Ibid, 27.
13. Augustine, *De Nuptiis et Concupiscentia*, I, 19.
14. *Gaudium et Spes*, art 13.

Chapter 7. Creation and Alienation, pp. 131-47

1. P. V. Tobias cited in J. C. Eccles, *The Human Mystery*, London 1984, 97.
2. See P. Schoonenberg, *Man and Sin: A Theological View*, London 1965. Rahner's views are conveniently set out in *Sacramentum Mundi*, IV, New York 1969, 328-34.
3. On A. Vanneste see G. Vandervelde, *Original Sin: Two Major Trends in Contemporary Roman Catholic Reinterpretation*, Amsterdam 1975, 259-88.
4. P. Tillich, *Systematic Theology*, II, Welwyn 1968, 36.
5. Tillich, *S.T.*, 50.
6. E. Neumann, *The Origins and History of Consciousness*, London 1954, 267.
7. E. Cassirer, *An Essay on Man: An Introduction to a Philosophy of Human Culture*, New Haven and London 1962, 81.
8. Cassirer, *Essay*, 82, original italics.
9. Neumann, *Origins*, 268.
10. P. Ricoeur, 'Evil, a challenge to Philosophy and Theology', *Journal of the American Academy of Religion*, 53/3 (1985), 640.
11. Augustine, *De Civitate Dei*, XIX, 13.
12. Augustine, *De Civ. Dei* XIX, 14.
13. See T. Dobzhansky, *The Biology of Ultimate Concern*, London 1971, 69.
14. Dobzhansky, *Biology*, 79.
15. C. G. Jung, *Answer to Job*, London 1984, 87. See also his *Analytical Psychology: Its Theory and Practice,* London 1986, 3-38.
16. See J. Burnaby, *Amor Dei: A Study of St Augustine's Teaching on the Love of God as the Motive of Christian Life*, London 1938, 92-100.
17. Augustine, *De Vera Religione*, XXXV, 65.
18. Augustine, *Ad Simplicianum de Diversis Questionibus*, II, 21.
19. Augustine, *In Joannis Evangelium Tractatus*, XL, 10. *Desiderium sinus cordis* resists graceful translation; but if *sinus* is translated as 'core' and

allowed to suggest a nuclear reactor, the figure, for all its anachronism, would faithfully render Augustine's thought.

20. Augustine, *De Trinitate*, IV, 15, 20.
21. Cited in R. May, *Love and Will*, London 1972, 122.

Chapter 8. The Dark Enigma, pp. 148-68
  1. P. Toynbee, *Towards the Holy Spirit: A Tract for the Times*, London 1973.
  2. Toynbee, *Holy Spirit*, 8.   3. Toynbee, *Holy Spirit*, 9.
  4. Toynbee, *Holy Spirit*, 75.
  5. *The Observer*, 16 December 1973, 32.
  6. F. Dostoyevsky, *The Brothers Karamazov*, Harmondsworth, 1958, I, 276-88.
  7. P. Ricoeur, 'Evil, A Challenge to Philosophy and Theology', *Journal of the American Academy of Religion*, 53, no. 3, 635-48.
  8. Ricoeur, 'Evil' 635.   9. Ricoeur, 'Evil', 636.
 10. C. G. Jung, *Answer to Job*, London 1984.
 11. Jung, *Answer*, 25.   12. Jung, *Answer*, 34-5.   13. Jung, *Answer*, 55.
 14. Jung, *Answer*, 67-8.   15. Jung, *Answer*, 74.   16. Jung, *Answer*, 86.
 17. Jung, *Answer*, 87.
 18. Ricoeur, 'Evil', 640.
 19. Augustine, *De Civitate Dei*, I, 9.
 20. Augustine, *Civ. Dei*, I, 8.
 21. Augustine, *Enchiridion*, VIII, 27.
 22. Cited by J. Butt in his introduction to Voltaire, *Candide, Or Optimism*, Harmondsworth 1947, 9.
 23. P. Hazard, *European Thought in the Eighteenth Century*, Harmondsworth 1965, 344.
 24. I. Kant, *Religion within the Limits of Reason Alone*, New York 1960, 28.
 25. Kant, *Religion*, 38.
 26. K. Barth, *Protestant Theology in the Nineteenth Century*, London 1972, 294.
 27. Barth, *Protestant Theology*, 269.
 28. Ricoeur, 'Evil', 645.
 29. Ricoeur, 'Evil', 647.
 30. Ibid.

Chapter 9. Redemption in Scripture and Tradition, pp. 169-93
  1. J. H. Newman, *An Essay on the Development of Christian Doctrine*, London 1878, 337.
  2. P. H. Pearse, *Political Writings and Speeches* (Dublin, 1917), p. 99; cited in F. X. Martin, '1916—Myth, Fact, and Mystery', *Studia Hibernica*, 7 (1967), 109.
  3. Martin, '1916', 109.   4. Martin, '1916', 110.
  5. R. de Vaux, *Studies in Old Testament Sacrifice*, Cardiff 1964, 93.
  6. For analysis of this and other Eucharistic theories of the pre-Vatican II

period see F. Clark, *Eucharistic Sacrifice and the Reformation*, Devon 1981, 243-68.

7. J. Ratzinger, 'Is the Eucharist a Sacrifice?', *Concilium*, IV (April 1967), 37-8.
8. Irenaeus, *Adversus Haereses* [to be cited as *A. H.*], V, xvi, 3.
9. *A. H.*, IV, xiv, 1.   10. *A. H.*, IV, xxxviii, 1.   11. *A. H.*, IV, xiv, 2.
12. *A. H.*, III, xxiii, 6.   13. *A. H.*, III, xx, 2.   14. *A. H.*, III, xxii, 3.
15. *A. H.*, III, xviii, 7.   16. *A. H.*, IV, xxxviii, 2.
17. Origen, *Comm. in Mathaeum*, XVI, 8.
18. Gregory of Nyssa, *Oratio Catechetica*, 24.
19. Tertullian, *De Pudicitia*, 2.
20. Tertullian, *De Poenitentia*, 5.
21. G. Aulén, *Christus Victor: An Historical Study of the Three Main Types of the Idea of the Atonement*, London 1970.
22. Aulén, *Christus Victor*, 59.
23. R. W. Southern, *The Making of the Middle Ages*, London 1953, 219-57.
24. R. W. Southern, *St Anselm and His Biographer: A Study of Monastic Life and Thought, 1059-c. 1130*, Cambridge 1966, 94.
25. Anselm, *Cur Deus Homo*, I, 21.   26. Southern, *St Anselm*, 113.
27. P. Abelard, *Expositio in Epistolam ad Romanos*, II, 3.
28. St Bernard, *Letter 190*, analysed in A. Victor Murray, *Abelard and St Bernard: A Study in Twelfth Century 'Modernism'*, Manchester 1967, 72-88.
29. H. Rashdall, *The Idea of Atonement in Christian Theology*, London 1919, 360.
30. R. E. Weingart, *The Logic of Divine Love: A Critical Analysis of the Soteriology of Peter Abelard*, Oxford 1970, 205.

Chapter 10. Redemption in Contemporary Perspective, pp. 194-215.
1. Plato, *The Republic*, Book II, translated and with an Introduction by H. D. P. Lee, Harmondsworth 1955, 93.
2. Tadhg Gaelach O Súilleabháin, 'Duain Chroí Íosa', translated by Thomas Kinsella, in S. Ó Tuama, ed., *An Duanaire, 1600-1900: Poems of the Dispossessed*, Mountrath 1981, 193.
3. E. Schillebeeckx, *Christ*, 758.
4. M. de Unamuno, *Tragic Sense of Life*, New York 1954, 144.
5. See H. Peukert, *Science, Action, and Fundamental Theology: Towards a Theology of Communicative Action*, Cambridge Mass. 1984, 206-10.
6. F. R. Barry, *The Atonement* London 1968, 183.
7. J. P. Mackey, *Modern Theology: A Sense of Direction*, Oxford 1987, 185.
8. World Council of Churches, Faith and Order Paper no. 111, *Baptism, Eucharist and Ministry*, Geneva 1982, 10-11.

Index

228